GenAdmin

WRITING PROGRAM ADMINISTRATION
Series Editors: Susan H. McLeod and Margot Soven

The Writing Program Administration series provides a venue for scholarly monographs and projects that are research- or theory-based and that provide insights into important issues in the field. We encourage submissions that examine the work of writing program administration, broadly defined (e.g., not just administration of first-year composition programs). Possible topics include but are not limited to 1) historical studies of writing program administration or administrators (archival work is particularly encouraged); 2) studies evaluating the relevance of theories developed in other fields (e.g., management, sustainability, organizational theory); 3) studies of particular personnel issues (e.g., unionization, use of adjunct faculty); 4) research on developing and articulating curricula; 5) studies of assessment and accountability issues for WPAs; and 6) examinations of the politics of writing program administration work at the community college.

BOOKS IN THE SERIES

GenAdmin: Theorizing WPA Identities in the 21st Century by Colin Charlton, Jonikka Charlton, Tarez Samra Graban, Kathleen J. Ryan, and Amy Ferdinandt Stolley (2011).

GenAdmin

Theorizing WPA Identities in the Twenty-First Century

Colin Charlton, Jonikka Charlton,
Tarez Samra Graban, Kathleen J. Ryan,
and Amy Ferdinandt Stolley

Parlor Press
Anderson, South Carolina
www.parlorpress.com

Parlor Press LLC, Anderson, South Carolina, USA

© 2011 by Parlor Press
All rights reserved.
Printed in the United States of America

S A N: 2 5 4 - 8 8 7 9

Library of Congress Cataloging-in-Publication Data

Charlton, Colin, 1971-
  GenAdmin : theorizing WPA identities in the 21st century / Colin Charlton ...[et al.].
       p. cm.
  Includes bibliographical references and index.
  ISBN 978-1-60235-236-0 (pbk. : alk. paper) -- ISBN 978-1-60235-237-7 (hardcover : alk. paper) -- ISBN 978-1-60235-238-4 (adobe ebook) -- ISBN 978-1-60235-239-1 (epub)
  1. English language--Rhetoric--Study and teaching. 2. Report writing--Study and teaching (Higher) 3. Writing centers--Administration. I. Title.
  PE1404.C477 2011
  808'.042071--dc23
                         2011030631

1 2 3 4 5

Cover design by Colin Charlton.
Printed on acid-free paper.

Parlor Press, LLC is an independent publisher of scholarly and trade titles in print and multimedia formats. This book is available in paper, cloth and Adobe eBook formats from Parlor Press on the World Wide Web at http://www.parlorpress.com or through online and brick-and-mortar bookstores. For submission information or to find out about Parlor Press publications, write to Parlor Press, 3015 Brackenberry Drive, Anderson, South Carolina, 29621, or e-mail editor@parlorpress.com.

Dedications

To my mentors, especially Pat, Shirley, Bud, Linda, and Nancy, who taught me that my questions mattered, to my coauthors who taught me that questions are richer when asked and answered together, and to Karl for being the best one.

—AFS

To my feminist mentors—Elizabeth, Hepsie, Nancy, and Jody—for teaching me early on about the need for balance. To my coauthors for making me think and laugh. To Cima and Eva for their furry friendship. To John for everything else.

—KR

To my mentors—Pat, Victor, Shirley, and Bud—for being steadfast and humane in their guidance, and for treating their students as full-fledged participants in the field. To A, C, J, and K for taking this project on. To Eric, for always making space for me to write.

—TSG

To Shirley, Dick, Donna, Bud, and Gerry, for living what this book is about before I could articulate it. To those who have or will have the passion and conviction to embrace administrative work, most especially my four coauthors. To my mom and my sweet loves, Duncan, Ian, and Colin, who remind me what matters when I need it most. And especially to my dad, who would have told everyone he knew about his baby girl's book.

—JC

To Mom and Dad, for the Zen of it all. To my partners in crime, for the comingling of voices. To Shirley, for asking me why I was here. And to J, for being the best answer I will ever think of.

—CC

Contents

Acknowledgments *ix*
Prelude *xi*

1 Toward a Philosophy of Generation Administration   3

Interlude: On Choice   23

2 Listening to and Rewriting History   35

Interlude: On Empathy   57

3 Constructing Professional Identities   62

Interlude: On Expertise   99

4 Becoming WPAs   104

Interlude: On Strategizing   129

5 Enacting GenAdmin Discourse   133

Interlude: On Advocacy   165

6 Re-Theorizing a GenAdmin Ethics   172

Afterword   201
    Jeanne Gunner, Joseph Harris,
    Dennis Lynch, and Martha Townsend

Notes   213
Works Cited   223
Index   241
About the Authors   247

Acknowledgments

We are indebted to many people on the completion of this book. We would specifically like to thank our Parlor Press publisher, David Blakesley, our reviewers, and the WPA series editors Susan McLeod and Margot Soven, who were quick to respond to the idea of this book and who made the process smooth from start to finish. Nancy DeJoy gave us formative, substantive suggestions for revision, and Dana Anderson, Christine Farris, Joan Linton, and John Schilb each read portions of the earliest draft that helped shape our thinking. A 2008 research grant, awarded for *The Assemblage Project*, from the Council of Writing Program Administrators allowed us to gather and index other WPAs' stories and to rethink how those stories can be circulated and retold.

We also thank those individuals who encouraged us as we wrote, in small and large ways, and who gave us reason to believe in this project's exigence and audiences. Collectively, we are indebted to the participants at our "GenAdmin: Making Sense of/for a New Generation of Writing Program Administrators" session during the 2008 CWPA Conference in Denver. The crosstalk that occurred during and after that session has shaped the final version of this book in more ways than one. For the years they invested in our well-being—personally and professionally, either in the classroom or as colleagues in a dynamic discipline—we are also indebted to Shirley K Rose, Irwin Weiser, Janice Lauer, Thomas Rickert, Dick Fulkerson, and Donna Dunbar-Odom, whose commitment to rhetorical traditions, past and present, has influenced each of us and impacted this book. For the less obvious, sometimes implicit, ways they interacted with us, tracked our careers, provided opportunities to collaborate, modeled for us the kinds of intellectual engagers we hoped to become, or challenged (sometimes chastened) us throughout this project, we thank Linda Adler-Kassner, Joe Janangelo, Marty Townsend, Thomas Miller, Hephzibah Roskelly,

Kate Ronald, and Elizabeth Chiseri Strater. We thank Jeanne Gunner, Joe Harris, Dennis Lynch, and Martha Townsend for their dialogic thinking about our book, for offering us responses, reactions, and feedback as we drafted it, and for beginning the conversation we hoped that it would. And we thank this book's readers—for taking on the task of thinking philosophically about writing program administration in an institutional climate that may not explicitly invite it, for not succumbing to the weariness that clouds all we do, and for recognizing that we do not struggle against depictions of the job or of our institutions, but rather struggle *with* them. Our need for *becoming* among today's contingencies seems ever more pressing.

Finally, we mention important personal debts. Jonikka and Colin would like to thank Moriah McCracken, Larry Dambreville, Robert Reitz, Shoney Flores, Theron Francis, Gary Schneider, Kyoung Lee, the Coles, Dalel Serda, Bonnie Garcia, Valerie Oritz, Brittany Ramirez, Jordan Guerra, and Sharon Fulkerson for reminding them that there can be joy in their work and in their play. Tarez would like to thank Pat Sullivan and Shirely Rose for modeling—in her generosity, perseverance, and patience—a work ethic that drives most of Tarez's collaborations, at Indiana University and elsewhere. Amy would like to thank her colleagues at Saint Xavier who have given her an institutional home that is far more homey than institutional; they've graciously made space for her to ask questions about writing and generously supported her efforts to find answers. Kate would like to thank Rebecca Jones, Deb Dew, Beth Howells, Amy Ratto Parks, Nancy Cook, Bruce Ballenger, Janet Bean, Kelly Webster, Doug Downs, and Duane Roen for valuing writing program administration and believing in her commitment to and capacity for doing that work.

Prelude

ON LOCATION

Somewhere in the swirl of life, each of us ponders three essential questions: "Who am I?" "Where am I?" and "What am I supposed to do?" We often consider the first question in isolation, as if it were the true key to our existence—as if the matter of who we are could be resolved independently of the two remaining questions. But all three of these questions must be answered in consort, as together they articulate the totality of the human condition. We do different things with varying degrees of understanding and purpose. We are born, live, feel, think, act, move, settle, and die. Questions of our existence and action are separable neither from each other nor from place—but it is place that we have most often ignored.

—Robert L. Thayer, Jr.

Robert Thayer's insight is an appropriate opening to this book because his questions are also our questions and because his questions prompt another: *Where to begin in defining this project?* The idea of GenAdmin—a group or generation of writing program administrators whose graduate careers prepared them to do WPA work in some form, who came to see administration as a core component of their professional and intellectual identities, and who pursued or accepted administrative roles before tenure to satisfy personal or professional needs—emerged for each of us as we experienced substantially different lives, interests, and courses of study. But any portrait of an artist or collective, specifically with writing program administration as a subject, calls for a frame, no matter how untethered its edges may seem. And so, we offer one of place—or, perhaps more accurately, we offer

xii *Prelude*

a frame constructed of locations, meta-narratives, memories of places where the book began for each of us, where the questions and desires that led to the book began to solidify.

In Memories of Emerging Identities: Jonikka's first national conference presentation was in July 2002 at the Council of Writing Program Administrators (CWPA) conference in Park City, Utah. She was on a panel with Shirley K Rose, her WPA mentor, and they were making the case for the professionalization, specifically the intellectual preparation, of future WPAs. It was the first time Jonikka articulated the idea that she felt somehow different because she had *chosen* writing program administration, not only in terms of the various roles and responsibilities that come with a WPA position, but also in terms of embracing WPA as her emerging professional identity.

As the years passed, she took several writing program administration seminars, and, in other courses, wrote papers with a WPA perspective, all of which culminated in her dissertation, in which she began to articulate what it might mean to think of the WPA as an updated version of Quintilian's *vir bonus*. While she has moved in and out of WPA *positions* ever since, she has maintained her WPA *identity* through a preoccupation with theorizing that identity—for herself and for others, specifically thinking about what marks writing program administration expertise and how one can *learn* to think and act from a WPA perspective.

One of her clearest memories of stepping into her new role as a WPA scholar is when Marty Townsend approached her at the end of that 2002 conference presentation and said something to the effect of, "You know, I chose WPA work, too. If you ever want to write about that, let me know." That moment validated Jonikka's experience and thinking and gave her the encouragement she needed to pursue her questions of WPA identity: What difference does it make when we *choose* WPA work? How might that one factor change the ways we do our work and the ways others see our work? And what happens when more and more of us begin to choose writing program administration as the focus of our scholarly identity? Over time, Jonikka saw in Amy, Tarez, Kate, and Colin a desire to ask similar questions, all borne of a hope to do meaningful work in often cynical places. Part of what brings us together is a conviction that WPAs can do ethical work, can entertain vital ideas, and can promote change without letting fear overwhelm them. The book emerged for Jonikka from that desire to theorize what makes us able to think, believe, and act as we do.

In Memories of Thinking Together: Between 2002 and 2007, Tarez had collaborated with Jonikka and Colin on one project, and with Kate on one or two others. She had also worked with Amy on course projects during their PhD program. In that five-year span, each of them had already been thinking, together and apart, about mentoring, pedagogy, and the discipline, and this thinking had been sustained and challenged by institutional challenges such as job relocations, institutional resistance, and curriculum upheaval. What these solo and collaborative projects held in common for Tarez was evidence of a willingness and an aptitude to write from different sites or approaches to administrative work—i.e., to problematize the *expert*, to theorize the *feminist/pragmatic*, to rethink the *gaze* on graduate student WPAs (gWPAs). But these collaborations also signaled transformative and reciprocal experiences for Tarez, and they signaled the reasons why she first became interested in WPA work.

Early on in her tenure-track job, Tarez realized how difficult such collaborations were to come by, how rare they were to achieve, and how much they needed to be nurtured and maintained over time. She also realized that transformative collaboration would probably always define her role as both a WPA and a rhetoric and composition practitioner. For her, this project emerged from a desire to engage each other in a larger scale collaboration where we were all at its center, but a collaboration that was powerful enough to invite (or provoke) ideological disruption in our different institutional contexts.

In Memories of Listening to Others: In Chattanooga, Tennessee, site of the 2006 CWPA conference—in a hotel topped with a marquee train suggesting history, motion, and the "you are here" appeal of a landmark—Colin was hauling around tripods and microphones. He didn't know anything more about WPAs than what he had picked up from Jonikka's classes in that specialization and was trying to understand writing programs through video documentaries of students, teachers, and the work that emerged when they collaborated on public writing projects. He was trying, as an outsider, to collect enough tape to create an audio documentary. He and Jonikka found Tarez at a table and literally took a load (of equipment) off.

For Colin, the idea for this book began to emerge at that table, where Amy and Kate eventually happened by, talking about the panels we had attended. Juxtaposed with the strangeness that accompanies recording others, Colin sensed a familiarity of energy around that accidental table as we asked each other questions about what was happening around us, why we did or didn't belong. We were people watching, physically lurking amongst names we knew for which we still did not have faces.

In Memories of Interrogating Assumptions: In 2007, Amy was struggling with her decision to take a non-tenure-track WPA job her first year out of graduate school. She felt good about her decision because it allowed her to live in the same city as her husband rather than resorting to the long-distance marriage so many dual-career academics are forced to choose, but she also wondered if she had made a mistake in disregarding the oft-repeated advice that pre-tenure faculty who took WPA positions were doomed for failure. She came to the book project wanting to interrogate the assumption that all pre-tenure WPAs are doomed, and she wanted a space to talk about how her decision to take such a job made her feel like she was being disobedient or naive, disregarding the advice of those with more professional experience in favor of what felt right for her whole life, not just her professional life.

As she moved from that first non-tenure-track WPA job to a tenure-track WPA job early in the life of this project, Amy became more aware of the professional/personal dichotomy her earlier thinking had created, and she wanted to write towards a new understanding of WPA work that blended the personal and professional in a more nuanced way. Her job change caused her to shift her approach to the project, and she experienced a felt need to move beyond simply resisting those dire advice narratives to imagining new ways that we could tell our stories of WPA work and new ways of thinking about our shared histories.

In Memories of Resistance: Two thousand and six found Kate at the end of her fifth year as a WPA, and the end of her first year as the Director of Composition in her second tenure-track job. As a pre-tenure WPA she had felt, on the one hand, the excitement of developing composition curricula on two campuses and working with TAs and instructors on their development as composition teachers, and, on the other, the frustration of being a composition specialist making arguments she was surprised to find still needed to be made, like those about the need to hire qualified adjunct instructors to teach composition, to understand that writing is a complex and rhetorical process rather than a simple matter of skill mastery, and to recognize the limited value of rising junior exams. She wished that accepted disciplinary ideas were more welcome across campuses. At the same time, she struggled with resistance to a prevalent notion circulating among WPAs, namely that being a pre-tenure WPA is untenable and should be undesirable. She wished the CWPA could find ways to move past arguments about whether or not there should be pre-tenure WPAs and towards discussions of power, agency, and positioning for all WPAs, including those who chose to be WPAs pre-tenure. Conversations with Tarez, Amy, Colin, and Jonikka at the 2006 CWPA conference were well timed, as Kate was ready to offer her perspective on these tensions. She entered this project with a readiness to speak and theorize publicly about these issues instead of just feeling frustrated and unproductively resistant to them.

Our conversations throughout 2006 and 2007 became an ongoing discussion on the nature of administration before tenure, the philosophies of writing programs, the energies that communities create, and the unavoidable distances that demarcate where we are and what we were hoping to individually accomplish. We began listening to each other intensely. As we listened, we heard about the different ways in which our work was our life, about why we had been professionally tapped to innovate while also being discouraged from wandering into unfamiliar territory, about what we needed and what we could live without, and about which ideas we gravitated towards as people who desired change, as abstract as that desire for change can sometimes seem.

Through these conversations, we realized how our lives were each marked, albeit differently, by common points of tension. We were all programmatically invested in what our home campuses were fostering, perpetuating, inventing, and constraining, but we were not necessarily sketching bumper sticker designs on napkins that read "Honk if you're GenAdmin." We had not yet coined the term, although words like *hybridity, becoming, optimism, pragmatism, responsibility*, and even new words like *multiplicinarity*, came up in our discussions of our students, our ways of learning, our colleagues, our ways of being in the world, our programs, our plans for food and friendship at future conference meetings.

Energized by these interactions, we proposed a panel for the CCCCs in New York, where we planned to synthesize these conversations and share them with others, specifically to explore the tensions between our administrative identities and the emergent writing programs in which we currently worked or had played a part. Although the panel proposal wasn't accepted, our enthusiasm for the project had already grown, and our commitment to the project—and to each other—demanded that we give voice to the ideas we were building together. As teachers with administrative identities, we wanted to theorize the various ways and contexts in which we present ourselves as mentors, program developers, teachers, and scholars. We wanted to work through how other people interpret and represent our identities largely in light of their own locations and commitments, and often with misunderstanding or resistance. Finally, we wanted to demonstrate that part of our role as administrative teachers is recognizing areas of resistance as productive sites for bridging communication gaps, to find ways to engage with those who resist or are silent/silenced, not just to console ourselves or convince them, but to arrive at a shared commitment to the intellectual work of composition. In other words, we wanted to articulate how such a re-presentation could open and close epistemic opportunities for the field at large.

Somewhere between a brief conversation in Park City and a planned panel in New York City, a space had emerged where we found a voice, both individual and collective, that spoke through hundreds of emails, Google chats, panel proposals, conference dinners, and a videoconference. We learned that collaboration is more difficult, more satisfying, and more epistemic than going it alone. We found that, in thinking together, we arrived at more nuanced understandings of our experiences because of the multiplicity of perspectives we had to accommodate. We realized, in fact, that we had sketched an early but viable portrait of a generation of writing program administrators. Back in 2008, as embedded as we were in the Presidential campaigns, we could not disguise our interest in and connection to a historical moment rich with volunteerism, activism, and dialogue. Such a groundswell, complete with generational analyses and attempts to frame small movements as movements of larger significance, still could not quite capture how we were thinking of our "generation" of writing program administrators.

But we had been generated, we were generating, and we were sensing and thinking through shifts in the reflections, identities, and goals between us and some of our WPA predecessors.

We sought an umbrella for our shared terms and experiences, one that had the hope and promise of a new perspective on what it means to compose a writing program among students, teachers, administrators, publics, and families, without dividing our administrative selves off from other works that engaged us, letting our administrative responsibilities and relationships smother us, or dissociating ourselves from the WPAs who had trained us. To articulate who we were, to have a name and a place, was a necessary philosophical, practical, and social act, as we continued to discuss how our identities didn't exist, or weren't necessarily experienced, as stable and teleological. We chose GenAdmin, short for Generation Administration, since both *generation* and *administration* are value-heavy and convenient frames for imagining how we belong to and/or stand apart from a world we keep trying (with infinite shortfalls) to understand. But in talking with each other, we wanted to give shape to the sense we had of each other as complex people who do not always seek to separate out the one voice from the many, the academic from the real, or the intellectual from the administrative.

By theorizing WPA identities in the twenty-first century, particularly GenAdmin, we articulate our goals for writing program administration, our writing program visions, and our conception of stakeholders in WPA situations to legitimize writing program administration as a chosen and creative site where we live, work, think, act, and promote intellectual change. These are the questions that drove our invention and theorizing as we lived through our examples, expanded upon our theories, and revised our practices:

- How does GenAdmin define itself in relationship to principles and beliefs inherited from previous generations of WPAs?
- How does GenAdmin disrupt assumptions about WPA identity that are often tacitly, or in some cases explicitly, forwarded by official organizations?
- How do we further define ourselves in relation to often competing principles and visions?
- What are the possibilities afforded to scholar-teacher-activist-administrators in various WPA roles?

- How might the answers to these questions change the nature of administration for those who follow and the thinking of those who came before?

In pursuing these questions, we talked frequently about what we did not want to come together as a group and write. We did not want to write a book about the emergence of a small support group for recent PhDs in rhetoric and composition with WPA identities. While we certainly did share stories, support each other, and learn from one another, we each felt an urge to do more than simply share our experience. We wanted to think about it, problematize it, theorize it, and make new knowledge out of it.

Our ongoing GenAdmin experience is a theoretical, practical, and potential assemblage of the WPAs we become, gravitate towards, and fail to represent; of the physical, administrative, pedagogical, emotional, and theoretical places we desire and where we actually end up; of the ways we act amongst ourselves, our colleagues, our mentees, our students, and those who might define themselves administratively much differently than we do. At one of our final working meetings, we discussed how our thinking has evolved since we started writing this book, becoming less dualistic, more complex, *and* more specific. Ultimately, we found ways to exchange our dis-ease with traditional narratives about WPAs for a project that articulates alternatives. This is a book about dissensus and consensus among colleagues and friends who had interlocking philosophies of how writing programs and life develop, of how we should perceive our administrative identities and engage our administrative responsibilities, and of how we might articulate and further enact our ways of being and becoming in a world that is simply too complex for us to find one way of *managing* it, one map appropriate to all navigable situations. We hope that what follows at least complicates and at best offers viable alternatives to narratives that emphasize tales of disappointment, loss, and grief in unwelcome jobs, that create binaries of writing program administration whereby we are either doomed as junior faculty WPAs or destined to succeed as senior WPAs, that posit us as either scholars or managers, and that quite simply limit possibilities for all WPAs.

GenAdmin

1 Toward a Philosophy of Generation Administration

As they read, write, and practice administration, students and faculty try on wildly divergent self-images of the WPA.

—Louise Wetherbee Phelps

Using landscaping as a metaphor for disciplinary knowledge-making offers a mechanism for understanding two provocative challenges. One is to recognize that whatever we currently know about rhetorical history as a disciplinary landscape is situated on a larger terrain of developed and undeveloped possibilities. A second challenge is to understand on an operational level, rather than just a theoretical one, that knowledge is less truth for all the time, space, and conditions than it is interpretation.

—Jacqueline Jones Royster

It's not about choosing the job or not choosing the job. That's a false and binary understanding of the choices we face for employment and academic responsibility. It's about not letting the job choose you, and not letting it alone define your identity.

—Conversational nugget from the authors

What is Administrative Identity?— Generating a Generational Frame

The identity of writing program administration has historically been varied, complex, and marked by periods of tension, out of which new temporal and theoretical moments continually grow. Where writing program administration was once largely perceived as a much-needed service role for corralling large numbers of composition sections and their teachers, it has since become a discipline and profession performed by tenured, tenure-track, and non-tenure-track faculty, as well as graduate students taking on such roles as part of their educational training. To the five of us writing this book, GenAdmin refers to an historical positioning that isn't bound by chronological placement or cultural positioning as much as by an intellectual posturing towards the work. For that reason, we have two main goals for this book, and readers will see us frequently negotiate some tension between them: (1) to articulate an administrative positioning that we have seen emerge in the theorization and practice of writing program work in the last two decades; and (2) to illustrate how that positioning reflects a philosophy of writing program administration that impels us to retheorize a discipline of writing program administration, even as we rethink disciplinary parameters.

This undertaking is rich with the complications that arose as we learned to write together through our differences, highlighting both the shared characteristics of and the disparity among our roles. Fundamentally, we have three experiences in common: (1) we have had explicit preparation in one or more aspects of writing program administration that our predecessors did not; (2) we have directly benefited from groundwork laid by the CWPA (e.g., in terms of guidance for evaluation of the intellectual work of the WPA); and (3) we have all at one time or another expressed a difference between our understandings of our beliefs and goals as untenured WPAs and common expectations for junior WPAs (jWPAs) even endorsed by the CWPA. These commonalities still leave room for flux: we do not all have the same expectation of our roles as WPAs; we were not all hired into departments where our work is acknowledged, valued, or understood; and we did not all come to our roles via the same understandings of what it means to choose a career in writing program administration. But throughout our ongoing conversations, we return again and again to the idea that what we experienced in our first years as WPAs was different than what we were told to expect. We found that our relationships with colleagues need not be agonistic, that effective program work could be done without the power afforded by tenure, and that being an untenured WPA need not require that we forsake a domestic or extra-academic existence. The narratives peppering the scholarship of writing program administration told us we should expect otherwise, as did some of our mentors. When our collective and individual experiences did not match those stories, we began to wonder if we were a part of a new generation of WPAs—one for whom the conventional WPA narratives do not necessarily apply, or for whom they could be more deliberately disrupted.

In the course of this book there are many terms, like jWPA, that we do not privilege as identifiers because of our desire to position and understand WPA work and workers in relationships that are complex alternatives to ones defined as junior/senior. Of course, we realize that some positionings will always be institutionally unrealizable or unproductive, revealing both the ends and the beginnings of concepts even as we name or categorize them. We suggest GenAdmin, instead, as a placeholder. As a generational placeholder, we value GenAdmin for what it makes visible: how we moved into the roles we now play as writing program administrators, and how this identity played out in other areas of our work. This visibility, in turn, complicates other notions, such as what it means to choose WPA work (something we will take up in greater depth in an interlude to Chapter 2), what is at stake in abandoning traditional arguments against this work on the basis of institutional naïveté (which we address in Chapter 3), whether and how well other forms of disciplinary knowledge or authority can serve pre-tenure WPAs (which we take up in Chapters 4 and 5), and what WPA responsibility might mean when responsibility is refigured as ethic not task (which we explore in Chapter 6).

We recognize that, as material conditions on many campuses cause WPA roles to be more creatively defined, expanded, or shared, the benefits afforded those roles do not always follow suit. The possibilities of the job and for the role are still constructed differently according to a constellation of factors. In "Ethics and the jWPA," although Alice Horning offers what we see as uninterrogated assumptions[1] about power and responsibility in speaking for junior WPAs, we realize she makes an argument that cannot be wholly ignored—it is unsustainable to have untenured faculty do program work in some institutions because of the ways in which the jWPA is practically, theoretically, or technically situated within that environment. For example, the untenured faculty member doing WPA work at a college or university that lacks a way of recognizing the work as commensurate with reward is at risk of not getting her needs met in the form of resources, course releases, or research support. A solo WPA who is the only rhetoric and composition faculty member or a WPA facing high publication expectations that don't accommodate her administrative service will also be vulnerable, as WPAs in those roles may find it difficult to be fully functioning members of the faculty. But because both the limits and the sources of support are determined by complex rather than single factors, we also realize that choosing pre-tenure WPA positions well (insomuch as this is possible) is important, as is being savvy rhetoricians on the job. Nevertheless, being intellectually shaped by a disciplinary landscape in which writing program administration is a legitimate scholarly enterprise can create an unavoidably different climate, one that disrupts the categories dominating debates in the field for the past two decades.

Applying a generational frame to the changing nature of WPA work, and the professionals who inhabit those positions, is not new to WPA studies. In their multivocal article, "The Progress of Generations," Anthony Baker, Karen Bishop, Suellyn Duffey, Jeanne Gunner, Rich Miller, and Shelley Reid identify themselves as members of two generations of WPA professionals—those who paved new territory in their departments and institutions as the first officially trained WPA to hold the position and those who take up the work after a first-generation WPA has moved on to a different role. They write of ghosts who haunt the second-generation WPAs as these newer professionals attempt to develop and lead already established programs, but they do so "carrying the professional DNA of earlier generations," forcing them to comply with or fight against their genetic predispositions (Baker et al. 55).

Our ghosts, or at least the ones we try to lay to rest in this volume, are less institutional and more disciplinary, in part because we see our identity as WPAs separate from our institutional contexts, even though our practices are always informed by our institutional and theoretical locations. We are a generation of WPAs whose identities are emerging from a philosophy of life and work that is more portable than earlier discussions of WPA work focused on institutional context would suggest. Instead, our generational frame offers us a new way of thinking about our identities as WPAs, identities that are, indeed, marked with the DNA of earlier generations but that are shaped and moved forward by different political, personal, and disciplinary forces. What we offer here is not a dismissal or a critique of the work of previous generations of WPAs; on the contrary, we are well aware that we would not be able to do this work without the efforts the WPAs who came before us and successfully argued for the professionalization of WPA roles and for the intellectual nature of WPA work. We use generational differences as a starting point for highlighting the ways in which the material reality and the intellectual nature of WPA work has changed.

We acknowledge differences in our WPA roles and those of prior generations, made possible by the increasing disciplinarity of the field and demonstrated in part by a rise in rhetoric and composition doctoral programs with writing program administration emphases; the slowly growing presence of WPA curriculum or seminars; professionalizing efforts by the CWPA; the increasing number of collections focusing on writing program administration; and the shifting material conditions of our universities which lead to part-time or full-time positions as graduate student WPAs, or that necessitate shared administration and lead to multiple WPA roles on one campus. These shifts are well documented and have been theorized by a generation or more of active and retiring WPAs who have worked hard to improve the conditions in which we now work, and who have themselves adopted writing program administration as more than an occupational identity. We see ourselves as taking earlier work in new directions, particularly on such intertwined issues as disciplinarity and identity; power, authority and positioning; and the place of rhetoric and ethics in writing program administration.

In this new intellectual climate, what does and can it mean to be teachers and scholars, especially pre-tenure, with an administrative identity? How does this positioning translate as a way of being a scholar, teacher, researcher, and citizen? We do not necessarily posit writing program administration as a subdiscipline of rhetoric, composition, or English studies, but rather acknowledge its *multiplicinarity*,[2] especially inasmuch as it concerns all of us with the articulation of particular theoretical orientations for the instruction each of our programs provides (Gunner, "Ideology" 7), thus setting itself apart from any number of fields to which it "belongs." By the same token, we do not only posit GenAdmin as a specific population within the WPA community, but also a philosophical perspective that we see emerging from the ongoing theorization of this field.

We hope this book helps account for the thinking of a generation of rhetoric and composition practitioners who were in some ways trained to think ideologically or philosophically like WPAs, whether or not they were seeking a traditional WPA role. We contribute to the emergent historical picture of who WPAs are but also who they can be, and in some part to assuage our own dissonances with taking on various aspects of the job. Our mentors taught us to think certain ways with the full knowledge that they were sending us out into a different field, a different job, a different historical and epistemological context, even if they didn't know exactly what those would be. Here, we explore consequences of educations embraced, jobs taken, lessons learned.

Even still, a project like this comes with the following risks:

- contextualizing our work only in terms of what we wish to change about our individual circumstances;
- coming across as simply being "dis"—dissatisfied, disempowered, disenfranchised—while trying to explicitly avoid a they say/we say binary;
- perpetuating metaphors and narratives of loss, victimization, and grief;
- sounding so neutral that our message loses impact;
- sounding so specific that we over-criticize the institutions where we live or have lived;
- subjecting our real message to erasure in our attempts to be well-intentioned with every audience we wish to reach; and
- romanticizing pragmatic hopefulness.

In fact, none of these is our goal. Readers of this book will find that we offer GenAdmin not as a homogeneous identifier, an essentialization of any set of characteristics, or a polemical suggestion, but as a theorization—a concept for the WPA community at large, a core philosophy that can actually be mobilized in spite of (or because of) the complexities of our different roles, and a movement towards a new kind of agency for those who do WPA work. We hope this book will be useful for its larger philosophical breadth. We hope it will be read and valued by people who didn't originally self-identify as WPAs according to stock definitions of power and profession, but who recognize in administration a vital intellectual identity—one that is never only parlayed into serving the immediate needs of particular tasks, courses, or programs.

Ultimately, we theorize administration as an open identity that is (we hope) more productive than some of the narratives that have shaped our field. The narratives of grief, fear, victimization, extraordinary empowerment, and heroism that have helped us to understand the evolving WPA experience are not unproductive in themselves, but neither are they always told with the intention of enacting discursive power, shared understanding, or change. Like others before us, we reject the dichotomous thinking that posits WPAs as either administrators or intellectuals. But a rejection does not fully justify how and why this dichotomy is unnecessary. In the same way that Christy Desmet elides the "accommodation-resistance" (40) binary among new teachers in a writing program, we hope to elide a rhetoric-administration binary among all program participants that causes them to position the classroom, the WPA, the students, the teachers, and the curriculum in static positions that shape not only their work, but also their identities. Where this binary operates, it usually implies that, by virtue of our filling a role, we must stand in for a subset of ideologies that others assume the role carries with it. We also see this binary at work whenever professional rhetoric and composition identities are formulated at the exclusion of other personas, rather than understood as preparation for "adopting myriad and shifting professional personas" that our roles may need us to take up (Anderson and Romano 3).

SITUATING GENADMIN HISTORICALLY

Reading through the past fifteen years of literature in WPA scholarship, we see assertions of writing program administration as a legitimate discipline in the twentieth century and the recognition in the twenty-first century of writing program administration as a protean and diverse discipline.[3] We also see a good deal of attention paid to the WPA and an emphasis on sharing experiential narratives. Such writings often consider how issues of power, authority and responsibility intersect and diverge, often related to the existence of untenured WPAs and a lack of disciplinary recognition and respect from administrators and colleagues within and beyond our "home" departments. The identities of WPAs have evolved to include an understanding of the multiple roles and personas a WPA might adopt—and adapt differently in different situations—to succeed on the job. As a discipline and an endeavor, writing program administration is marked regularly as a space of tension—between crisis and change, discord and direction, promise and peril—because of the political, ethical, and programmatic challenges of both being an endeavor attached to a simultaneously poorly respected discipline and one that involves stakeholders with varying degrees of commitment to this discipline and its theories, practices, and interests. With the WPA often at the center of these tensions, the notion of the WPA as a change agent, established by Susan McLeod in 1995, has coalesced into a professional totem, though what that entails is varied and complex. These evolutions position writing program administration as a particularly rich site for institutional change and the WPA as a catalyst of change. For the five of us, one circumstance of our inherited WPA identity, and one impetus for ongoing change, has been the underlying conviction that our work is creative, intellectual, and has activist potential within and beyond our programs. In committee meetings we find ourselves regularly trying to creatively reform beliefs and practices about writing and writing instruction that have currency on our campuses and in our departments. We rhetorically frame data so that different stakeholders will support our program developments because of their extra-programmatic concerns and values. We invent and experiment with new feedback strategies that bridge our understanding of best practices with local student needs, values, and anxieties. When we create public events around the work our students and teachers do, we try to shift the culture of degree requirement into a culture of intellectual accomplishment. Even upholding program policies and negotiating student-instructor disagreements demands creative and intellectual efforts that may in fact lead stakeholders to new understandings. And these programmatic acts keep aggregating to create new, hopeful representations for employers, parents, public organizations, and more about what exactly it is that we do in writing programs. It is the conviction behind these examples that caused us to seek out jobs with different iterations of programmatic responsibility right away, and we see this coalescence of conviction and artistic action as an interesting historical moment to explore.

In *Resituating Writing: Constructing and Administering Writing Programs*, editors Joseph Janangelo and Kristine Hansen collect arguments that claim, from multiple angles, that the administrative work of WPAs is an expression of disciplinarity. GenAdmin follows this argument in new directions, largely because we represent a generation of administrators who became administrators in this climate of professionalization, who chose writing program administration as a career pre-tenure, or who became interested in writing program administration as an intellectual pursuit. In other words, our WPA disciplinary identification is strong, though our discipline still contends with those who see administration as purely managerial and entrepreneurial. Texts such as Stuart C. Brown and Theresa Enos's *The Writing Program Administrator's Resource* and Irene Ward and William J. Carpenter's *The Allyn and Bacon Sourcebook for Writing Program Administrators* mark the disciplinary terrain Janangelo and Hansen's collection explores, establishing guideposts that offer handy resources for practicing WPAs, particularly new WPAs seeking knowledge from authorities in the field to help them solve problems and gain background knowledge in the diverse disciplinary terrain. Additionally, Brown and Enos's collection extends the conversation of WPA disciplinarity by emphasizing the importance of WPAs adopting a reflective stance towards writing program administration, something the five of us have thoroughly embraced as an important methodology for making sense of our WPA experiences (as teachers, scholars, activists, and researchers). Each of these texts argues, in different ways, that writing program administration is its own discipline, one marked by thoughtful planning, problem solving, communication, and reflection.

Shirley K Rose and Irwin Weiser's *The Writing Program Administrator as Theorist* extends the recognition of writing program administration as scholarly to "develop our professional understanding of the role of theory in writing program administration" (1). "Raised" as we were studying rhetorical and literary theory, this discussion of how WPAs develop and use theory and theorizing is an inherent part of our educational history and positioning, for it confirms our understanding that writing program administration is not just something that we do; rather, it is something we think about, write about, and live. *Discord and Direction: The Postmodern Writing Program Administrator*, edited by Carolyn Handa and Sharon James McGee, focuses on postmodern theory and how it impacts writing program administration, particularly given the claim that composition studies "sides itself more with modernism" while postmodernism "aptly characterizes the world in which WPAs must function every day" (2). Their collection considers how postmodern actions, like challenging hierarchies or resisting master narratives (Handa and McGee 2), play out in the context of writing program administration to determine how WPAs and their programs can move from discord to direction. McGee and Handa's position is a thread that informs our entire collection, for in arguing that WPA work, and GenAdmin in particular, is a becoming, we negotiate the theoretical tensions between what we want for our programs and the environment in which our programs exist.

Current WPA research adds to this rich body of work that has established writing program administration as a theory-based discipline in its own right by exploring the ways that WPAs enact their identities, problematize their work and role as administrators, and chart new paths toward pragmatic, ethical program leadership. In *The Activist WPA: Changing Stories about Writing and Writers*, Linda Adler-Kassner identifies the need for WPAs to link ideas with strategies to reframe the predominantly negative stories about writing and writing instruction that circulate publicly, drawing largely on principles and practices related to grassroots organizing. Moreover, Adler-Kassner cites *tikkun olam*, a Jewish practice of "healing and restoring the world," and prophetic pragmatism as motives and means that guide her activism as a WPA (169). Like Adler-Kassner, studying identities and ethics motivates and grounds our own work, although we focus more closely on academic WPA communities because we also see a need for activism and reform within these contexts. We value Adler-Kassner's call to shift frames, a move we also make, though our focus is more often on changing the stories WPAs tell about themselves.

A reading of the essays in Theresa Enos and Shane Borrowman's *The Promise and Perils of Writing Program Administration* causes us to reconsider the belief that writing program administration is a discipline built on solid ground. This collection offers survey data about WPAs and their living/working conditions and situates WPAs as caught between tensions related to a disrespect of our disciplinarity and jobs that entail large responsibilities but little authority, largely because of the number of untenured WPAs. An important argument

Skeffington, Borrowman, and Enos make is that writing program administrators need to extend their understanding of the legitimacy of writing program administration beyond their sphere or work: "we have convinced ourselves that writing program administration is legitimate, important, and theoretical work. We now need to convince faculty members in our departments, colleges, and across campus" ("Living" 19). The tensions that WPAs negotiate, they argue, are often the source of much peril, but also create the possibility for much promise. Debra Frank Dew and Alice Horning's recent collection, *Untenured Faculty as Writing Program Administrators: Institutional Practices and Politics*, more fully explores the ethics and politics of jWPA positions, a discussion close to our hearts and minds as we all hold or have held WPA positions as graduate students and as pre-tenure faculty. This collection begins to re-landscape writing program administration in significant ways, and our work responds to their concerns, for we go further to disrupt accepted WPA narratives and frameworks that claim that jWPAs should not ever take on WPA jobs, a stance that the five of us find to be practically untenable and philosophically limiting given the many complications related to job choice.

Virginia Anderson and Susan Romano's collection, *Culture Shock and the Practice of Profession: Training the Next Wave in Rhetoric and Composition*, turns a critical lens on the position of WPA by examining how the decisions WPAs make and the philosophies they enact as WPAs, combined with the changing issues of disciplinarity and professionalization happening in the field, challenge rhetoric and composition graduates' identity development, practices, and beliefs about graduate student preparation. As a whole, the book critiques "luck-of-the-draw, true-grit" professional narratives in favor of rhetorical understanding (2). In their introduction, Anderson and Romano characterize the essays in this collection as "ask[ing] implicitly and explicitly for preparation in *rhetorica utens*, in the arts of deploying disciplinary knowledge and the skills of establishing relationships and ethos, from programs that have listened to and acted on news from the field" (3). We likewise use critique to construct new thinking about our profession. In this book, we build not only on "news from the field" to develop our arguments, but also on our collective (though disparate) experiences as WPAs in order to establish GenAdmin as an identity that includes, among other things, *rhetorica utens* and the notion that taking on shifting identities rather than seeking a fixed positioning is not only strategic (Anderson and Romano 3) but also a part of how we understand and experience identity.

In Lynn Z. Bloom, Donald A. Daiker, and Edward M. White's two edited collections on twenty-first century WPA identities—*Composition in the Twenty-First Century: Crisis and Change* and *Composition Studies in the New Millennium: Rereading the Past, Rewriting the Future*—the various chapters complicate a new WPA role and WPA work in the market-driven university by revitalizing their convergences with and their divergences from composition studies on issues like disciplinary origins, epistemology, and methodology. Framed around questions explored at an October 1993 conference by the same name, the first volume focuses on crisis and change by anticipating the kinds of practical and theoretical re-definitions that WPAs will need to make, not only to understand and teach the discipline but also to identify stakeholders in the discipline and what that identification means, to rethink assessment, to ask questions about politics, to understand and enact activism, and to consider how research will affect teaching. The second volume, shaped very much by the shadow of the September 11 attacks on the World Trade Center and Pentagon, offers multiple readings of composition's past in order to compose arguments for the future. In these collections, the editors and their contributors were as focused on an historical moment as we are now.

We build on the promises of texts like these because doing so yields a more complex understanding of WPA identity and disciplinarity. Most recently, Donna Strickland and Jeanne Gunner's *The Writing Program Interrupted: Making Space for Critical Discourse* examines where WPAs have been, where they are, and where they are going in their abilities to critique the cultures, discourses, and subjectivities that ensue, reminding us again of the critical urgency to locate the WPA among vital and current theoretical dilemmas. Where previous work helped WPAs to see and rely on "admin" as a position, GenAdmin views administration as an orientation towards creating new conditions and, hence, for choosing the work. Rather than replace "admin" in our work, we hope to define it more robustly.

These texts, and any number of articles from the pages of our journals, especially *WPA: Writing Program Administration*, have been instrumental in the development of writing program administration as theory, as practice, as scholarly pursuit. Although these are not the only texts that have influenced the disciplinary emergence of writing program administration or our own beliefs as WPAs, we cannot underscore enough their importance in establishing writing program administration as a scholarly discipline in creating a body of texts, establishing research methods (narration, theorizing, reflecting, studying local practices and programs to offer useful generalizations), and in imparting means of constructing and revising programs rhetorically and thoughtfully.

Changing Perceptions About Administration

Our intent is not to talk back or aggressively reject criticisms that are directed towards our perceptions of WPA work, mainly because these are no longer the only speech acts that have shaped our thinking, but also because we are well aware of the diversity of our mentoring and training—that where we are is a direct result of the committed and longstanding work of many people in writing program administration specifically and in rhetoric and composition more broadly. As GenAdmin, we position ourselves within the dimensions of a broader evolving WPA identity that has been shaping the field since Donald Bushman's recasting of the WPA as humanist intellectual in "The WPA as Pragmatist: Recasting 'Service' as 'Human Science,'" including the WPA as activist, scholar, and change agent. Although in Chapter 4 we discuss the inefficacy of laying claim to metaphors, we realize that the evolving WPA role has been critical to our identity study. Furthermore, we invite extra-academic connections, again because of how related roles have challenged stable definitions of WPA work.

To clarify, this book is not a statement of identity or an essentialist manifesto, a simple acknowledgment that the tenor and shape of the job is changing, therefore so must we, or a confession of entitlement, difference, or being caught unawares. This book is an exploration of WPA identity in the twenty-first century; an identification of GenAdmin as a subject position for WPAs in the twenty-first century; a narrative of choice, hybridity, and/or emergence; an opportunity to locate WPA work within larger systems of activity and to reinvent the parameters of those activity systems; and an occasion to disrupt some of the binaries that have caused tensions between how past, present, and future WPAs perceive one another to work and to think, perhaps even to help them arrive at a more nuanced understanding of one another's positionings in the field. In taking up the questions posed by our Prelude, we arrive at the following understanding of GenAdmin: it is an always emergent identity, a position from which we can destabilize and disrupt prevalent binaries in writing program administration scholarship to, consequently, represent and enact administration as rhetorical theory and philosophical practice.

CHALLENGING HISTORY AND "DOING PHILOSOPHY"

At this point it is useful to mention that in challenging perceptions about administration and in clarifying the purposes for our book, we both build on and build away from Jacqueline Jones Royster's idea of "disciplinary landscaping" for rhetoric and composition. On the one hand, we recognize that knowledge in rhetoric and composition studies (in writing program administration, specifically) is an interpretive enterprise and social construction ("Disciplinary" 149) that can be collectively "historiciz[ed] based on new perceptions" and "reenvision[ed] . . . in more dynamic ways" ("Disciplinary" 163). Royster makes this point in the context of challenging rhetorical history to disrupt the understanding that African women's rhetorical participation began in the nineteenth-century United States when we can reasonably situate it three to five centuries earlier by being more inclusive with our collections across genre, space, and time—more inclusive of the terms of their "participation" ("Disciplinary" 151). It is useful to remember that historical situatedness is a matter of geospatial location and rhetorical context, and not merely of temporality. On the other hand, we suggest alternatives to or disruptions of the perpetual mapping and landscaping metaphors that probably inspired Sidney I. Dobrin to charge the discipline of writing program administration with having "foregone the freedom of space in favor of a guarded conservatism to protect its place" (57). That is, of being so preoccupied with legitimation and place that it has "renounced not only critical perspectives of its work . . . but has succumbed to a false security bound up in a mythology of administrative power that fails not only to question the very safety of that place but to deny the potential critical, theoretical, and political work that can be done beyond the borders of WPA-place" (Dobrin 57-58). Whereas maps and landscape images can serve to fortify borders and boundaries (to totalize or imperialize), we disrupt and make more fluid these boundaries as spaces and places to move towards as we chart out new epistemologies for our work.[4]

Even in our theorization of GenAdmin as a disciplinary identity, we aim to reasonably disrupt the various histories that GenAdmin inherits as well as to consider how such an identifier challenges (or stretches or expands) "disciplinary" history. Like Royster, the larger point we make is that when you shift rhetorical subjects and challenge perceptions, you can reform disciplinary histories beyond geographic and historical scope ("Disciplinary" 152) towards a more nuanced recovery of both self and history. But unlike Royster, we do not strive for self-and-historical recovery as much as we provoke what have traditionally been seen as stringent theoretical (and historical) divisions that limit perceptions of our work. In other words, rather than unsettling past narratives of WPA work so as to more accurately say what GenAdmin is, we strive to enact what GenAdmin does, and to redefine the terms of this en/action in the process.

This move in turn puts a compelling question to our book: What are our explicit interventions in WPA's theory and history if we do not wish to re-landscape, correct, or totalize in return? What does it mean for us and for GenAdmin to "theoretically disrupt"? In her article "Sp(l)itting Images," Karen Kopelson poses a similar question, asking readers that if theory need not be applicable, if it need not be justified as a mode of inquiry, and if in fact there is no real need to overcome the theory/practice split (or what she calls the "use/do" divide) (764), then what are requisite roles for praxis in rhetoric and composition? While practice need not be consciously informed by theory, praxis, or "action *driven by* and *resulting from* theory" (Kopelson 764), it necessitates a more urgent recognition of a theory/praxis split, since practice is an "explicitly theorized, politicized intervention" (Kopelson 764). To make this new errand explicit, Kopelson argues for a redefinition of "terms such as action, intervention, service, and use" (765), a movement that aligns with how we see GenAdmin praxis being taken up.

Although we may be less concerned than Kopelson's subjects that our discipline will be seen as a user-doer-producer for others, rather than as a producer of our own knowledge field, we do benefit from Kopelson's characterization in five dimensions of what she calls a "living rhetoric and composition" (775). We extend these five dimensions towards GenAdmin to consider the tenets that make GenAdmin a living philosophy and that differentiate it from other theoretical subject positions. First, a living philosophy aligns action, intervention, service, and use with politicized intervention rather than with group identification. Second, it links identity to becoming rather than to stability, where participants may be defined less by the spaces they occupy than by how they move between and among them. Third, it is productive—it makes itself, feeds on itself, could itself be seen as a field rather than as in servitude to some other field. Fourth, it relies on both the study of and deployment of language uses, in turn acknowledging the significant role of discourse in its enactments. Finally, it offers a spaciousness around which "an array of disciplinary inquiries and pursuits might best coalesce" (Kopelson 772), including those concerned with ethics and change.

At the heart of a living philosophy we see an illumination and enactment of principles that can themselves carry meaning as useful abstractions, and a flexibility to imagine and respect other people's truths even as we pursue alternatives. Thus, we do not posit that none of the difficulties raised by our critics is unprecedented or real. However, we do argue that these difficulties create vital gaps in WPA theorizing that push us to reject helpless notions of power for more helpful notions of disciplinarity and agency. They also push us to embrace the non-universality of our experiences without arriving at an unproductive, unpragmatic, relativistic set of principles from which to practice.

Even still, this philosophy has its limitations. It need not stand in for perfect understanding, perfect rhetorical persuasion, or universally accepted principles of program management—hallmarks of the analytic philosophical tradition rather than a more feminist epistemology that privileges context and subjectivity. It may be a universal enough assumption to acknowledge (by now) that our lives would be easier in some ways if we were not WPAs. However, an overarching value of GenAdmin for us isn't finding ways to make things easier day to day, but rather making ways to build the discipline by negotiating daily realities in the enactment of rhetoric and writing, whether or not those realities directly pertain to the construction and maintenance of a college writing program. In an attempt at re-orientation and enactment, we have arranged this book around six chapters that both describe and argue for an administrative philosophy embodied in a new generation of writing program administrators by addressing interrelated questions about WPA identities and actions. Both the conflation of rhetoric and composition with writing program administration, and the positioning of them as subsets of English studies are, we think, serious problems; as much as possible, the reader will find that our philosophy elides either conflation or subjugation in favor of other positionings, as we use narrative, reflection, and theorizing to study WPA identities and provide examples of how this theorizing impacts the work that we do.

In so doing, the five of us assign new meaning to the narratives we inherit to articulate our understanding of WPA work within the context of new identities and experiential realities in order to build new knowledge about WPA identities and work. This book follows discussions of how we, as writing program administrators, and as teachers, scholars, spouses, parents, gamers, painters, foodies, hikers, yogis, crafters, birdwatchers, and more explore such questions as, *Who do we think we are?*, *How do we conduct our work?*, and *What difference can that make?* Because those discussions involved tracking our movement between past, present, and future locations and our positioning in those locations, each chapter in this book represents one of these locations or positionings, even as it articulates how a GenAdmin philosophy repositions us.

In organizing the book, we found no perfect ordering to the chapters, as each chapter is a bit of a microcosm of what was, is, and can/should be. Even so, the order of our chapters is best described as a movement from past to future in terms of how GenAdmin relates to the domain of writing program administration. In Chapter 2, we illustrate the ways in which GenAdmin both inherit and challenge the conventional history of WPAs and their work by problematizing the perception of WPAs who take the job before tenure through a historical re-interpretation of WPA beliefs. We respond to and reframe the negative victim narratives that have shaped the field of WPA studies so consistently. We discuss how history and disciplinary memory influence writing program identities and work, for all program participants and stakeholders, and we begin to address the question of why this philosophical practice is sustainable day to day.

In Chapter 3, we consider how GenAdmin is prepared for its work, focusing specifically on what WPA education looks like now and what it might look like in the future. We discuss the fear of professionalization grounded in a limiting suspicion of managerial specialization, the processes by which we studied or trained to *become* WPAs, and a possible future for disciplinary professionalization. We also consider what it means to be marked by multiplicinarity and the possibilities that WPA education affords our various roles.

In Chapter 4, we discuss various iterations and implications of seeing ourselves as people in the process of becoming WPAs, and how withholding fixed identification affects theorizing, collaboration, training, and the value of expertise. This chapter performs a detotalizing of certain binaries, especially labels like s/j/gWPA, which we eschew for their association with tasks and preset identifiers. In disrupting staid and hierarchical notions of expertise, we better realize that the contexts in which those hierarchical relationships first emerged have changed and are changing. The same structures aren't in place to support this kind of master/learner relationship; thus the relationships are being reconfigured.

In Chapter 5, we consider another turn in WPA theorizing by presenting GenAdmin discourse as inherently rhetorical and pragmatic (which we in turn understand as temporal, contextual, and shifting). This chapter explicates what we have come to understand as the arts of discursive participation, focusing on redefinitions of *pragmatic activism*, *civic discourse*, and *communicative ideology* as essential components of how we further our work. GenAdmin discourse occurs at the intersection of three areas: feminist rereadings of classical American pragmatism, rhetorical theory, and discourse studies. At this intersection, we find new models for enacting a discursive power—rather than settling between the dichotomous models of centered/managerial power and decentered/shared power—in order to participate in ideological conversations where our institutions might see or feel them the most quickly and urgently.

We end the book with a chapter that helps us consider GenAdmin philosophies for retheorizing other aspects of the university and profession. In Chapter 6, we offer a concomitant ethics for GenAdmin that relies on hope as a collective and critical endeavor. Part of theorizing a GenAdmin identity for WPAs means replacing stories of reluctance, disappointment, default, or defeat with those of *eudaimonia*, or flourishing. A GenAdmin identity helps the five of us to construct and enact an ethics that recognizes our potential as change agents and reflects our desires to have a productive impact on our worlds. This ethics is characterized by agency and by a reconsideration of responsibility as more than a set of tasks attached to a job description but rather as part of a scholarly, administrative ethic. While we respond to the daily challenges or practical demands of the job (and try to come up with ways to solve them), it is not this practicality that drives us as much as it is a desire to do the job humanely, creatively, reflectively, and critically.

CONVERSATIONS AND INTERLUDES

Because this is in every way a collaboratively written book, we do not present a singular perspective about the philosophy or practice of WPA. In fact, the five of us are a small model of dissensus in action. We agreed to write together, to work through ideological differences and to challenge each other's definitions, in order to try to arrive at something *after* understanding. One dimension of our interactions that a coherent theoretical text cannot replicate is the dimension of anecdotal dialogues or the power of narrative. As five friends, colleagues, and collaborators working on a book project, we have talked at length through email, extended conference meetings, and document creation and revision activities using interfaces like Google Docs. The consequence of these dialogic sessions is the interstitial philosophy and explication that is *the* book—one voice derived from many. But we do not want to lose the flavor of our differences and dialogues and how individual anecdotes lead to ingenious connectivity and invention, especially since these dialogues are a major force in keeping our ideas in oscillation rather than stagnation.

One way we juxtapose the necessary univocality of our book with dialogue is to include shorter extended illuminations or interludes between the major chapters where we have noted fault lines in our theorizing. These interludes are culled from a range of texts to (1) serve as interesting and thought-provoking bridges between chapters and their main ideas and (2) illuminate the way that GenAdmin enjoy thinking and rethinking about the daily issues we face. In the development of this book, we noted particular hotspots or contact zones regarding the complexities of *choice*, *expertise*, and *empathy*; the definitions and ways of *strategizing* in WPA work; and the practice of *productive advocacy* in the administration of higher education. In contrast to the rest of the book, each interlude is singly voiced and individually written (or compiled in the case of the first interlude "On Choice") to represent how one of us has navigated a contact zone by theorizing individual experiences. We have left the authors of the singly voiced interludes unidentified to keep the emphasis on the individual experience while demonstrating the near arbitrariness of the narrative "I."

While working on this book, we also began circulating Flip Ultra HD video cameras to WPAs and those with WPA interests around the country in order to collect responses to the questions driving our book in a kind of unscripted and aggregating conversation. We have created a supplemental website (www.sites.google.com/site/assemblageproject) where we have been and will continue to collect and index these clips. We call it *The Assemblage Project* to connote any number of texts, objects, or pieces gathered into a single set and context. This site will allow us to illuminate the book's text with particular videos or sets of videos that extend conversation on an idea or topic. As a public site, other contributors will also be able to create original assemblages for any number of projects. Our purpose, other than experimenting with new ways of collecting and connecting knowledge, is to put our questions and ideas into play with a larger set of voices by creating an archive of interaction, providing either a quick entrance to the conversation or a more extensive source for research by our colleagues. Such a dialogical practice is commensurate with our understanding that GenAdmin, both as a working identity and a philosophical practice, never rests. As we live out the theorizing of GenAdmin, it remains explicitly under construction, allowing for the connections, inventions, and unforeseens we thrive on.

Interlude

On Choice

Jonnika: I live with the desire to both fit in and be different. I left my home and parents to go back to graduate school, picked up and moved with Colin and our then-two-year-old son Ian over eight hundred miles away to a place that, compared to where I had spent the last twenty-six years of my life, was cold, gray, and huge. It was an extremely difficult choice to make, one I agonized over for the first few years of school, but one I knew would make a significant change in the trajectory of my professional life. But it was the reason I was leaving almost everything I knew and it was breaking my parents' hearts, so I clung to a vision of myself as a WPA as a way to justify my choice to move.

I like to think about the big picture, and I love the viral potential of doing administrative work. It must be linked to my desire to do something big with my life, always seemingly unfulfilled, that makes me want to be a WPA, a *real* one, a *respected* one. I had been the interim writing center director at the university where I got my MA, and while I knew my colleagues had confidence in me, I also knew they wanted the position to be tenure-track, which meant I would not be able to keep it. I had to go back to school. I chose my graduate program because of its secondary area in WPA, and I immediately embraced what that program had to offer—a commitment to the intellectual nature of WPA work. I knew that was my path towards respect.

Colin: While Jonikka defined and chose a path for a PhD, I went along for the ride. I knew I wanted to teach writing, and I knew that, unlike a range of couples we would meet in our doctoral program, Jonikka and I would be together, working together, even if I eventually went outside of academia for a job. So moving to Indiana, for me, wasn't a choice I ever had to make. But I did choose to have a programmatic voice, even though I struggled with the definition of rhetoric and my role in a rhetoric and composition program for many years. And that started from day one when I met with our incoming graduate student mentor group. Shirley K Rose asked us pretty directly, "Why are you here?" I couldn't answer that question, and she bugged me about it until I could. In fact, she kept asking until I had incorporated it into my internalized reflections, my ways of thinking about teaching and learning, about being anywhere.

At the time, I didn't know that asking such a question would lead me to learn about an area connected to administration. But that word wasn't a bad word to me. I think I was in middle school when my dad was promoted to being in charge of a lab at a government contractor, and I remember his prep-work including reading Miyamoto Musashi's *The Book of Five Rings*, which I read in turn. Such a self-education taught me several things about what my dad called management: (1) administration doesn't circumvent creativity and should in fact stimulate it; (2) assessment isn't useful or relevant if you can't give a five (on a one to five scale) to your people—it's just a rationalization for financial choices that will be made at an administrative level higher than yours; and (3) interdisciplinary reading should increase exponentially with your pay-grade, while management-related trend texts were barely worth a library card and a quick read for main points. In short, a classic book on the way of the samurai can be quite a relevant read for anyone in a position of authority and responsibility if you're not asking questions you already have the answers to.

Amy: Like Jonikka, I'm a big picture-thinker and I'm a planner. I like to think about what could be and what has to happen in order to make the *could be* what *is*. While I like thinking about and reading theory, I'm a practical person by nature, and WPA work gave me the chance to take the theories of rhetoric and composition and put them into practice in ways that supported student writers and their teachers. To me, it felt like work that mattered. I could see the outcome of my writing and thinking as a WPA that I couldn't see if I tried to imagine myself as a *theorist*. I don't support the theory-practice divide that seems to pervade much of the field because I think that writing program administration is a blending of both, but I was drawn to WPA work because of its practicality—it suited my interests and strengths and my desire to contribute to the programs in which I work. I'm also a collaborator; I work best when I can talk through ideas with others, and that seemed to be a particular offering of WPA studies. This could be because I was doing my work in a big program with lots of WPAs who worked closely together, so I saw the collaborative work environment I desired modeled by the faculty in my program. Taking what I knew of myself and what I wanted and how I worked best, I really didn't see any other option than making WPA studies a central part of my graduate work.

Kate: For me, becoming a WPA never felt like a big, life altering choice but rather the unfolding of decisions and choices along the way that, while substantial, weren't a direct path to writing program administration. I chose to leave my first doctoral program because I felt a huge disconnect between my teaching and prospective dissertation research and wanted to spend more time teaching before outlining a research trajectory that would likely map my career. A few years later I chose to leave my high school teaching job because I understood many of my beliefs about teaching and felt driven to return to graduate school to earn the PhD that might make my beliefs about teaching and learning matter more than to a few sections of composition or literature classes, that might have larger impact on students stuck learning five-paragraph essays and thinking they have to guess what the teacher wants. I also went back because I knew that as a woman I didn't get listened to that much when it came to raising concerns about writing, agency, and gender in the high school I taught in. I wanted to have more influence on designing curriculum and helping students gain a sense of agency from learning about writing and rhetoric. As a doctoral candidate, I learned how WPAs use their disciplinary knowledge to design, develop, and teach curricula that engage students in thinking and learning in potentially powerful ways. My commitment to writing program administration became a commitment to rhetoric and often a commitment to reform.

Jonnika: During that first year of my PhD program, I took two WPA courses, and it was pretty clear to me early on that many of my peers were in those courses because they knew that one day they might *have to be* a WPA. Only a few of us were there because WPA work was our passion. That summer, I presented at my very first CWPA conference, and I began my paper, an argument for WPA professionalization, with a line that has been at the heart of my work ever since: "I choose to be a WPA." In that statement was the idea that drives this book for me. The fact that I *choose* to be a WPA, that I *am* a WPA even when I don't hold an official WPA position, defines a large part of who I am.

I took four WPA classes, I wrote a WPA dissertation, and when I went on the job market, I sought out WPA jobs. Advice to steer clear of those jobs until after tenure were deeply offensive to me since, emotionally, that advice registered as an affront to my worth as an academic, to my education and experience as a WPA, to my professional identity.

Kate: I never took any WPA classes, and I wrote my dissertation on the rhetorical canon of memory. Honestly, it didn't occur to me to write a WPA dissertation. I simply hadn't read enough WPA literature to realize I might want to make that choice. My doctoral institution was small, and we didn't have courses about WPA work. Instead, I came to WPA through service and my interest always in the big picture: I was the assistant director of the program, co-taught the TA practicum, and found I really liked teaching and mentoring teachers, and I wanted to make that central to my daily work. When I went on the job market the first time, I chose to apply for both WPA jobs and non-WPA jobs, and my first job cemented my WPA career. I'm not sure I could have chosen other than a WPA job and gotten it in a geographical region my partner and I wanted to live—the so-called more desirable route to tenure—but since I wanted a WPA job, I was happy to get one. And I really enjoyed working with TAs, collaborating with colleagues, and contributing to developing an undergraduate composition program. I wasn't advised to steer clear of WPA jobs, though I was advised to carefully consider the do-ability of any job. When I left my first WPA job, in part because it felt untenable—too big, too many worries that I couldn't get tenure because of its scope (I had worries of my own and didn't feel comfortable with other people's worries on top of my own)—and because we wanted to live in the west, I chose to step into an actually bigger WPA job—a directorship—at a smaller school. While we can never know what we choose when we choose a job, on that search I felt like I was choosing—a certain kind of WPA in a certain kind of school, in a particular place. I already had a job, and felt like I could choose a new one or stay at the old one. The first time on the market I felt like I had to take the best job offer rather than the best lifestyle choice for me.

Tarez: I was drawn to WPA coursework and projects because I enjoyed the kind of intellectual engagement they provided, had been a WPA prior to my PhD program, served as a gWPA in graduate school, and in many ways think like a WPA. I identify with the role and its potential for institutional and social reform because it seems like a natural outgrowth of (or parallel space to) my identity as a rhetoric and composition scholar and practitioner, not because I felt inclined to identify with a subject position or a group called WPA. Writing program administration problems and questions are the discipline's problems and questions, just as much as other theoretical or historical or methodological commitments become the shared property of us all. (Here, I don't mean to forward the argument that one is a sub-field of or supra-field to another, simply that I do not view my work in histories and theories of rhetoric and composition as cut off from the same intellectual onus that drives the work I do with course administration, TA mentoring, and curriculum development. And vice versa.)

This may be why I have been drawn to Generation Administration as a historical and geospatial identifier more so than to WPA as a label or a subject position. I did not leave my doctoral program hoping for a WPA job, but simply hoped and expected that I would continue to mentor teachers and develop curriculum in a dynamic program, at the hub of core issues and trends that shaped or disrupted the broader university context.

Amy: The WPA courses that I took as a graduate student taught me how to think like a WPA. I began graduate school with an interest in language and grammar (having spent two years working as a copy-editor for an investment company before beginning my PhD), and while my dissertation was about grammar instruction, it had a particular WPA bent, examining the ways in which decisions made by WPAs in TA training and curricular development push grammar out of the first-year writing curriculum. I could have focused my study on classrooms alone, but because I was trained to think like a WPA, I knew that what happened in the classroom was directly influenced by how a program was constructed, so for me, writing about grammar pedagogy necessarily meant that I had to talk to WPAs, too.

Colin: I was actually able, in retrospect, to overlap all of my final classes and my dissertation with programmatic questions that emerged for me as our writing program underwent a massive change from a two-semester sequence to a single five-hour course that had a serious rhetorical-technological dimension. I worked with professors, new teachers, and students at the undergraduate and graduate level to try to understand the dynamics we were putting in place, from conferencing to computer classroom pedagogies to my obsession with challenging expert-novice narratives of education in writing classrooms. Without taking any WPA classes (though I did occasionally peek at Jonikka's course packs) and with a position as a graduate mentor, WPA concerns emerged in all aspects of my doctoral experience. But this was in large part due to my desire and choice to work with particular people and not a connection to an area of study.

Jonnika: My relationship with the concept of choosing WPA has not always been an easy one. When I took my first tenure-track job, I still *felt* like a WPA, I *wanted* to be a WPA, but I wasn't *the* WPA, and that hurt my feelings. One of my new colleagues had taken on the WPA position in a pinch the year we came in, and while he certainly proved himself to be a capable steward of the program, his true interests lay elsewhere, and, emotionally, that was hard for me. I didn't take over the position for a couple of years, and in the interim, I had a bit of an identity crisis. If I wasn't the WPA, who was I? A WPA scholarly agenda, a strong WPA mentor, and WPA friends helped me see that my WPA identity was more complex than I had realized. I will always be a WPA no matter the circumstances.

Kate: At my current job, I am *the* WPA. I try to both resist and deploy the notion that *the* connotes for me—the only one. Technically, I'm not, as there is a Basic Writing Coordinator, a Composition Coordinator, a Writing Center Director, and an Associate Writing Center Director, all of whom are committed to their jobs. But I am the only one with a doctorate, the only one with a doctorate in rhetoric and composition. My love of collaboration also urges me resist the *the* even as I have invoked my role as it pertains to my responsibilities for writing and writing students and my disciplinary affiliation that shapes my beliefs and arguments on campus. I also resist the phrase because for many people it's seen in quite a reductive way, as little more than a manager of multiple composition sections and their teachers, mainly TAs and adjuncts. As *the* WPA, I'm also a WPA for life even though I imagine not being the only WPA because I think the WPA is too conflated with the program, and I want to see it diversify and entail more of a shared programmatic commitment. As the WPA, I'm in the position of needing to try to define and imagine what else that could mean.

Colin: I usually don't think about a class, a teacher, or a curriculum apart from a program. Makes for complicated negotiations, but I adopted the mantra *don't teach what you love* early on. That just leads to disappointment. I'd rather *teach what I don't know (yet)* under an umbrella or vision for the smaller pieces—like a first-year writing class—as a smaller part of a greater sequence. As someone obsessed with invention in senses beyond rhetoric and composition, I still can't function without a map. Some would say that explains why Jonikka and I are together. Anyone who goes off the reservation needs a map. But her involvement with WPA never seemed programmed. Our discussions always gave me a sense that, for my own personal style of teaching and philosophy of learning, I had to know about, think about, and live with the larger structures of power, persuasion, invention, and functionality that surrounded me in any job. My obsession with invention morphed into a desire to change what I perceived as detrimental dependence on expert-apprentice models for learning in rhetoric and composition. But you have to be in the administrative mix to change that particular dichotomy, or at least you have a better chance to promote significant change. So when I had an opportunity to coordinate developmental courses at my current university, I felt compelled to choose it, to become officially a teacher-scholar-administrator. But you really have to just keep adding hyphens, especially in terms of what I have come to see as GenAdmin. I have a willingness to engage, and a need to not rely on another class of people to take care of what I do or don't do in the set of classes I'm responsible for, in my classrooms, or in my writing.

Tarez: I think that what sets GenAdmin apart is its intellectual orientation to the work, i.e., having been brought up under the onus that one can do the work willingly, prepared, and excitedly, that doing the work is likely intrinsic to all the other dimensions of our selves, and that doing the work carries multiple forms beyond the lone writing program director. There is something exciting in the realization that what brings us together for the writing of this book—and what may have brought some of us together to do WPA coursework in graduate school—is our need to theorize and to articulate our theories as fundamental, not only to the daily operations of the courses or the programs we direct, but also to the epistemic fissures and openings that drive the field forward. There is also something hopeful about knowing that there do exist collaborative models for program direction, and that one need not always be *the* WPA to carry influence on campus. Before and throughout graduate school, it had always been my experience that the writing program was one of the most dynamic, fluid, and contentious systems of activity on campus. When its players were committed to that contention and oriented towards that dynamism, the work felt rewarding indeed.

Amy: The year that I applied for my current job, the university had two rhetoric and composition lines open—one for a rhetoric and composition specialist and one for a rhetoric and composition specialist who would be the WPA. At the time, I was in a non-tenure track WAC job at the institution where my husband had been offered a tenure-track job. WAC wasn't my forte, and at the time I believed I wanted a tenure-track job that didn't have administrative responsibilities, so I applied for the non-WPA rhetoric and composition job. Because of budget shortfalls, they were only able to hire one position, and although I didn't officially apply for it, they offered me the WPA job because of my experiences as the Assistant WPA in graduate school. I chose to take the job because I wanted to work toward tenure, and I knew that I could do the WPA work they required, but I was nervous about being *the* WPA before tenure. Now that I've been in the job for two years, I can't imagine not being *the* WPA (even though, like Kate, I don't like the article). I came in to the job while the university was in the midst of a major general education overhaul, one that necessitated a revised first-year writing course. I have been able to enact the curricular development, collaboration, and big-picture thinking that originally drew me to WPA studies in my job, and I feel fortunate that while I certainly have WPA tasks that seem, at times, managerial, I'm supported by my department in doing the intellectual work of writing program administration that I desire.

Jonnika: I feel like I have been the most adamant in pursuing the idea that what sets GenAdmin apart is our choice to be WPAs, but saying that doesn't mean that we do so blindly or that we will always choose to be *the* WPA at our given institutions. We know enough to make wise choices based on the information available to us. And we know the perils of WPA work—of any kind of meaningful work—but we choose to do our best to realize the potential of our individual contexts. I know that I don't want to be the WPA every day, but whether I am the official WPA or not, I will continue to think and act as WPAs do because that's how I see my professional world.

Kate: I find I often see choices by the choices I've chosen against. I chose not to be X or do X, which means I chose Y. That doesn't make Y a default choice, but a way of getting to Y by refusing to be or do X. I know what I didn't want, in other words. I didn't want a doctorate in literature. I didn't want a job focusing on technical and professional writing. I wanted a degree in rhetoric. I wanted to be a WPA. Of course, what we choose and how it works out doesn't necessarily match up. We choose careers and jobs with information we have at the time, and sometimes we realize our choices come with constraints we would not have chosen or possibilities we wouldn't have sought out. Choice for me is both agentive and strategic and somewhat imaginative and serendipitous. I make choices and not-choices to make my way in the world, but I'm cognizant of how choices might lead to limits but also open to how choices might liberate and inspire me. Part of my commitment to writing program administration derives from knowing I could do otherwise, but I choose to be a WPA.

Tarez: I guess the bottom line for me in how we're defining GenAdmin isn't "people who choose the work in spite of the consequences," but "people who do not see subjectivity as something that has to be overcome." So the notion of choice, for me is not a simple one or a moral one either, but requires much disruption beyond whether untenured junior faculty should take on WPA roles. Choices can be both freeing and constraining.

Amy: There are days, often those when I look at the calendar and mark the second consecutive week that I've been unable to turn my attention to my research, that I question my decision to be a WPA. I find it hard to balance my research and administrative responsibilities; though I receive incredible support for my research from my colleagues, I find myself more drawn to the work that allows me to engage with other people, which for me, is administrative. And there are days when I wish I weren't the WPA because then I wouldn't have to care about the curriculum or the position of adjuncts in the program or how to handle another grade appeal. I sometimes look longingly at my colleagues who spend hours writing in their offices, undisturbed by e-mail or meetings or decisions that need to be made. But I am the WPA because I care, and I find that I work better when I care about what I'm working for. My first job didn't engage me—people didn't fight about writing or pedagogy or curriculum because it wasn't a priority for them. I was left to work on my own, but I've realized, since I've changed jobs, that I need the emotional engagement in order to do my job well. I need people to want to discuss, and sometimes argue, about what is best for the writing program. I want to get worked up about the program, I want to be an advocate, I want to fight for what I believe is right. What I know now, though, is that emotional engagement takes its toll—psychically, intellectually, emotionally—but it also makes me present and engaged and allows me to do the intellectual work that is central to writing program administration. Caring about my job and the people I work with and the students we work for makes me a better WPA.

Jonnika: When I started writing about what choice has meant for me, I couldn't get a line from the first of the *Lord of the Rings* movies out of my mind. Arwen is telling Aragorn that she is not leaving Middle Earth with the other elves, that she is forsaking her immortality to be with him, and she says, "I choose a mortal life." Though our choices have been much less life altering and romantic, they have changed our paths in perhaps subtler, yet still significant ways, and they have led us to commit to think together about what it means to be a WPA and do WPA work. Our choices have led us here, to this moment, to this book, to these types of lives.

Tarez: I think our GenAdmin orientation bears a certain kind of responsibility—more specifically, the responsibility to look at whether and how our discipline has actually made writing program administration viable and feasible and fair in the institutional contexts in which we work. Like Kate, my own experiences before, during, and after graduate school tell me that we have not yet penetrated these institutional contexts sufficiently enough, ideologically enough, to make WPA work equitable everywhere. While visibility is important, making WPA work more visible isn't necessarily a panacea if there is no way to valuate the work. This is really nothing new, and in a way I merely echo how Andrea Lunsford has been challenging and encouraging rhetoric and composition (as a field) to look carefully at its positioning, to ask itself critically whether its gains represent the best kinds of progress— i.e., field status and recognition, collective vision, intellectual growth, and material support for writing programs—each time she is invited to speak at a national conference.

Colin: While preparing our first full manuscript for the book, I took on another administrative position. Because of shifts above me in positions, I was asked to take over the vice provost's responsibilities for university-wide program review, in part because of my work as chair of the program review committee at my university for two years. I was untenured and, of course, nervous about meeting with the new president to discuss this opportunity. But I never thought about not doing it, or how much time, energy, and expertise it would take. At some point in the meeting, he said that he expected the job to take 25%—and only 25%—of my time, and he would be fair in determining how that would affect my other responsibilities. I couldn't quite wrap my brain around the idea that this translated into two course releases (since course releases were being snatched back at a record pace), or that this would take away from my teaching or my writing and research projects. I write and teach and learn in almost every aspect of my work at a university. The distinctions between the types of work we do are, in the end, obstacles to invention, to making choices possible.

Tarez: I don't think it hurts us to consider whether we are enacting and promoting choice in the best possible way for the current health and future growth of writing program administration and of GenAdmin. For example, if our efforts to ensure compensation and an authoritative voice for the untenured WPA inadvertently create the expectation that a lower tier of WPA-laborers should not have access to these things (because they carry lesser roles), then we have not persuaded our departments or institutions of the long-term viability, reputability, and complexity of the work, or done our part to prove that it takes on many forms, and in all forms is difficult. If our need to relinquish ourselves from harmful "protective" measures keeping untenured faculty from playing *the* WPA role inadvertently cuts off other WPA-laborers from this protection when they do need it, then we have not increased our market value on campus. Instead, we may still be offering ourselves as too cheap a solution to the symptomatic problem that most university structures still lack an ideological space for valuating any kind of administrative work as substantive, intellectual, commensurate. We may be inadvertently making promises to ourselves and to other junior faculty that the work we do, if quantifiable and justifiable, will be enough to not only get us tenure but also to cause our colleagues to embrace us as intellectual partners, when in fact the more zealously we do the work, the less they tend to embrace us.

I don't think I am arguing that we should not do the work or should not choose to do it (mainly because I do the work and choose to do it well), but that we realize the opportunity for GenAdmin not only to complicate choice as a generational identifier, but also to heighten and deepen our understanding of all the players in our activity system whose lives and theoretical orientations are affected by our choices. We need to know what they need "choosing" to be. If we can pull it off, this interlude (and the larger book project it serves) may well represent a way of doing institutional critique—a way of pushing for greater ideological disruption. If GenAdmin does not do this, then who will? If GenAdmin cannot help position WPAs in alternative relationships than simply junior/senior, inside/outside, privileged/underprivileged, spoken for/spoken through, then what can?

2 Listening to and Rewriting History

> *When our present vocabularies prove inadequate for describing the world, a new vocabulary is necessary . . . [and] is the result of conscious questioning of the existing order. . . . [This] new vocabulary allows for different modes of expression than current language allows.*
>
> —Valerie Renegar and Stacey K. Sowards

As our experiences in the composition classroom have taught us, the problem of audience is a common one for those entering into an academic discourse community with well-established norms, patterns, and rules. The discourse patterns employed when writing about writing program administrator identity are fairly well illustrated by the titles of volumes that explore these issues, like *Kitchen Cooks, Plate Twirlers and Troubadours*; *The Promise and Perils of Writing Program Administration*; or *Untenured Faculty as Writing Program Administrators*. When we review these narratives and think of our own, the five of us imagine that if we could only find a metaphor to illustrate our experiences, we would have a way of talking about the work that reflects our lived experiences. If we could place ourselves on a continuum between two descriptive poles, either promising or perilous, we would have a foundation for our WPA identities. If we could define ourselves by rank alone, we would know how to place ourselves within the conversation. But because we think of our work—and ourselves as we do the work—more fluidly, there doesn't seem to be much space for our stories in the narrative patterns established by the field; our stories do not fit the existing narrative patterns. And we expect we're not alone in this thinking.

The work of this chapter, then, is to position GenAdmin within a context of history and inheritance, to attempt to carve a new narrative space for WPAs whose lives and work cannot be expressed easily in old metaphors, along binary continuums, or by the identification of rank. We seek a new vocabulary with which to discuss WPA work, its historical roots, and its potential to accommodate a wider range of views and experiences. We find agency in our historical positioning, which necessarily includes understanding how certain ideas have been taken up from past histories, reclaiming other ideas that have been neglected or left behind, and acknowledging the narratives we have inherited. We expose and come to terms with our own frustration at being viewed as naive or unprepared in understanding the kairotic moments that inspired past histories and stories. Most importantly, we offer a new way of imagining a history both collective and diverse in order to shed the notion that WPAs are victims and to create a new space for thinking about administration as capable of creating new conditions.

WPA Narratives as Situated Histories

Telling stories is a way of "doing history" (Lerner 199), and this narrative historicization becomes a useful site for the co-construction of WPA identities (Campbell, "Agency"; Howard, "Reflexivity"). Because they help establish norms and values that shape individuals' behavior and thinking within a community, narratives develop a shared history that functions as a touchstone for later generations as they negotiate their present and imagine their future. This imagining, in turn, gives individuals the opportunity to claim ownership over their own lives and experiences and empowers the community to exercise control over its own self-perception. In the ways that narratives "give messages and instructions; they offer blueprints and ideals; they issue warnings and prohibitions" (Stone 5), they offer powerful representations that legitimize certain ways of being in the world that shape who we were, who we are, and who we are becoming.

Storytelling has become an integral component of WPA professional life and identity, as conventional a part of scholarship as citing sources or participating on the WPA-L listserv. At the 2008 WPA Conference, Amy listened to the ways that presenters used storytelling to frame their public discourse about WPA work. Out of the eighteen speakers she attended (including four panels of three presenters each, and three plenary speakers), seventeen told stories in one form or another as a way to frame their scholarship. The prevalence of these stories may be explained by the fact that narratives provide WPAs an opportunity to move between theory and experience and to anchor the hermeneutic inside/outside moves Donald E. Hall describes in *The Academic Community: A Manual for Change*. As Thomas P. Miller notes, "Stories help us make the imaginative leap back and forth between our lived experiences and abstract speculations" (Anson et al. 80).

Stories may also help us move from isolated self-definition to a sense of shared community. As graduate students, Amy, Jonikka, and Tarez wrote professionalization narratives in their WPA seminars that were modeled on published narratives in the field. They each adopted a genre or metaphor that shaped their story—Amy wrote a fable and Tarez wrote a creation myth, while others wrote a fairy tale, a victim narrative, or a children's story. Given the opportunity to tell stories in their own way, seminar participants were able to articulate and share their experiences while also entering into a community—as both actor and listener—from which some members had previously felt excluded. Seminar participants drew on these narratives not as experts in each genre but as rhetoricians interested in how their composition provided insights into the communal values they tried to represent, whether certain genres best represented the epistemic potential of writing histories, and how the process of constructing narrative histories asked them to reconcile their "mixed heritages" and "complex pasts." These narratives were a discovery of how to proceed, and their writing revealed much about how WPAs can see and approach the labor of reconstructing their own intellectual migration. Their writing also revealed that professionalization narratives have great potential as an ethnomethodological practice that—in their construction and analysis—can align writing program administration with knowledge-making, especially by helping new WPAs or WPAs-in-training to understand and reflect on the work of writing programs as emergent, their role in them as productive, and their representations as situated and complex.[1] In a way, narratives position writers and readers as co-creators of productive knowledge, revealing how we use story in an ongoing maintenance of social order.

While narratives function in very particular ways for *members* of a given community, they can function just as powerfully for those *outside* of the community. Chris Anson's claim that "experiential narratives set up a Bahktinian multivocality that rarely leads to a sense of resolution" is apt here (Anson et al. 79). In the same way that we posit GenAdmin as a broader reaching philosophical practice, we do not just think about what we gain personally by telling our stories, but rather we consider how these stories could work in the world: What do our colleagues in other disciplines make of our stories? How do these narratives shape the understanding of the field for pre-service WPAs or graduate students? Are we perpetuating an administrative philosophy, a way of being and working, that limits new opportunities for thinking about administrative work? How do these stories include and exclude, liberate and oppress? The weight of these questions, and the implications of their answers for the future of the field, calls us to interrogate the narratives that have shaped our WPA community by critically examining *how* they are told, *why* they are told, and how and why they might be told *differently*. To that end, we offer a discussion of the different ways in which WPAs tell their stories with an eye toward understanding what these stories say about this community, our notions of our community's history, and the possibilities for its future.

A Spectrum of WPA Stories (or Beyond "The Promise and the Peril")

The available WPA narratives seem to fall within a spectrum that places the victor's story of success on one side (White, "Use It") and the victim's tale of suffering on the other (Bishop and Crossley, "How to Tell"; Bloom, "I Want"). These two poles offer very few avenues by which GenAdmin can enter into WPA discourse and claim authenticity: if we are successful WPAs, it is because we know how to read people and institutions and use the power we have. If we fail, it is because the system has in some way failed us. The extremes these two story types represent—the superabundance of power on the one hand and the lack of agency on the other—do not serve our visions of ourselves, and we're not sure they serve WPAs as agents in the twenty-first century, in part because they are so extreme.[2] Like other historians and theorists of rhetoric, we understand that what gives agency can also threaten it; that is, whatever is resource is also restraint (Campbell), and what some see as opportunity can be seen by others as impediment. Thus, examining the narratives we have inherited may help us to realize what aspects of WPA work and identity GenAdmin are compelled to adopt.

The Hero's Story

On one end of the spectrum, we have inherited the hero's story, demonstrating that when faced with seemingly impossible institutional constraints, colleagues, or budgets, the hero WPA perseveres. Edward M. White's 1991 article, "Use It or Lose It: Power and the WPA," offers a clear example of the hero's tale and the tropes such stories employ. White begins his narrative with a credible scenario: his writing-across-the-curriculum budget is cut in favor of other, more powerful departments, and while the Dean offers consolation in a "soothing" voice, he refuses to support the program or to support White as the WPA. By mobilizing his contacts, White is able to convince the new dean of undergraduate studies to take the WAC program under its umbrella (an umbrella with a more fluid budget), and, in so doing, he "discovered a kind of power that does not appear in flow charts, power that most WPAs have, and [he] was able to use it to save the program" ("Use It" 5). In this tale, White wields heroic power in defense of his program, and the experience taught him that in the face of adversaries who will not support writing instruction, writing programs, or WPAs, "only one answer will work: sheer power" ("Use It" 8). "It is futile to argue with them," he continues, "for you cannot pierce the hidden source of their beliefs. The most difficult part of being a WPA is combating those who have only scorn for our enterprise, for that means assessing and using the forces at our disposal" ("Use It" 8).

What is notable about White's argument is the extent to which he acknowledges WPAs' apparent lack of power. In his opening paragraph, he offers this exhortation: "Recognize the fact that all administration deals in power; power games demand aggressive players; assert that you have power (even if you don't) and you can often wield it" ("Use It" 3). Two important premises of White's argument are that power is owned and is inherently tied to outwardly aggressive acts, and that in order to be successful, the WPA must wield whatever power he has (or doesn't have) with a ferocity that matches the power department chairs, deans, provosts, chancellors, and presidents have through title and position alone. White's rally cry offers a seemingly more heroic solution than the victim narrative for WPAs under siege—if we use or create power when we feel we have none, we might be the victor of our story, successful in our efforts to save our program, our faculty, our students, and ourselves.

The Victim Narrative

On the other side of the spectrum, we have inherited the victim narrative detailing the situations of those WPAs who suffered at the hands of institutional whims, vindictive colleagues, tight budgets, or unrepentantly selfish teaching assistants. Lynn Z. Bloom's satirical "I Want a Writing Director," written in the style of Judy Syfer's iconic piece, "I Want a Wife," offers a victim narrative that exemplifies the genre. Writing in the voice of the exacting male department chair, Bloom describes the unreasonable expectations he has of his (always) female WPA: manage writing program faculty, establish curricular guidelines, handle student complaints, and care for colleagues. According to Bloom's chair, the ideal WPA is a female who "will keep the writing program out of my hair" (176). On top of the administrative responsibilities the chair asks her to assume, Bloom also explores the demanding expectations placed upon the WPA who not only has to manage the program, but also has to "meet [the] department's rigorous criteria for tenure," all the while remaining invisible, someone "who will not demand attention when [the chair is] preoccupied with [his] scholarly work, and who will remain faithful to [his] needs so that [he does] not have to clutter up [his] intellectual life with administrative details" (177).

We can only hope that Bloom's essay blends her experiences with stories other WPAs have shared with her, that it's not just one person's narrative of a good job gone horribly wrong. For many WPAs, at least one element of her narrative is familiar, and this sense of the collective, shared suffering Bloom describes allows us to tap into the comfort Bishop and Crossley describe when WPAs discover "that others share their experiences" (74). We can think, "If nothing else, at least we don't have it as bad as the WPA Bloom describes," but that positioning leaves unchallenged the assumptions about WPA work that the narrative perpetuates. While Bloom's narrative creates empathy in her readers, she concludes her essay with a vexing question: assuming WPAs were everything her fictional Chair hoped for, she wonders, "My God, who *wouldn't* want a Writing Director?" (178). Yet for some readers considering WPA work, this closing raises a different question: My God, who would ever *choose* to be a WPA?

Bloom's text may work in different ways for different audiences—for seasoned WPAs, it may elicit a knowing nod and a resigned sigh; for pre-service WPAs, graduate students, or non-WPA colleagues, it may raise warning flags about the nature of the work or the priorities of those who willingly take on the job. For GenAdmin, specifically, it reasserts the feminization of composition and the alignment of writing program administration with mere service, in turn reinforcing a research/service binary that we and others wish to disrupt.

Wendy Bishop and Gay Lynn Crossley's meta-narrative about their attempts to construct a story of WPA work highlights another feature of the victim narrative we wish to interrogate: bringing stories to voice in a discipline that is sometimes critical of the narrative form itself. Their text is a hybrid of journal entries, reflective response, and critical discussion that explores the ways in which Bishop, a principled WPA—one who is committed to developing a "'strong' writing program . . . staffed by teachers educated to work toward the objectives of a coherent, theoretically-informed, student-centered curriculum"—was silenced by her colleagues (Bishop and Crossley 71). When Bishop's attempt to preserve her "strong" writing program caused her to make administrative decisions that went against the graduate director's desires, her expertise was belittled and her influence ignored because her priorities were not in line with the department's or the university's. Not surprisingly, Bishop resigned early from her position, frustrated, exhausted, and alienated by the experience.

In an effort to comment on the institutional and political constraints that made their work almost impossible, Bishop and Crossley also include comments from early, anonymous reviewers of their essay who claimed that the authors (1) were naive to the critical distance, the separation of personal and professional lives, required of WPAs or (2) were simply telling "another victimization narrative that you hear so often in accounts of composition, WPAs, and even women WPAs" (74). Bishop and Crossley bristle at the critique, claiming they made efforts to avoid both of those criticisms, and yet their early readers still assumed they were either unprepared for the work or too self-affected to look critically at their own experiences.

The WPAs of Bishop, Crossley, and Bloom are destined for failure because of the expectations and constraints put upon them, a theme which highlights another function of the victim narrative in the construction of WPA identity from which GenAdmin hopes to dissociate. If we construct ourselves as victims, as hapless females or males unable to act on our own behalf, we are able to tell the stories of our failure without accepting professional responsibility or personal blame for those failures. This isn't to say that the overt reason WPAs tell victim narratives is to shirk responsibility or place blame, but it does illustrate the ways in which narratives about oppressive forces (whether they are institutional or individual) hold particular sway in academe. It may be the case for many WPAs that their training as progressive, open-minded academics leads them to side with, rather than blame, the victim, and while victim narratives certainly emerge as a way of naming the intellectual, personal, and professional violence done to us as WPAs, they also emerge as evidence of institutional power run amok, narratives told not just by WPAs or even English faculty, but faculty in disciplines across the university. The victim narrative justifies why WPAs are unable to succeed, and those justifications often go unchallenged within university culture writ large.

The narratives by White, Bloom, and Bishop and Crossley have shaped many WPAs' notions of what it means to be a WPA and do the work required of the position, and yet they present only one side of the story, one aspect of the job that does not take into account the many successes we have found at the institutional and disciplinary levels. Furthermore, they impose an unnecessary constraint on the generative potential of what narratives *can* do. Shirley K Rose and Irwin Weiser's edited collections, *The Writing Program Administrator as Researcher* and *The Writing Program Administrator as Theorist*, present different WPA stories, making a compelling argument about how much intellectual, rhetorical work writing program administration requires. Collections like these offer a welcome counterargument for those whose tenure committees would dismiss administration as service equivalent to other committee work, and their texts make the case that writing program administration is a valid site for scholarship, functioning as a theoretical response to the difficulties some WPAs discuss in their narratives of having people understand, respect, and acknowledge the work that they produce. Moreover, Rose and Weiser offer ways to reframe WPA identity as something not defined by a university or department, but rather by self-reflective inquiry.

The jWPA and the Advice Narrative

While many WPA narratives help to support the belief that significant work has been done to establish writing rogram administration as a serious, intellectual, legitimate field of study (and by extension, that those who labor as WPAs should be perceived as inquiring intellectuals rather than entry-level managers), the hero/victim spectrum invites different conclusions about the nature of writing program administration and the qualifications of those who do the work. One such conclusion, which some of us heard often as graduate students, was that an untenured faculty member should under no circumstances take on a WPA role, even if he or she had the requisite graduate preparation suggested by the Portland Resolution. Alice Horning's essay, "Ethics and the jWPA," exemplifies this kind of advice narrative that seeks to use other WPAs' experiences as the basis for generalized summaries of what WPA work is, who should do it, and how WPA tasks should be approached. For those pre-tenure faculty who still write, collaborate, and think like WPAs, yet who were strongly discouraged from *being* WPAs, these advice narratives may harm more than they help. They often write GenAdmin out of a job by reinforcing the stereotype that we are unprepared—intellectually, personally, and professionally—to take on a WPA role successfully, when they could focus collectively on how to rethink models of *protection* and *power* so that GenAdmin can more quickly (i.e., sooner in their careers) do what they were trained to do in graduate school, which is to think, talk, and write about writing programs.

We find ourselves in a fundamental disagreement with arguments that claim we should play it safe, and we find this rationale for not accepting jWPA positions to be paternalistic: "Just as no parent would give children a steady supply of treats just because kids want them, no administration should give junior faculty members writing program administrator positions just because new graduates want them, not withstanding their training, energy, and experience" (Horning 48). The subject position that these arguments create doesn't leave us much room to respond because our critique of these arguments can be dismissed as naïve, unaware, or unwilling to accept the gravity of life as a jWPA.[3]

In many ways, the tension we have just described that exists between generations of WPAs is mirrored by the often unspoken conflicts that exist between second- and third-wave feminists. In their book, *ManifestA: Young Women, Feminism, and the Future*, Jennifer Baumgardner and Amy Richards describe the ways in which critiques by third-wave feminists have been silenced—either by those in the second wave, or more problematically, by the third wave writers themselves—because the younger feminists are perceived to be "unmindful of [their] foremothers" (224). Baumgardner and Richards explain that in many feminist organizations, if a third-wave feminist critiques or problematizes the organizing practices, strategies, or conceptions of feminism promoted by second-wave feminists, then she runs the risk of being seen as someone who doesn't understand the lessons of the feminist movement and disregards the advancements the second-wave fought so hard to achieve.

Rather than participating in the conversation about how to be a feminist in the twenty-first century, Baumgardner and Richards note that many third-wave feminists feel they are not welcome in the conversation unless they toe the line. As Diane Elam noted, "Daughters are not allowed to invent new ways of thinking and doing feminism for themselves; feminists' politics should take the same shape that it has always assumed" (Baumgardner and Richards 224). In their own experience and their observation of others, Renegar and Sowards argue that many third-wave feminists feel disconnected from the feminist community because, while they acknowledge and enjoy the victories previous generations of feminists achieved, "our experience as feminists . . . leave us feeling angry, hopeless, and confused as to where we are supposed to go, how we are supposed to get there, and what battles we are supposed to wage as part of a feminist movement" (330). Members of GenAdmin may feel the same sense of frustration—as if caught between second-wave and third-wave goals and means. Now that some of the major WPA battles have been declared—arguing for WPA studies as part of the discipline of rhetoric and composition, fighting for clear job descriptions for WPAs, making the case that WPA studies is an intellectual pursuit—it can sometimes seem difficult to know what our next "declaration" can be on an organizational level. That is not to say there is no longer a need to keep fighting these battles, particularly with recession cutbacks. Yet, as we have discussed, these efforts begin to build a monolithic view of what *WPA* is (as an organization, a job, and an identity) that doesn't leave space for differing, resisting views.

We see this kind of stance in our discipline in moments when generational conflicts impede our efforts to build on the past and reimagine the future of WPA work. In his preface to *Untenured Faculty as Writing Program Administrators*, Edward M. White notes, "When a jWPA takes the job, the center of gravity shifts somewhat. The traditional tasks remain, but the younger faculty has less stake in tradition, in keeping things running as they have been, in exerting authority over the program. . . . The jWPA may be more interested in challenging than maintaining the way things are done" (Preface viii). White acknowledges a shift in the way WPA work is conducted by junior faculty, but his reluctance to embrace this shift whole-heartedly illustrates a tension that jWPAs feel as well: we are torn between the received wisdom of experts—much of which has been transmitted through narrative warnings—and our own experiences and hopes for ourselves as WPAs. But we also recognize in this quotation an assumption that tradition and maintenance are privileged terms and that changing may be viewed as merely disruptive rather than directed productively. Here, we see evidence of different values emerging between generations of WPAs, values that we have often learned from our mentors but are enacting differently as GenAdmin.

When we argue that there is space in the academy for untenured WPAs, we feel we are perceived as undercutting the argument that WPA work requires institutional and professional maturity that senior WPAs have, and we seem to show disrespect for the efforts of previous generations to gain institutional and disciplinary legitimacy for WPA work. When we make arguments in favor of a balanced professional and personal life, we are accused of promoting an "unattractive combination of disappointment and entitlement," just as Kristen Kennedy was for early drafts of her essay outlining the struggles she had in finding a career that satisfies her desire for both a meaningful professional and intellectual life and contentment in her personal life (527). In many ways, it would be much easier to stay quiet and follow the advice of our predecessors, and as Debra Dew points out in her discussion of the jWPA role, many young WPAs do subscribe to the party line, and their propensity for "groupie behavior" makes them "eager to flatter successful WPA professionals, both our local mentors, and national superstars, who deservedly appreciate the fawning of wannabe WPAs" (115). So when, as junior WPAs, we offer a different view of

WPA work and identity, we run the risk of appearing disrespectful to both our peers and our senior colleagues.

For those who have lived experiences similar to those outlined by the victim and hero stories we discuss, GenAdmin may resemble a group of upstarts who are unwilling to heed the advice generated by those stories. By no means are we arguing that all junior or all senior WPAs think in these ways; instead, we recognize an opportunity to articulate some of the tensions we have felt when accounting for our differences, tensions that have been brought out, in particular, by the binary narratives that have shaped the advice sometimes given to those who aspire to WPA jobs. We realize GenAdmin can fall into essentializing traps just as easily as any social movement or category, and we recognize that generational misunderstanding can go both ways, but our disappointment rests with arguments such as Horning's, which diminish the value of the jWPA, stop the dialectic conversation between different generations of WPAs and may cause our collective ideas about what it means to be a WPA to stagnate.

Although GenAdmin may, at times, feel reticent to contradict senior WPAs with whom we disagree, we still feel the necessity to consider new ways in which to tell WPA stories that resist the old binaries and create space to come to new understandings of WPA work for a generation of administrators who perceive new challenges for the field. These efforts shape, in part, our GenAdmin ethical stance as we work to develop a new vocabulary that resists assumptions about the field, since, just as in the feminist movement, when conflicts over WPA work "are viewed from a different perspective, a dialectic arises to connect the members of the various . . . factions" (Renegar and Sowards, "Liberal" 335). It is in this dialectic that we see opportunity to reach a new understanding of our shared history and to chart new paths for our collective future.

Promoting a Different WPA Narrative: The Resistant WPA as Historically Situated

As we have argued, conceptions of WPA work may have been built and perpetuated by victim and hero narratives, but these narratives do not paint a comprehensive picture of what it means to be a WPA. One way of seeking agency is in developing power within boundaries and constraints, in this case, looking to the resistant narratives in WPA history for a fuller understanding of the diversity of WPA histories, cultural memories, and cultural norms, even as the conditions surrounding our programs seem to stay constant (McLeod, *Writing*). In suggesting that these narratives resist "settled histories" and encourage alternative, localized renditions of what might otherwise become grand narratives that could limit our field, Richard Miller mentions the need to disrupt WPAs' interactions with each other, their institutions, and the discipline as a whole, to complicate the notion that composition work is merely the perpetual training of novices and newcomers ("From" 26). In doing so, Miller seems to suggest that writing program administration is upholding a master narrative that limits what we want to achieve as scholars. Rather than narrating our histories as stories of marginalization and struggle (what he deems the intellectual wasteland), he suggests reseeing (and rewriting) ourselves into the center of the university's intellectual sphere. His method is to adapt a discourse that builds our work as "resource-rich"—knowledge-centered, interdisciplinary, and deeply theoretical yet very public, even activist— and to perform for different audiences and organizational structures ("From" 37). In short, his goal is to challenge the rhetorical sovereignty of certain types of metanarratives by introducing a new vocabulary with which to discuss administrative history.

Miller works to reframe this vocabulary by linking writing program administration (and its history) with the discipline of composition, but a historical reading of writing program administration illustrates a new component of this vocabulary—the vocabulary of resistance. If we look at the history of composition, and the role that WPAs played in the evolution of the teaching of writing, we see that the history of the WPA is actually one of active resistance to (or in some cases, anticipation of) institutional and disciplinary shifts that could have victimized the WPA. More often than not, these shifts provided an opportunity for growth, not just in a given writing program, but also in the field of rhetoric and composition as a whole. The resistant WPA is neither a victim of the powers that be, nor is she a hero who solves every problem. Instead, if we trace her role through the development of the field, we find her to be a stalwart advocate for the relevance of writing instruction, the potential of student writers, and the integrity of the faculty who teach them. By reading our shared administrative history in this way, we heed Min-Zhan Lu's argument in "Tracking Comp Tales" for the value of telling and retelling our disciplinary stories to "bring to crisis established conditions of that world and established understandings of and relations to those conditions, so that with each crisis, opportunity is molded in danger, and danger becomes a form of opportunity" (226). In this case, the opportunity we recognize is the need to tell different WPA stories, in part by critiquing stories that do not map onto our world so satisfactorily.

The first glimpses we see of the resistant WPA appear in the way Sharon Crowley resituates an oft-cited origin story of American writing programs, the development of Freshman English at Harvard in the 1870s, around Adams Sherman Hill's professorship. Crowley's origin story argues that Hill, Harvard's assistant to the Boylston Professor of rhetoric (and de facto WPA), had to "make English strange" (Brereton 324) to argue for its institutional importance and to justify why studying the vernacular had to be learned rather than merely assumed in the study of literature. For Hill, learning principles of style, usage, and editing comprised an art of pure and efficient communication, wherein "pure" meant what was "universally understood" . . . by "reputable, national, and present use" (Brereton 324), a belletristic aim with somewhat political dimensions. Crowley explains that Hill and Harvard took three steps to accomplish this aim: "The first step in the process was to define English as a language from which its native speakers were alienated. The second step was to establish an entrance examination in English that was very difficult to pass. The third step, necessitated by the large number of failures on the exam, was to install a course of study that would remediate the lack demonstrated by the examination" (60). These moves paved the way for a new way of thinking about writing instruction, making the case for a course in composition as a material necessity for incoming college freshmen. While Crowley recounts this history as evidence for why first-year composition should be abolished (because it offers neither the students nor the discipline appropriate agency), we recognize the work of a resistant early WPA who made his beliefs about language and writing reflected in his administrative efforts, albeit in a context that limited composition's intellectual force.

Susan McLeod's *Writing Program Administration* offers a history of resistant writing program administrators whose efforts may seem more familiar to present-day readers than Hill's attempts to "make English strange" (Brereton 324). Building on the histories of the field written by earlier composition historians (including Albert R. Kitzhaber, John C. Brereton, James Berlin, Robert Connors, and Donald C. Stewart, among others), McLeod points to Fred Newton Scott at Michigan, Gertrude Buck at Vassar, and Regina Crandall at Bryn Mawr as early models of composition faculty whose work included administrative responsibilities familiar to the contemporary WPA. Their work can also be seen as sites of resistance against the status quo in composition pedagogy and institutional politics. As Barbara L'Eplattenier and Lisa Mastrangelo note, not all of these individuals were WPAs per se, but they "required an administrative space within which to function" and within that space they extended their colleagues' understanding of what composition curricula could and should be ("Why" xviii). Scott, for example, labored to move Michigan's curriculum away from the current-traditional model prevalent at that time in favor of teaching "rhetoric in a social context" (McLeod, *Writing* 47), and connecting "writing to real experience" (McLeod, *Writing* 37). Scott's graduate student, Gertrude Buck, extended his project of revising composition curricula to emphasize what, in current nomenclature, would be a Deweyian student-centered pedagogy. Her classes included "few lectures and quizzes . . . ; instead there were discussions of the literature they had read, individual and group interviews with the teacher on the themes they had written, and group work in class for discussing and critiquing themes" (McLeod, *Writing* 52). Suzanne Bordelon understands Buck not just as a purveyor of Scott's democratic rhetoric, but as a theorist of argumentation that stemmed from middle-class feminine activism (and was subsequently sparked by Progressive-Era forces from outside of the university).[4] Finally, McLeod presents Regina Crandall as a WPA who sought to improve the working conditions of the writing faculty at Bryn Mawr: even though she had "no authority over the curriculum or the hiring of faculty in the program she directed, [Crandall] fought back in a number of letters lobbying for better pay and working conditions for her faculty" (*Writing* 55).

The histories of Hill, Scott, Buck, Crandall, and the programs they shaped illustrate the ways in which early composition history is also a history of writing program administration, because, as McLeod notes, "To understand the history of writing program administration and to understand the politics still surrounding the position of WPA, one must go back to the beginnings of this unique course [composition]" (*Writing* 23). These histories illustrate that it is a part of WPA identity to labor for progress, including reframing our understanding of WPA work as one characterized by a progressive stance we choose for ourselves, rather than a heroic or victimized stance foisted on us by the beliefs, decisions, or actions of others. Even in our achievement of certain milestones or signs that we have arrived—the acknowledgement of administration as scholarship by our colleagues in other fields, a resolution to the English/composition tensions in our departments, an equitable policy for the use of adjuncts to teach writing courses—there will always be sites within the discipline, institutions, departments, and classrooms that compel WPAs to resist common assumptions about the work they do and drive them toward more ethical and effective administrative and teaching practices.

For the purposes of narrative reconstruction, our understanding of the resistant WPA is further solidified in histories of rhetoric and composition as retold by James Berlin, Robert Connors, John C. Brereton, and Stephen North, out of which emerge five particular moments in rhetoric and composition's history that represent the work of the resistant WPA. These moments of resistance map directly onto the contemporary history and trends of writing instruction in general, as the history of composition and writing program administration are intimately intertwined.

Moment One: The Resistant WPA as Researcher and Theorist

The influx of knowledge being generated about the writing process through cognitive psychology during the 1980s is directly related to the notion of the resistant WPA as a researcher and theorist. The resistant WPA argued that writing was a recursive, intellectual process that needed to be practiced (with feedback) rather than something that could be mimicked by exposure to "good" literature and model texts.

The process movement required that WPAs resist the once dominant belief that teaching writing is teaching grammar and/or literature. WPAs had to resist pressure from colleagues in other disciplines who bemoaned the "lack of writing skills" students displayed in their classrooms. They had to resist the resistance from teachers who didn't want to change their pedagogy based on "some new theory." And they had to resist critiques that composition teachers weren't doing their jobs because they were no longer providing their "service" to the university.

In many ways, the process movement has been a defining moment for the field of rhetoric and composition as a whole because, as Maxine Hairston argued, it created a "paradigmatic shift" (76) within the field that changed the way we thought about—and taught—writing. Therefore, it seems necessary to include the process movement as a moment of resistance for WPAs, as well, because a paradigmatic shift demands a curricular shift, and the resistant WPA has historically had to continually defend process as a meaningful approach to the teaching of writing.

Moment Two: The Resistant WPA as Collaborator

As the process movement took hold and the teaching of writing turned its attention away from the final written product, faculty in other disciplines began to complain that writing teachers "weren't doing their jobs anymore" because the writing classroom no longer fit their memories of their own educations in writing. At the same time, public discourse about a "literacy crisis" became common, which necessitated entire university communities to consider how and when to teach college level writing (Bazerman et al. 31). Writing Across the Curriculum, Communication Across the Curriculum, and Writing in the Disciplines all illustrate moments when WPAs resisted that claim by changing the nature of the debate, demonstrating through scholarship and collaboration with their faculty colleagues that students learn to write by writing not just in their English classes, but at all stages throughout their academic careers.

The WAC movement is perhaps the most successful WPAs have had in articulating the changing theories of composition theory to those outside of the discipline, because these resistant WPAs were able to respond to a complaint with an intelligent (though not perfect) solution that shared responsibility for writing instruction. Moreover, the WAC movement illustrates a moment that resistant WPAs advocated for and initiated and one that achieved significant institutional change.

Moment Three: The Resistant WPA as Politico

The Council of Writing Program Administrators' 1990 Portland Resolution illustrates the best example of WPAs' response to their own resistance to the preponderance of sub-par working conditions for WPAs. The Portland Resolution, initiated by Christine Hult's article, "On Being a Writing Program Administrator," outlined the institutional changes required for more humane working conditions for WPAs—job descriptions, job security, institutional resources, and administrative autonomy. The Resolution has been used as a sort of "expert argument" by WPAs to resist the less hospitable working environments they find themselves in, and the document has also been used as support for non-tenured or pre-tenured WPAs' arguments for changes to their contracts.

The reform efforts made by the Portland Resolution provide an interesting contrast to Hill's original attempts to "make English strange"; rather than placing the burden on the students to argue for better working conditions for writing teachers and WPAs, the CWPA put the onus on the institutions who employed and benefited from the work of the WPAs. This rhetorical shift illustrates progress in our institutional stature because the CWPA perceived that there was an institutional audience who would recognize the authority of the organization and (perhaps) find it more persuasive because it came from a recognized organization of individuals rather than a few composition instructors at a given institution. More importantly, perhaps, the rhetorical shift employed by the Portland Resolution shows that the field's way of thinking about students has become more ethical—rather than making English strange (to the detriment of our students) in an effort to improve our institutional stature, the CWPA created an ethical, logical argument that didn't objectify students.

Moment Four: The Resistant WPA as Technologist

In 1983, Bruce Herzberg published "A Primer on Computer Literacy for WPAs and Writing Instructors," in which he provides useful strategies for WPAs who wish to incorporate computers into their writing programs. Herzberg's essay identifies a growing awareness among WPAs that developments in technology were changing the process of writing, and he recommends that WPAs educate themselves about computers to determine whether or not they would be useful in their writing programs. As institutions slowly recognized the potential of technological resources as a recruiting tool for new students, Herzberg began to articulate a way for WPAs to make the argument that writing is a sort of technology in itself, one that needs technological resources in order to thrive, and, as such, he suggests ways for WPAs to strategize for computers, lab space, and software, issues as timely now as they were in 1983. While Herzberg's text outlines practical and political strategies for WPAs interested in integrating computers into their programs, he also predicts the ways technology could change our students' and our own conceptions of writing: "In short, the word processor makes writers—and not only freshman writers—aware of new possibilities in their writing" (26).

The move to incorporate computers into the field of composition more thoroughly is one that clearly revolutionized the teaching of composition, but it also exemplifies the resistant WPA's flexibility as she correctly anticipates institutional shifts toward technology while positioning herself as a stakeholder in the discussions surrounding those changes. The role that technology plays in many introductory writing programs—and the way that technology has become an inevitable and integral core of what it means to teach writing—is due in good part to a WPA's ability to anticipate technological changes and act rather than react accordingly.

Moment Five: The Resistant WPA as Activist

The resistant WPA as activist is motivated by the resistance she feels when the WPA hears yet another story about why Johnny can't write. She is focused on mobilizing WPAs to lobby local, state, and federal governments to enact legislation that promotes sound pedagogical practices in teaching literacy and writing, but she is also encouraging people to act on the basis of principle. She sees political activism as a way of thinking and re-thinking previously held beliefs about the teaching of writing, and her work fosters a move from a defensive position of protecting our programs, curricula, and pedagogy to one of engaged advocacy for our students.

This moment is noteworthy because it represents a shift in our notion that WPA work is either program-based, worked out in our institutional homes, or theoretical and shared with readers in article and manuscript publication. Instead, texts such as Adler-Kassner's *The Activist WPA* and Eli Goldblatt's *Because We Live Here* position WPAs as active participants in local and national political movements, specifically as they relate to literacy education in our communities. Activist WPAs are not tied to institutions or disciplinary sites; instead, they are motivated to perform their scholarly expertise in public, for the public.

While these moments cannot fully illustrate the complex history of composition and writing program administration, we hope they productively point to different roles the resistant WPA has taken on over the years. Whether acting as a collaborator, researcher, or technologist, the resistant WPA engages in challenging rhetorical and hermeneutic work, making the familiar strange or the strange familiar as ways to persuade others to embrace new ideas about writing instruction. These moments clearly blur and extend into the present. Susan McLeod's "The Foreigner: WAC Director as Agents of Change" brings together the WPA as collaborator and WPA as politico, while *Computers and Composition Online* and *Kairos* challenge us to rethink writing instruction and publication in an electronic age. These important acts of interpretation and persuasion have shaped the history of writing instruction on such topics as access and what it means to teach writing. Moreover, they suggest that a resistant WPA both responds to and creates opportunities for developments in writing instruction because the resistant WPA is both a composer and an interpreter of texts and contexts—an agent not merely a reactor in the story of writing program administration.

Rewriting GenAdmin

GenAdmin's position within the discipline of writing program administration is best read through narrative histories that are not causal but rather extra-moral and imminent because they lead the writer and reader away from polarizing binaries toward a more nuanced understanding of the complexities of WPA work and WPA identities. The WPAs of such historicized narratives embody conflicts on behalf of larger groups and make them visible to others, and they provide the opportunity for WPAs to reshape the field, or as Malea Powell says, to "reflect, rethink, and revise the stories that create who we are" (428), because they are not stories of individual struggles but of disciplinary emergence. The narrative's subject blurs the lines of authority and control and helps to redefine programs, not as fixed sets of stable practices, but as fluctuating entities that act and are acted upon in contexts requiring change (Gunner, "Collaborative" 257). In "Poetics and Narrativity," Philip Eubanks calls the study of narratives the "study of cultures" and makes the case for story-based writing as argumentative texts (34). More than just literary devices, narratives and metaphors are rhetorical figures that provide WPAs means to inquire into the social processes of their own contexts by teaching them to develop a "pedagogy of listening" and a consciousness of "being present." They are ongoing, emergent, and participatory, leading WPAs to create chapters and interchapters that must constantly be reread, retold, and rewritten for their purposes to be clear. They provide ways to reconceive organizational contexts by acting as constituents of changed and changing social and disciplinary relations. As a result, we can consider more emergent histories and theories of our discipline, align our work with knowledge making, and derive tales that position WPA work as "imagination" (Powell 399) not legitimation.

While the five of us certainly prefer the narrative of the resistant, proactive WPA, we do not choose it merely to promote one set of stories over another; there are more far reaching implications for an alternative history of the WPA. First and foremost, while their institutions and their colleagues have mistreated many WPAs, any narrative on the hero to victim spectrum constructs a vastly incomplete profile of WPAs. Most acting WPAs know this, but those whose only insight into WPA work is through such narratives may not. The images of suffering can be overwhelming; likewise, the conclusions put forward by "advice narratives" that are built on the perilous premises of the victim and hero narratives establish generalized knowledge that we find too limited in their assumptions about what WPA work is and who should do it. If we focus instead on the resistant WPA as a lens through which we can view their roles in forming the discipline, we might see an administrator who is engaged, responsive, and proactive rather than one who is disenfranchised or reactive. We might also recognize the power of writing history, and recognize how the stories we tell about our past inform the perspectives we have on our present and future possibilities:

> What we remember, what we stress as significant, and what we omit of our past defines our present. And since the boundaries of our self-definition also delimit our hopes and aspirations, this personal history affects our future. If we see ourselves as victimized, as powerless and overwhelmed by forces we cannot understand or control, we will choose to live cautiously, avoid conflict and evade pain. If we see ourselves as loved,

> grounded, powerful, we will embrace the future, live courageously and accept challenges with confidence. (Lerner 199)

Quite simply, we find hope in considering those moments where WPAs are proactive agents, not victims or heroes, working towards changing our programs for the better.

In the majority of our administrative experiences, programmatic change is neither sexy nor groundbreaking nor even revolutionary. The fairest and most productive way of delineating such change is to say that it is aggregative. Layer after layer of local assessment, scholarly research, pedagogical theory and lore accumulate until the necessary amount of time and pressure on just the right points causes something new to happen, and change eventually emerges. Binary frames—and we want to stress here that we are talking about overarching narratives and not the details that underlay many of our metaphoric profiles of WPA life and work—like the victim narrative, want and need the revolution. When we walk back to our imaginary and collective office space after our department chair has misrepresented our reasons for maintaining (an already high) course cap of twenty-five in our first-year writing classes, we have multiple choices: reactionary resentment, passive acceptance, resistance, deferral, strategizing, analysis, etc. When colleagues do not value our views because we require so many teachers to cover our classes, or because writing is a set of skills that can be taught within the first year of university work, we will most likely feel like victims of our own making because we are hierarchically positioned to catch the boomerang of information passed from source to source, from one set of experiences to another set of ears, and so on, unless and until they can be paradigmatically replaced.

What we suggest as a direction here, and what the rest of the book will provide examples of, are administrative philosophies that give voice to a variety of resistance models so that we can dislocate the binaries—victim/hero, jWPA or gWPA/senior WPA, research/service, program maintenance/upheaval—we have come to expect with a range of complex behaviors. This is an example of pushing through rather than making the metaphors we have work for our experiences.

Interlude

On Empathy

From my vantage point at a research-extensive public university, *empathy* has become a vital site for humanistic inquiry. It has been taken up as the topic of interdisciplinary symposia, featured in undergraduate courses with empathy as their focus, has emerged in scholarship about its role in navigating academic cultures in rhetoric and composition, and has been used as a vehicle through which we publicly resituate communities to their pasts.[1] In all these contexts, empathy seems to require much more than an enhanced ability *to understand one another*; rather, empathy requires an enhanced understanding of *how we position ourselves* as interpreters of and participants in ongoing experiences.

Our emphasis throughout this book on the active and creative nature of theorizing GenAdmin necessitates an equally active and creative ethic of caring—caring for others not according to how we want care for ourselves, but according to how they need or desire to be cared for. This ethic in turn holds some of the critical and hermeneutic potential that drives our articulations of GenAdmin as a philosophy. It is not simply charity, although we recognize charity as a complex act. It is not simply compassion (even though compassion drives much of what I do in my professional life, as in my personal life). I prefer to think of empathetic caring as a willingness to put aside one subject position in order to allow another one to come forward, or—in more concrete terms—to let someone else be right, and to let their needs be paramount to my own.

A rhetorician is likely to understand *empatheia* (ἐμπάθεια) as a partiality that comes from "passion or suffering" ("empathy"). Yet I understand empathy—and its derivative "feeling into"[2]—not as something native to how we feel but rather as something linked to how well individuals imagine an "other," whether that other is a state or a motive or a position, and how adeptly our imagining translates itself into response or to action that speaks right to the heart of that state, motive, or position. In other words, a projected or commonly understood felt sense need not be concerned only with emotion but can be concerned with the kind of reasoning activity that is cultivated and then practiced. By this definition, empathy seems as essential to GenAdmin as the generational positioning we have inherited that has equipped us to approach the work critically and willingly.

Empathy has come up at so many different junctures in our theorizing that it is difficult for me to know, now, what we intended it to mean, or to remember the conflict it was meant to illuminate. To some extent, this interlude bridges Chapters 2 and 5 by connecting our need to historically reposition ourselves with our need to perform the difficult but necessary interpretive acts we call GenAdmin discourse. To some extent, this interlude bridges Chapters 4 and 6 by explaining how our *becoming* identification can drive a hopeful pragmatism from which we enact what we call a GenAdmin ethics. For example, say we find ourselves in an irresolvable context, as we often do in the context of our own writing programs, created by a lack of will or talent to negotiate, resulting in some one (or some ones, including ourselves) not willing to budge, but with a pragmatic goal that must be obtained somewhere in the middle. How do we arrive at this goal when not only are we not going to budge from our positions, but neither will we change our perceptions of one another because we are embedded in histories that cause us to see each other in certain ways? What is there to this art of reaching temporary resolution—a temporary suspension of disbelief—to make a writing program run well? How can we not revert to policing, capitulating, being aggressive, avoiding conflict, etc.?

No matter how we approach it, empathy for GenAdmin signals an agentive potential and a pragmatic action simultaneously. It signals a response to (our own and others') resistance, and a way to be responsive and proactive rather than simply reactive. It signals a way to stop being hurt and to stop hurting others. As we write this book, we are aware of potential criticism or skepticism toward our efforts to disrupt, to become, to discourse, and to change. We have experienced (or witnessed and understood) the institutional contexts and material conditions that may cause others to disbelieve our work, especially in the present institutional climate, perhaps because it is difficult to prove that such a philosophy *works*, and that may cause us to resist others in turn. But at this juncture in our theorizing—at this juncture in the profession—it isn't a matter of whether GenAdmin philosophy *works* but rather, what GenAdmin philosophy *is*, *does*, and *has been* or *done*. In other words, our interest in this skepticism—as in most aspects of the philosophy we articulate—is less suasory than it is descriptive.

We seek no converts, but rather, spaces to dialogue. We seek to make those spaces visible and accessible to any or all persons who need them, desire them, or have been routinely denied them. For me (and for the five of us) empathy bears on how to make these contextualized spaces discursive, and thus transformative, where the discourse doesn't work *through* the spaces but rather *is* those spaces. In other words, the goal of empathetic discourse with others is not often to lead them to a suasive end (although we do see suasory ends as compatible with our discourse), but rather to convince them that the act of engaging and staying engaged in the conversation is useful because it requires us to define our subject positions as unstable and contingent, a condition of being and *becoming* for which we argue in Chapter 4.

However, knowledge is only made when we dwell in these contextualized spaces (e.g., committees, classrooms, meeting rooms, roundtables, departments, and programs) with willing participants, when they see and value the contingencies, too. By "dwelling," I mean agreeing to see parameters not as closures or borders that cut off one's experiences from another's in the interest of one person getting what s/he wants, but as places to move towards in order to chart out epistemologies. Rather than me inviting someone to come and dwell in my belief, or someone else convincing me to step inside his shoes, we locate a position, conviction, or ideological state in which we can dwell together for a time, long enough to accomplish some objective.

Empathy bears on what makes these locations reciprocal and, thus, epistemological, but only if that knowledge is captured via reflection and is collectively witnessed or agreed upon. This is probably why we find ourselves very often *not* making knowledge from our empathetic actions towards others. We may not have chosen the best position to occupy with others. Or, others may not feel as if we are being empathetic. Or, locatability may seem too abstract for others to consider on a daily basis. Or, instabilities may seem too evasive to embrace as outcomes and goals. And yet, because our scholarly preparation has taught us to consider and embrace them, we will continue to strive for this reciprocity.

The demonstration of multiple empathies already defines the roles we get assigned and our responses to these roles, for example, in the way that graduate students seek out which academic advisor they need at a given moment, or TAs will seek out which WPA they think will serve a perceived need. They may assign me a role that doesn't reflect the role I think I play (or could play, or even desire to play) and overlook me for roles that I should be playing. Colleagues may do the same, assigning me a role that does not reflect the whole of what I can do (or have done) and threatens my own sense of viability. Yet if I remember that this assigning comes from their positioning as much as (or more than) my own, I might spend less time being hurt, upset, feeling slighted or excluded by their choices. Eliding the misidentification that often ensues when others assign us (roles, values, or worth) may be one small step in reversing or halting a pattern of misunderstanding, especially if it helps us elide the blaming assumptions we may make in return. And then when (or if) we manage these elisions, other possibilities might open up in turn for vulnerability to become shared.

This vulnerability is necessary to our theorizing, and in fact is a core element in our interdisciplinarity. The five of us have introduced, defined, and will use the term *multiplicinarity* throughout this book because we found it a more appropriate term to describe our intellectual emergence than *disciplinarity* or *interdisciplinarity*. Rather than thinking about GenAdmin identities as being rooted only in certain faculties (or fields of knowledge), and hence only representing the methodologies or epistemologies that those fields invite, in using this term, we consider the ways that GenAdmin identity is epistemological itself. In other words, the kinds of negotiations we undertake in defining GenAdmin, tracing its origins, justifying its usefulness, and describing how to enact its empathy require that we constantly let go of disciplinary placeholders. This may be because GenAdmin as a philosophical identification seems to disrupt the notion of disciplinarity at all. It may also be because we (the five of us, and also more broadly the "we" of the profession) have not yet used "interdisciplinary" to its fullest potential. Sometimes we are aware that we have to be willing to argue for a quasi-disciplinary position, or a position that represents the fusion of our disciplinary stance with another, revealing that there may be spaces between "WPA" and "rhetoric and composition," for example, and revealing the questions that make those middle grounds visible to us as we argue.

In the same way that we define GenAdmin not according to a job but according to our rhetorical attitudes and motivations towards the job, our notion of empathy as a kind of rhetorical agility includes the *recognition of* and *movement between* the material conditions that bear on our work. Because recognition without movement is not knowledge-bearing, one final aspect of how empathy plays a role in the unfolding of GenAdmin as a philosophy is in how it affords us rhetorical agency. In a featured session entitled "Rhetorics and Feminisms: The Remix" at the 2010 CCCC, the speakers oscillated between an epideictic account of how far the discipline of feminist rhetorical studies had come and a cautiously optimistic account of how far we have yet to go. Of them, Jacquelyn Jones Royster urged us to ask the hard question of "What comes next beyond recovery and inscription?" in historical studies of feminist rhetors. Andrea Lunsford called for a more "robust theory of reading"—a way to get over disciplinary straitjackets and to influence other fields and disciplines without losing sight of our core beliefs. Although they did not use the word "empathy" to describe what they proposed, Royster and Lunsford did suggest that rhetoric and composition scholars adopt certain interpretive postures that involve taking in new information and putting it to use based on their understanding of how information *can be*, *has been*, and *will be* used.

3 Constructing Professional Identities

> *Time was when directors were rank amateurs. An assistant professor took on the odious job of directing freshman English for tenure's sake. He (always he then) had some interest in teaching composition but none in constructing and managing a durable program, and the only theory he knew was in Aristotle. I exaggerate a bit. There were dedicated directors about. I knew some. But the un-tenured assistant professor coerced by senior professors was more common. From this estranged figure came mismanagement, or none at all. . . . That was the Dark Ages.*
>
> —Dwight Purdy

While there may exist material and emotional resonances between the WPA of the "Dark Ages" and today's WPAs—we all feel overwhelmed and in unfamiliar territory on any given day, and some of us still take on administrative work grudgingly—much has changed significantly and for the better since the days of the "rank amateur" director. While each of us has come to our WPA lives via very different paths and we may see and experience our WPA-ness in significantly different ways, the richness and diversity of the WPA identities we collectively enact is possible because of the professionalization not only of rhetoric and composition, but also of writing program administration. GenAdmin would not exist if there had not been the Harvey Weiners, Kenneth Bruffees, Christine Hults, or the countless others with or without national or institutional recognition who helped to shape WPA as a profession, as an area of intellectual work, inquiry, and ways of being.[1] A result of this professionalization has been that even though some

WPAs do work on campuses where the Dark Ages still exist, most WPAs, to use Purdy's phrase, have "come in from the cold" (794).

So, what has been the path of professionalization for WPAs, and how has that professionalization affected WPA identity for the twenty-first century? In Chapter 2, we looked at narratives of WPA history, focusing specifically on the narratives that the field has used to describe its work, and we offered a new way of framing that history through resistance. In this chapter, then, we'd like to focus more on WPA identities and how they can be shaped and created over a professional lifetime, how members of GenAdmin are prepared to act and think as WPAs, as well as the consequences of purposefully preparing future faculty to do so, even as junior faculty. While much of our book is dedicated to fleshing out just what GenAdmin means in theoretical and lived terms, in this chapter we focus on how we got to this place in our professional history—specifically, how the education and preparation we received helped us consider our WPA identities in more philosophical terms rather than as tied to particular job titles—and how the historical "shifts" outlined above give us alternative positionings from which to theorize our work. Because these shifts have provided spaces for seeing meaningful acts of writing program administration as disciplinary, GenAdmin are able to think and act with a sense of multiplicinarity.

In the past ten years, there has been robust interest in constructing WPA histories, and a project like ours necessitates looking back in order to figure out how we have come to be at this particular historical moment, a time of reflection on what it means to be a WPA and what it might mean for the future. Susan McLeod's history in *Writing Program Administration* offers us one way to tell a story of our professionalization, which we recount briefly here as a way to help us trace a genealogy of GenAdmin.[2] One version of the timeline might look like this:[3]

- 1949: WPAs first began to organize at CCCC.
- 1960s: There was a rise in professional journals and doctoral programs in rhetoric and composition, specialized professional organizations, and "increasingly sophisticated job descriptions" for WPAs in the MLA *Job Information List*.

- 1976: Harvey Weiner decided (at the annual MLA meeting) to form a national organization for WPAs; the CWPA constitution and bylaws were approved in early 1977.
- 1979: The *WPA: Writing Program Administration* journal premiered.
- 1982: CWPA and Northeastern University partnered to offer the first workshop for new WPAs, led by Harvey Weiner and Tim Donovan, at Martha's Vineyard.
- 1986: The first CWPA conference was held in Oxford, OH, at Miami University (Horner 5).
- 1980: With the help of an Exxon Education Foundation grant, the CWPA initiated the WPA Consultant-Evaluator service (Weiner).
- 1989: CWPA began to award WPA research grants.
- 1991: David Schwalm started the WPA-L listserv.
- 1992: The CWPA Executive Board adopted the Portland Resolution.
- 1996: The Evaluating the Intellectual Work of Writing Administration document is published (adopted in 1998 by the Executive Board).
- 1998: Purdue began offering the first PhD secondary area in writing program administration.
- 2000: By 2000, at least thirteen doctoral programs offered WPA courses (Enos, "Reflexive" 62).
- 2002: The CWPA began offering a targeted one-day Assessment Institute prior to the annual conference (Yancey 7). In subsequent years, additional institutes have been added, including Technology Institutes, Research Institutes, and, in 2009, a WPA Renewal Institute and a Writing Program Administrators as Writers Institute.
- 2004: The Graduate WPA (gWPA) Listserv and SIG are formed.
- 2004: A group of WPAs form the jWPA SIG at CCCC.

According to McLeod's history, up until the 1940s, writing program administration was a "task rather than a position" (*Writing* 45); after WWII, millions of veterans returned to the university and English departments had to figure out how to "coordinat[e] the ever-multiplying sections of freshman English," a point at which McLeod argues the professionalization of writing program administration began in earnest (*Writing* 58-59). Still seen as a task, "those in charge of such programs sought each other out for workable solutions to pressing problems" (*Writing* 58-59), creating networks out of which CCCC was born and, later, the Council of Writing Program Administrators. "[P]erhaps the most important thing that the new organization did," McLeod writes, "was to coin the term that described the work: writing program administrator" (*Writing* 71), which Weiner believed would "[add] 'a dignifying occupational tag to the parlance' which 'bestowed a new level of legitimacy' to the job" (*Writing* 72). Thus, writing program administration shifted significantly from a series of tasks that someone—perhaps anyone—might perform to a *position* that, increasingly, those with specific expertise might hold.

WPA identity has become increasingly complex as the variety of roles and expectations for WPAs have expanded over the years, particularly since the 1980s. As McLeod tells it, "During the 1980s the position of writing program administrator became a revolving door at many institutions; new PhDs were hired to do administration and then told at the end of six years that their work only counted as service, and that they had not published enough to get tenure" (*Writing* 74). As English departments recognized the disciplinary expertise of those in rhetoric and composition, they "felt justified in assigning that person everything having to do with writing; the job definitions being generated as a result were so complex that no one person could possibly manage the position" (McLeod, *Writing* 75). By the 1990s, this situation was changing, as were WPA identities. WPAs had begun to focus on the intellectual, scholarly nature of their work, and, determined to legitimize their work in the larger academic community, they worked on creating the Portland Resolution, which offered guidelines, among other things, for "writing clear job descriptions, setting forth clear guidelines for the evaluation of WPAs, [and] establishing job security and stability for them" (McLeod, *Writing* 76). Rather than walking (or being pushed) through a revolving door or serving only until tenure's release, these WPAs were also sticking around, building programs based on disciplinary expertise and seeing them through, choosing to remain WPAs for a significant stretch of their careers.

This WPA identity McLeod portrays is one of a consummate professional, a confident teacher-scholar-administrator who draws on disciplinary expertise and hard-won respect from colleagues and other administrators to do important work in the university. But s/he was also a WPA who had learned everything on the job. S/he was the WPA of Sally Barr Ebest's 1992 and 1996 surveys who learned how to be a WPA "primarily through trial and error" ("Gender" 54), one of the many WPAs who led Ebest to conclude that "training in the skills and duties required of a WPA is, in most institutions, a matter of chance" ("The Next" 67). That WPA, however, need not be the only one representing the field's increased professional and scholarly profile, as we see a generation of teacher-scholars prepared to act and think from a WPA perspective as early as their introduction to the discipline in graduate school.

While our mentors (and some of theirs) witnessed a WPA identity shift from task to position, we now bear witness to another shift— from seeing WPA as a position that we might hold to seeing WPA as a way of being—a perspective from which we see, think, decide, and act, regardless of whether we are *the* WPA or not. As we explained in Chapter 1, this is a key element of our theorizing because a GenAdmin philosophy is not dependent on title or position alone but rather is marked by a more complex subjectivity. It is important to note, however, that newer jWPAs are not the only ones who experience this shift in WPA identity—senior WPAs (sWPAs) can experience it as well. As Martha A. Townsend notes in her chapter included in *The Promise and Perils of Writing Program Administration*, she has "never *not* been a WPA" (265). Faced with moving out of a long tenure in her WPA position and into non-WPA faculty life, she had to re-think her professional identity. We're sure she's not alone. In 2008, a message thread on "transitions" generated activity on the WPA-L listserv among several well-known WPAs, who were announcing retirements and/or moves out of their WPA positions. It was telling that one asked, perhaps tongue-in-cheek, whether she could still post to the list or go to WPA conferences since she was no longer technically a WPA. As our field matures, we will no doubt see more discussion about new roles for sWPAs, some of whom are moving back into teaching-only positions while others are moving on to other leadership positions on their campuses.[4] The 2008 WPA conference hosted multiple panels on WPA identity; our own GenAdmin roundtable was bookended by a "senior" panel in which Charles Schuster and Joe Harris pondered their own professional lives after administration.

Of course, most of these post-WPAs have never really stopped being WPAs. They may no longer hold official WPA positions at their home institutions, but they still serve as mentors for others in those positions, they hold leadership positions in our organizations, they post on our listservs, and they engage in scholarly activities directly related to the intellectual work of WPA, even after official retirement. It may be a normal reaction for them to equate writing program administration with a position, or even a set of tasks, because of prevailing attitudes about writing program work during their careers, but they live a WPA life even still.

As we have suggested throughout the book, in particular as we have noted both the differences among ourselves and the fact that GenAdmin is not an essentialist identifier, we recognize that the historical narrative of WPA professionalization is an uneven trajectory. To mindfully complicate this historical narrative of WPA professionalization, we want to insert two points. First, this history that tells the story of WPA evolution from "rank amateur" to professional director is not an even progress narrative because of the multiple contextual factors that make for different constraints and possibilities in different programs. Some institutions have WPAs who are not on the tenure track, who are seen only as managers, who do not receive course releases for their administrative work, who are not seen or perhaps not interested in positioning themselves as administrative scholars. Other institutions have collaborative writing program administrators who share and rotate roles or a WPA who sees her research agenda on writing program administration as vital to her position as Writing Center Director, WAC coordinator, Director of Professional Writing, or Director of First-Year Writing. Some WPAs are immersed in reading, writing, and theorizing administration, while others are more interested in teaching or pursuing other research agendas.

Second, the subjectivities of WPAs negotiating and living within particular programs and institutional contexts ensure that the history and future of WPA professionalization is not a uniform narrative, nor should it ever aim to produce one. It is unquestionably different to be a WPA at a university with doctoral programs in rhetoric and composition, at a small liberal arts college, or on a two-year campus. As such, we do not seek to standardize WPA professionalization for ourselves or others; we recognize and value the ways we have learned to become WPAs differently, and we recognize and welcome the reality that our administrative identities will always be in flux. But we also know that, whether or not we're in programs that recognize our work as we do or recognize our expertise as WPAs, we embrace GenAdmin identity because it articulates an agentive philosophy that merges what we do, how we do it, and who we are and reflects some agreed-upon values related to the teaching of writing and the administration of writing programs this book explores.

Professionalization Anxiety

> *Few graduate teachers think of leadership in that sense as a faculty competence to be cultivated in doctoral education. As for administration, it is stereotyped as the refuge of those less talented as scholars or past their prime. Narratives by faculty who have become administrators portray it as an accident that befalls an unsuspecting professor, drafted in reluctant duty and entirely naive about what it involves. Administration as intellectual leadership remains, for graduate students and young professors, almost unimaginable as a professional role they might aspire to as part of a faculty career. As a result, most faculty members are woefully unprepared for the complex challenges of program and departmental leadership that many will, sooner or later, taken on.*
>
> —Louise Wetherbee Phelps

GenAdmin is, perhaps, still in the minority in larger academic circles. We do not see administration as the "refuge of those less talented as scholars" since we recognize it as a scholarly endeavor that is not enacted as managerial, policing, or top-down, but rather as theoretical in its own right. Administrators—whether WPAs or not—are not our bogeymen, and we may even aspire to these roles. We may not be the first to find that administrative work is a calling—"to advocate, to reach back and help struggling writers along" by shaping writing programs with our leadership (Dew 111), to have a meaningful and viral influence on other educators' and stakeholders' views about the teaching and learning of writing. But one of the things that sets us apart from previous generations of WPAs is that we were purposefully prepared in graduate school to do administrative work, to think like WPAs do, from a "big picture" programmatic/institutional perspective as well as from an individual teacher-scholar's perspective. While it would be foolish to contend that the only way to become a "good" WPA is to take specialized coursework in writing program administration, we still strongly support graduate preparation through coursework which directly addresses writing program administration as an area of intellectual inquiry and through a variety of other curricular pathways and configurations which help students see their work in rhetoric and composition as part of larger programmatic, institutional, or cultural/civic enterprises. Whether we ought to think of graduate education in these ways, as preparation for thinking like a WPA, is up for debate. Each of us was fortunate enough to have our graduate education as scholars, thinkers, and teachers influenced by strong WPAs, so we know its potential for contributing meaningfully to our conceptions of administrative identity. But it is nonetheless important to ask a number of questions about the logic and consequences of such preparation.

Shirley K Rose and Irwin Weiser offer one such discussion of the major objections to and concerns about WPA professionalization in graduate school in their chapter "'Beyond Winging It': The Places of Writing Program Administration in Rhetoric and Composition Graduate Programs." The following list summarizes those objections[5]:

- Writing program administration is unteachable. WPA work is too situated and contextual to be taught well.
- Successful WPA-ing is "a matter of charisma and personality or innate ability to manage people" (163).
- WPA work is not worthy of study because it is "atheoretical practice" (163), a service for which no preparation is necessary.
- Experiential learning opportunities (like gWPA positions) cannot effectively prepare students for future work as WPAs since graduate students cannot have access to behind-the-scenes info, power, or decision-making authority that would help them really learn about WPA work (164).
- WPA professionalization is too linked to a specific position (like vocational education) and limits the career options for those who engage in it.
- WPA professionalization can privilege some rhetoric and composition people over others, which "may pose a threat to the presumed egalitarianism among composition specialists, but

- also delegitimize WPAs who do not have formal graduate preparation" (163).
- WPA professionalization leads faculty to WPA work too soon, particularly pre-tenure.

To Rose and Weiser's list, we would add a few more standard objections, some related to Phelps's quote above, others echoed several times during our GenAdmin roundtable discussion at the 2008 CWPA conference and in recent critiques of writing program work that have circulated in our scholarship and professional literature:

- Building attendant expectations for doing WPA work pre-tenure can set junior faculty up to fail in environments where the work isn't recognized.
- WPA work is mere service to the institution, or, relatedly, a PhD isn't necessary for doing WPA work.
- WPA professionalization can lead to the creation of a managerial class.
- "By introducing models of graduate education that center upon administration, composition is (short) leashed to that center, it's identity bound," thus limiting our recognition of the "need for wildly new approaches to how to talk about and enact administrative theories" (Dobrin 69).

We recognize that some read a commitment to writing program administration as complicity with the administrative side of the academic house; in this world view, administrators are always pitted against faculty, cast as disparate groups who hold diametrically opposed values. It's certainly fair to consider whether WPAs, particularly in their connection to required first-year writing courses and the often unfair labor practices associated with such programs, serves the larger discipline of rhetoric and composition well. Some of these critiques have been voiced by well-known scholars in our field (Mark Bousquet, Joseph Harris, and others) and are a legitimate and fundamental part of our larger conversations about academic work and administrative roles. Open discussion of these and other critiques of writing program administration are raised in Donna Strickland and Jeanne Gunner's recent collection, *The Writing Program Interrupted* (2009), particularly in the chapters written by Jeff Rice, Sid Dobrin, and Joe Hardin.

While we do agree that we should be cautious about how and why we prepare future faculty to be WPAs, we also think that writing program administration can—and should—be taught. Just as with any profession, no one ever graduates knowing everything one needs to know in order to deal with every situation. A writing program administration seminar cannot tell us the perfect thing to say to colleague X in department Y when we bring our new goals, means, and outcomes in for discussion and approval at a department meeting. But writing program administration courses can, along with other aspects of WPA preparation like experiential learning opportunities, help to inculcate a WPA way of being, give us the knowledge that our work will be contextual, offer ways of reading those institutions and situations, and help us situate our specific work in larger contexts. We can, as WPA educators and mentors, give future faculty members opportunities to see, think, and act as a WPA might, even if they never become an official WPA on campus.

If we spend time and coursework on administration (or computers and writing or cultural studies or any other specialty) in graduate school, we might feel compelled to look for jobs that utilize those specializations right away. Presumably, however, that is why we specialized in those areas in the first place—we *want* to do that work because that's where our experiences, lines of study, and interests lie. Again, it might be hard for some to imagine why anyone would *choose* a WPA job—and there are, most certainly, situations in which we would advise a new faculty member *not* to take a WPA job—but these are concerns that threaten to diminish an individual faculty's expertise, which they have worked hard to develop, just as it diminishes their opportunity to make wise choices informed by the contexts available to them. In one context, a WPA position might be the best option; in another, new faculty with writing program administration expertise may choose to pursue a WPA research agenda or serve on department assessment committees instead of taking on an official WPA position.

It is also possible, and understandable, that WPAs who did not explicitly *study to be WPAs* might feel threatened by the explicit marking of a new faculty member's writing program administration expertise through the credentialing that graduate preparation in writing program administration can provide, in the same way that the self-taught electrician with twenty years' experience might feel alongside a new graduate from an electrician's program at a local community college or vocational school. Credentialed WPAs may also exacerbate the feelings of anxiety that some doctoral candidates have while on the job market alongside counterparts from more prestigious programs. While we acknowledge the mistrust such a credentialing may create, it is important to point out that just because some WPAs were specifically prepared for WPA work in graduate school—or taught to think administratively—does not mean that they won't make mistakes on the job. It is quite likely, however, that they may be prepared to treat their administrative mistakes as an opportunity for reflection and theorizing because they see WPA work as an area of scholarly inquiry, and they will look to work collaboratively with their colleagues to build consensus and a stronger program than any one person could create. It is also important to recognize that there is no singular WPA expertise, no singular canon or curriculum through which one can become the ideal WPA—and not just because all WPA work is contextual. There are many ways that one can learn how to be and think like a WPA. WPA expertise gained through graduate preparation does not diminish WPA expertise gained through other avenues. Faculty with WPA graduate coursework, just like all faculty members, will continue to learn over the course of their professional lifetimes, often from those very WPAs who had no formal graduate WPA preparation.

Perhaps the most troubling objection to WPA professionalization are claims similar to those made by Lynn Worsham that administration is necessarily atheoretical (McLemee), and we hope that our own work here will add another piece in a long line of evidence to the contrary. For us, much of the work that WPAs do is scholarly, and GenAdmin's agenda is unquestioningly theoretical and intellectual, despite persistent stereotypes that administrators are merely bureaucrats, pencil pushers, enforcers of top-down decisions, and/or schedulers. As a field, we have certainly had a robust discussion in WPA literature of its managerial/bureaucratic/administrative nature in the past ten to fifteen years, most notably with the work of Marc Bousquet, Joseph Harris, Richard Miller, and now Joe Hardin, who has offered a particularly useful way of moving that conversation forward. But it is worth noting that WPAs differ from many other higher education administrators in that their administrative work is directly connected to their disciplinary expertise and commitment. To us, WPA work offers one opportunity to manifest the principles and theories at the foundation of rhetoric and composition in a way that benefits the students and faculty who make up our academic communities—an area of inquiry all its own with a growing body of scholarly work addressing a range of WPA-specific issues, including research on gender and administration and curriculum design for writing program administration courses. This larger body of work allows us to see "administrator" as a subject position we might inhabit. Like Joseph Janangelo, Linda Adler-Kassner, Eli Goldblatt, Richard Miller, and others, we see administration as an opportunity to do creative, inventive, rigorous, and engaged work—ranging from historical to theoretical to philosophical, and sometimes involving all of the above. We draw daily on our knowledge of rhetoric and composition to shape policies, design curricula, and articulate visions for our programs and centers, but writing program administration's theoretical work extends beyond applications of rhetoric and composition theory to practical problems like crafting an argument for lowering class size.

Almost fifteen years ago, Dave Healy reported on a survey of writing center directors he conducted, hoping to create a comprehensive profile of these professionals; he concluded his article, wondering how and why writing center directors entered the profession, with a question that also preoccupies our own work. He writes that:

> Outside the academy, we expect professionals to have sensed some kind of "calling" to their profession and to have devoted themselves with considerable intentionality and focus to their chosen specialty—whether in medicine or law or whatever. In the academy, those kinds of expectations apply to faculty members, less so to administrators. College and university administrators are often former faculty members who either got kicked, or kicked themselves, "upstairs." Their "call," their occupational socialization was typically to and in a particular academic discipline. They "end up" in administration—for a variety of reasons and with a variety of attitudes toward and kinds of preparation for the responsibilities they assume. (38)

Many of our WPA mentors and colleagues may well have "ended up" in administration not of a singular volition but of context or circumstance, and attitudes towards WPA work do still vary. Increasingly, however, more people can choose WPA work—in or out of official WPA positions—with a better attitude towards it because they aren't waiting for something better to come along, and that is, at least in part, because they have prepared for it.

Hopeful Professionalization in Action

> . . . [T]he nearly irrepressible urge that everyone feels is to blame the failure on bureaucratic malfeasance and the other ills that are imagined to plague higher education. . . . Get disappointed enough times, see two or three carefully thought out plans go down the drain and cynicism and despair seem like the only reasonable responses to have. And, once one has fallen into that mindset, all that's left to look forward to in the long walk to retirement is a life spent letting everyone else know that everything in the system works together to prevent innovation. That change isn't possible. That hope is for the young, the naïve, the foolish.
>
> —Richard Miller

> Hope is an emotional investment that we develop collaboratively; it is an act of mutuality that is nourished by our collective expectations. Teaching, learning and administration are not simply intellectual activities that one masters, but a complex blend of emotional and professional issues that involve the whole person.
>
> —Laura R. Micciche

Throughout the process of writing this text, we have grown accustomed to at least one of us sharing our experience of frustration, sadness, or even outrage during any given week. We are no Pollyannas, offering the future WPA panaceas for every problem she may encounter, or passing on enough rhetorical knowledge to have her colleagues and administrators eating out of her hands. But we also do not have to succumb to a long, cynical walk towards retirement that Miller describes. We are learning that hope is not just for the young in the realm of WPA work; it is for those who believe in theorizing and working actively for the long term while also living with immediate needs, constraints, and desires.

While writing this book, we have tried to imagine why it is that we can still have hope in the face of all we have experienced collectively. Certainly our relationships with one another and with our mentors and supportive colleagues have helped. But one thing we have realized in its writing is that, while WPA work may be one site for the kinds of learning and knowing we enjoy, our commitment to this kind of learning and knowing need not be restricted to just one site (or job). Our commitment to meaningful work compels us to resist the kinds of thinking that devalue writing program administration and, instead, to value the *potential* of our contributions. In 2002, Ann Austin reported on a four-year longitudinal study that followed a sample of seventy-nine graduate students from across the disciplines at doctoral-granting universities who wanted to be academics. What she found was that

> prospective faculty members today want "meaning" in their work. They want to engage in work that has a positive impact on the students with whom they come in contact or on the broader society and work that has personal significance for them. . . . Yet, these respondents do not view the faculty career as the only possibility for engaging in meaningful work. (107)

Like the respondents in this study, the five of us have broad understandings of our identities as professionals, as teachers and makers and knowers. At the 2009 CWPA Conference, Linda Adler-Kassner noted that when the frustration of the job becomes too much, she reminds herself, "We're not curing cancer here," and if the disappointment outweighs the joy, she can always leave the academy. While her mantra is a good reminder, we are able to maintain our hope because this is the work we have chosen to dedicate our intellect, energy, and passion to; we may not be curing cancer, but we do find significant meaning in our work by negotiating the waters of our academic communities to provide writing instruction that serves our students. We have a set of skills and abilities which the 2000 biology conference, "Re-envisioning the PhD," suggests are important to inculcate in doctoral education: the ability to "manag[e] complexity" and to "develop a philosophy about scholarship, education, and leadership . . . and understand how to continue to learn and adapt to changing situations" (Austin 101). This book is an expression of one such philosophy, this chapter one way of addressing how WPA professionalization and education might support a commitment to this kind of learning which can begin in graduate school and continue throughout a professional lifetime.

In this section, then, we explore more fully collective expectations for the education of a WPA to offer what we see as key components of WPA preparation. In doing so we consider what contributes most to the social, emotional, and intellectual education of a WPA, what curricular efforts in graduate school achieve, and what components of WPA education we can make use of to strengthen our abilities to do good WPA work. We draw on suggestions that have already been made in the body of work on WPA professionalization. However, rather than rehearse the long and familiar lists of everything the field has suggested WPAs should know (like institutional politics, budgeting, interpersonal communication, histories of the discipline, etc.), we focus instead on those elements (some of which were a part of our educational experiences, some of which weren't) that we believe can help us take on the "ways of knowing, questioning, and communicating that enable WPAs to do and understand their work, regardless of what [that] specific work turns out to be" (Rose and Weiser, "Beyond" 173). We take on that task to foster personal and professional hope and flourishing for WPAs.

The Explicit Curriculum

In the introduction to their collection, *Culture Shock and the Practice of Profession*, Anderson and Romano claim that "[E]ndowing students with stable identities as rhetoric and composition professionals is less crucial than preparing them to adopt myriad and shifting professional personas" (3) and that "the professional identity packed up with the china and furniture and books, the one polished and cosseted in seminars and with respected mentors, will seldom work" (6). Junior faculty members must be "prepared to reinvent themselves on the job" and be "prepared for difficulties of representation" with new colleagues (Anderson and Romano 6). They go on to argue that "these two 'Rs,' reinvention and representation, can't be 'taught' in any concrete sense. *How* a particular new hire will be required to reinvent herself and *how* she will be required to represent her professional self cannot be predicted until she is there" (Anderson and Romano 6). Like Anderson and Romano, we believe that what's most useful for future faculty is a *rhetorical* education, to "rethink graduate education as a matter of *rela-*

tionships: disciplinary/intra-interdisciplinary relationships; human relationships—hierarchical, labor, gender; and institution-to-discipline relationships" (7). We can't imagine being WPAs without also simultaneously being rhetoricians. While we don't want to focus here on the fascinating, but tangential, discussion of what rhetoric and composition graduate curricula should look like as a whole, we consider what might constitute vital curricular components of a WPA's education.

Big Picture Courses. It is customary to include a kind of professional literacy which reflects an understanding of institutional politics, a knowledge of how institutions work, and an understanding of histories of the discipline(s) in a long list of what WPAs should know before they take on their positions, but it is much less customary to find lengthy discussions of *how* to make these things an explicit part of the curriculum. Over ten years ago, Scott Miller, Brenda Jo Brueggemann, Bennis Blue, and Deneed M. Shepherd argued, after conducting a national survey of graduate students, that the field should "share more about what is involved in both the production and end product of a 'professional' in our field" (402). "Ensuring success," they write, "requires making the profession *as a subject* a part of the curriculum" (Miller et al. 402). Five years later, in 2002, Theresa Enos, made a compelling argument in the same vein that faculty should design professional development for graduate students that is "discipline based through the curriculum . . . so that students' transcripts reflect such 'credentialing' rather than having such work be perceived as part of 'service'" (59). At the University of Arizona, where Enos is the director of the Rhetoric, Composition, and the Teaching of English graduate program, they have designed their graduate curriculum to make good on that promise. Professional Studies is one of three areas in which students are required to take courses, alongside Histories of Rhetoric and Research, Theory, and Praxis.

In our own experience, such coursework has been valuable in helping us think about the larger goals of higher education institutions as well as think about inter- and intra-disciplinary relationships, important for all faculty, but particularly important for writing program administrators. Two of us took a course in graduate school called "The Rhetoric of Institutional Discourse," which examined the complex history and development of universities, humanities curricula, and the values that educators, theorists, and institutional critics deploy, critique, and revise as they operate in, through, and around systems of higher education. From reading and discussing texts alongside each other like Plato's *Apology*, Martha Nussbaum's *Cultivating Humanity: A Classical Defense of Liberal Education*, Martin Heidegger's *The Principle of Reason*, and Bill Readings's *The University in Ruins*, we gained a specific history of cultural missions for universities as institutors of belief and a broad understanding of the institutional players who may not be so easily categorized into students, teachers, and administrators. Together with texts like Ernesto Grassi's *Rhetoric as Philosophy* and Gary Olson's collection *Rhetoric and Composition as Intellectual Work*, we were led to think about the role of rhetoric in those larger cultural and institutional missions as well. We continue to shape our own philosophies about the relationships between our discipline, institutions of higher education, and larger purposes for education and work as they are reflected in our personal and professional choices about where to work, what kinds of relationships and programs we want to develop and nurture, what sorts of curriculum to design, and more.

Several of us also had coursework in the history of the profession/discipline(s) of English that provided rich context for reading institutional/departmental politics. Since Colin, Jonikka, and Kate took such courses in their Master's programs almost fifteen years ago, even more work has been done in this area, producing texts from which graduate faculty could choose, including Robert Scholes's *The Rise and Fall of English* and Bruce McComiskey's *English Studies: An Introduction to the Discipline(s)*. Courses like this are becoming more popular, even at the undergraduate level, as recognition of the interdisciplinary nature of English Studies increases as does specialization in these different disciplines. The more specialized we become, the fewer opportunities and incentives an English major has to take a sufficient number of courses in linguistics, literature, creative writing, or rhetoric and composition—just to name a few disciplines under the umbrella of English Studies—to really understand those disciplines in ways that would promote broader understanding of what each of these disciplines brings to a given department's mission and work. The same could be said of departments of writing in which faculty from professional writing, technical communication, histories of rhetoric, literacy studies, and pedagogy co-exist. The more faculty specialize, the more professionalized their discipline(s) become, the less they understand about one another as members of academic and extra-academic communities and the more they have to work on ways to communicate across our professional niches. Shirley Wilson Logan speaks to this topic in her 2006 article in *College English* on the future of English Studies.

Rhetoric and composition faculty at Colin and Jonikka's university have been offering a slightly different course, not one that focuses on the history or prospects of the profession, but one that seeks to introduce new rhetoric and composition graduate students to the different areas of inquiry their Master's program is organized around: rhetoric, composition, and literacy studies. In that course, as each rhetoric and composition faculty member visits to talk about his/her work, students are exposed to the reality that, even in the "same" discipline, we are not all preoccupied with the same questions, we don't use the same methodologies to arrive at answers to our questions, and we do not even all hold the same academic/philosophical values.

It is not hard to imagine how useful that kind of awareness might be in a rhetoric committee or department meeting, and without such a course, that awareness might have to be unnecessarily hard-won, often, frankly, at the expense of new faculty's emotional well-being. Lisa Langstraat and Julie Lindquist claim that "one of the most important features of graduate training is offering apprentice compositionists the opportunity to understand, and position themselves within, the histories of their field" so that they can "understand[] those histories not only in light of their material conditions, pedagogical causes and effects, or theoretical influences. We also need," they argue, "to explore those histories in light of shifting emotion cultures" (Langstraat and Lindquist 37). Introductory/Histories of the Discipline(s) courses are one way to *study* those disciplines and develop what Langstraat and Lindquist call a pragmatics of emotion which enables one to "historiciz[e] the emotion cultures of institutions and departments, encourag[e] a self-reflexive awareness of the ways affective lives intersect with our departmental emotion cultures, and forward[] a series of rhetorical approaches for both articulating and acting on those intersections" (36). These three approaches "can help students not only to read the ways in which the emotional underlife of an institution influences matters of administration and policy, but also to develop repertoires of ethical responses to everyday predicaments" (Langstraat and Lindquist 36).

WPA Seminars. Rebecca Jackson, Carrie Leverenz, and Joe Law make a compelling case for the value of graduate-level coursework in writing center administration in their chapter, "(Re)Shaping the Profession: Graduate Courses in Writing Center Theory, Practice, and Administration"; courses like these, they argue, can be seen as "marking a significant stage in the professionalization of writing centers, part of the identifiable pattern that can be traced in the evolution of most academic disciplines" (131). We would extend their argument to all WPA courses, whose existence, we and they believe, has led not only to a "sense of professionalization," but also to "a sense of disciplinarity, that is now being perpetuated in [WPA] graduate courses" (Jackson et al. 132). In 2002, Gail Stygall called for the certification of WPA knowledge, similar to the certification of other professionals like doctors and lawyers. One of her goals was to establish writing program administration expertise so that WPAs could "gain the kind of professional power necessary to work for progressive aims" (Stygall 80). Her article gives voice to the idea that not everyone can (or, perhaps, should) be a WPA. In other words, there is a disciplinary basis for work in rhetoric and composition and, increasingly, a disciplinary basis for work *in WPA*. That doesn't require a homogenized approach to WPA, but a recognition that WPA coursework offers one way of legitimizing and creating WPA disciplinary knowledge.

In some circles, it is now commonplace to say that WPA work is intellectual work. Formal study promotes WPA as a profession, and, if done well, can emphasize the role of research and scholarship *on* writing program administration itself (Rose and Weiser, "Beyond" 167-70). Course projects can be designed to encourage empirical research design and theory-building, all of which promotes the scholarly nature of WPA work and encourages future faculty members to consider a WPA scholarly agenda. Enos believes that "one effect of the WPA Intellectual Work document . . . is that more graduate students are *choosing* writing program administration as one of their areas of concentration in rhetoric and composition—rather than having it ordained by the job position itself" (64), and we believe that to be true. One in ten respondents to Shirley K Rose and Jonikka Charlton's 2007 survey of CWPA members cited writing a WPA-related dissertation as preparation for their WPA work (Charlton and Rose 138), and we suspect that number will go up as more graduate students are exposed to WPA scholarship and see possibilities for their own creative research agendas in the area. In Melissa Ianetta, Linda Bergmann, Lauren Fitzgerald, Carol Peterson Haviland, Lisa Lebduska, and Mary Wislocki's "Polylog," Bergmann noted that graduate students in her writing center administration classes "may [have been] attracted to the collaborative atmosphere and human caring of the writing center, [but] they are reading its now-canonical literature critically and asking difficult questions about our ideas and practices, such as 'do they work?' and 'how do we know?'" (33). As time goes on, more and more of us will be asking these kinds of questions and identifying ourselves not only, or perhaps not even first, as rhetoric and composition people, but as WPAs, because that's who we are as scholars.

In keeping with Anderson and Romano's call for a rhetorical education, Rose and Weiser also call for teaching writing program administration, through formal study, as rhetorical practice and inquiry ("Beyond" 173). They summarize what's been called for in writing program administration courses in the literature, including its role in "teaching students how to achieve a balance among administration, teaching, and research," "help[ing] us meet our ethical responsibility to reveal the benefits and hardships of writing program administration to students," and "prepar[ing] students to participate in institutional life more productively and with greater self-efficacy" (Rose and Weiser, "Beyond" 166). These are certainly lofty goals, and we can imagine skeptics wondering how these abilities could ever be *taught*. It may help to think of these as goals for a series of courses, as in the four-course WPA specialization Amy and Jonikka completed in graduate school. However, many of these issues can be addressed through readings and experiential learning opportunities even in a single course. In the WPA seminars which Jonikka, Tarez, and Amy took, several key groups of texts and role-playing activities were directly related to the first two goals above. Early on in the semester, they read, individually and collectively, a collection of current job descriptions, which advertised varying degrees of WPA work. In Jonikka's seminar, for most of the students in the class, it was the first time they had seen job descriptions of any kind, but it was clear early on that WPAs might have a special need to think carefully about how to balance administration, teaching, and research. When Amy and Tarez took the seminar, their group consisted of several current or past WPAs—from writing center directors, to assistant program directors, to core seminar coordinators—allowing them to focus on the ways that these descriptions and other genres critically mis/represented WPA work.

Another of their class meetings focused on reading and analyzing WPA narratives, a week which stood out clearly for them. As we recounted in Chapter 2, the force of these narratives in shaping conceptions about WPA work was powerful, and when Jonikka took the seminar, her professor hadn't anticipated the negative effect the narratives had on many students in the class, perhaps because, as an active, successful WPA for many years, it had been a long time since she had seen WPA work from an outsider's perspective. Because there was a curricular space for that conversation, they had the time and place to talk about the emotional toll of WPA work. When Tarez and Amy took the seminar, the professor's focus was more on critiquing the narratives for the ways that their writing reflected specific depictions or beliefs about writing program administration and provided venues for the students to critique these depictions and beliefs. They were all invited to imagine WPA narratives of their own, giving them the power to begin shaping those stories themselves. And they engaged in numerous situated role-playing activities, some of which they designed themselves based on their reading and their own fears and interests, finding a safe place to play those circumstances out, analyze their performances, and imagine alternatives to their actions—all without fear of long-term damage to their working relationships or reputations.

Amy's, Jonikka's, and Tarez's experiences in this seminar showed them that WPA work in all its permutations offers enough intellectual fodder for serious, formal study. Amy and Jonikka began their PhD programs knowing they wanted to get their specializations in writing program administration, which, at Purdue, consisted of four courses—a required WPA seminar, one WAC or assessment course, and two others selected from a list including second language writing, writing center theory, distance education, professional writing, and more. Jonikka even argued successfully for the inclusion of the "Rhetoric of Institutional Discourse" class as a WPA option. And while a student could easily stay in school for ten years taking WPA-related coursework, there isn't time enough or reason to think that one must learn everything before graduation. This kind of WPA seminar often plays the role of an introduction to WPA work; students who take it aren't always like Amy and Jonikka were, committed to WPA work and a WPA way of life or, like Tarez, interested in the intellectual engagement it provided. Some took it because they sensed what was coming for them and wanted to be prepared, like taking a flu shot. But those same people left the course with more respect for the body of work that WPAs have produced. As more theoretical and empirical work on writing program administration issues is produced, options for texts in these courses will continue to increase to the point where it will be increasingly difficult to choose which to use outside of specific program contexts.

We can imagine, however, a set of questions that WPA courses could attempt to address, questions which direct its participants to develop their own WPA philosophies, ways of thinking, and ways of pursuing questions about WPA work:

- What do we know about writing program administration and WPA lives? What else do we need to know?
- How does WPA identity get constructed and evolve?
- What constitutes WPA work? How does that work vary depending on contextual factors like institutional type and size, programmatic vision, and more?
- What are important areas of inquiry in writing program administration? What methods and methodologies do we use to pursue our questions?
- What are the conventions of writing program administration research? How do we distribute and share the practical and theoretical knowledge we build?
- What are our theories of administration? Our models?
- What do other disciplines and theories/ways of thinking have to offer our ways of understanding our work and purposes?
- What roles do WPAs play in program, departmental, institutional, and disciplinary life? What are the purposes of educational institutions, and what roles do writing and, thus, WPAs, play in those missions?
- What purposes do we imagine for our work in our own personal lives and in the larger cultural life of our communities and nation?
- What purposes do we imagine for our work within and beyond our discipline?

Doug Hesse once asked whether writing program administration should be "a curricular focus (e.g., a specific set of courses) or a curricular perspective (integrated into all graduate courses) or some combination of both" (Rose and Weiser, "Beyond" 169), and we wholeheartedly agree with the last. In the best of all worlds, it would be both. Those who know or think they want to hold WPA positions or pursue WPA scholarly agendas should take as many courses as possible with a focus on WPA issues. In WPA seminars, courses in assessment, writing center theory and administration, institutional rhetoric, and WAC, Amy, Jonikka, and Tarez entered into the WPA scholarly conversation and began to imagine the kinds of questions which they might pursue as WPA researchers and theorists, but in other classes—ones without an explicit WPA focus—they used that administrative point of view as a lens through which to view rhetorical history and visual rhetoric and feminist theory. In many places, we recognize it is not a curricular possibility to have WPA courses; in MA-only institutions, in departments focused solely on literary studies, or in small doctoral programs in rhetoric and composition, it is hard to justify the offering. But that doesn't mean that a WPA perspective or line of inquiry cannot be brought to bear in other courses or as a topic of study for directed readings and doctoral exams. We'd like to think it is possible for our curricula, no matter how they are configured, to "allow students to begin to develop identity as WPAs" (Rose and Weiser, "Beyond" 167) that will be nurtured and change over the course of a professional lifetime.

Engaged Program Work. One of the most vital contributions to our understanding of WPA (and faculty life) has been having multiple opportunities to engage in program work from very early on in our education, even at multiple institutions. It is easy to be a somewhat passive participant in program life whether in graduate school or in academic positions, teaching classes and going home to study or work on a project, complying with program rules for assessment without needing to know why or what the outcomes are. Each of us was, however, encouraged as graduate students to do work that offered us not only a glimpse at how departments work (however partial those glimpses inevitably are), but an opportunity to do real program work that helped us construct and reflect on our identities as participants in work of real consequence, and that taught us to see the ramifications of the small from a larger perspective.

As PhD students, Tarez, Jonikka, Colin, and Amy were deeply immersed in program life. They each sat on the Introductory Composition committee alongside six or more rhetoric and composition faculty, were involved in the development—and committee discussions about—new goals, means, and outcomes statements for the FYC program, and led efforts to build several syllabus approaches that were both disciplinarily sound and congruent with the goals, means, and outcomes statements. While the social benefits of such work are clear—they had to be able to articulate their own ideas, negotiate their desires with others, represent the concerns of their graduate student colleagues, etc.—the intellectual nature of this work was unmistakable. As part of their work, they had to articulate (in writing) the theoretical bases for their syllabus approaches, construct sample syllabi and writing assignments, and be able to present and defend their work to the fuller committee. They also had to consider how they might bring non-WPA collaborators on board and how to deliver their work as pedagogy, as Colin and Tarez did when they mentored new teachers in some of the new approaches.

WPA preparation is enhanced even further through engaged program work when we allow others to plan, conduct, and report on program research. Tarez, Jonikka, Colin, and Amy also had the opportunity as graduate students to design and carry out empirical research on required conferencing, a new facet of their first-year composition program delivery. As part of a graduate empirical research course, their professor used this project to help them learn not only how to design good empirical research, but also how empirical research can inform WPA work writ large. Efforts like these reflect a writing program administration-across-the-curriculum approach to that can be encouraged in many graduate programs, in turn lessening the burden of having one or two people responsible for doing all program research (as usually might be the case) and providing a meaningful application of theory for more than just students interested in writing program administration.

Of course, valuable administrative experience can be gained through opportunities to hold assistant WPA positions, as Kate, Amy, and Jonikka did. Kate was eager to participate in larger conversations and initiatives while at The University of North Carolina at Greensboro since she entered her program knowing she wanted to take part in discussions about curriculum design and program development. As the Assistant Director of Composition at UNCG, Kate participated in program administration related to scheduling composition courses, conducting meetings, co-leading TA orientation, and generally working closely with the Director of Composition on issues related particularly to TA education. This position not only gave Kate a chance to talk regularly with the director about what it means to administer a program, but she had lived experiences negotiating differential power dynamics, leading program meetings, and mentoring new graduate students. The explicit and implicit learning on the job was invaluable, particularly in a context that valued her contributions as a graduate student administrator. Though the most common way of gaining valuable administrative experience while in graduate school (as Rose and Charlton noted in their 2007 WPA conference presentation), 47% of CWPA members surveyed in 2007 attributed their gWPA positions to preparing them for WPA work), these positions are also scarce, too scarce for our discipline to rely too heavily on them as a major source of WPA preparation. While some programs are large enough to support five or more of these positions, most are lucky to have even one.

Of course, gWPA positions don't need to be limited to assistant directorships of composition programs. Kate served as a WAC research and program assistant at UNCG when the university was developing a speaking across the curriculum initiative and extending writing across the curriculum expectations beyond arts and sciences. She worked with the program director planning workshops, developing content for a WAC/SAC website, and attending faculty meetings and workshops related to the initiative. University projects like this one can be rich opportunities for graduate students to observe and participate in campus conversations about writing and faculty development. Kate also had an opportunity as a doctoral student to chair a conference for high school girls through the Women's Studies Program. Through this position, she developed an understanding of the negotiations and work it takes to lead and organize a local conference which involved faculty and instructors across campus. While not related to writing program administration directly, running a conference that served about seventy-five girls, helped her feel more confident about the prospect of taking on a WPA job after graduation. Working in this context enabled Kate to position herself professionally as a graduate student and reflect on that activity as it related to her career trajectory. Access to broader conversations and contexts such as these can help graduate students gain broader perspectives that resonate with scholarship, but also offer the advantage of lived, local context which reinforces the rhetoricity of writing program administration.

These same opportunities can be afforded faculty members as they take on projects born of any number of committees within and outside their departments. While it is important, then, to engage graduate students, especially, in program work, we have the opportunity and obligation to extend that invitation to our faculty colleagues as well; doing so will enrich our program work by inviting multiple, sometimes critical perspectives, into decision-making, and it will engage more faculty in thinking programmatically, like a WPA.

The Hidden Curriculum

Educators spend a great deal of time carefully designing curricula, articulating goals, designing reading lists and activities to encourage the achievement of those goals, and practicing assessment on the success of curricula to deliver on an explicit set of student learning outcomes. But we all know that we learned, and our students learn, a lot that is unintentional from the "hidden curriculum" of graduate school and beyond. We learn a lot about identity, especially, from being "keen observers and listeners" (Austin 104). Graduate students (and faculty alike) "listen carefully to formal as well as informal conversations with advisors and supervisors. They pay attention to casual, offhand remarks by professors and by more advanced students" (Austin 104). And they learn to read the emotional cultures around them in these ways, using their interpretations of these situations to shape and question their ideas of the purpose(s) and the possibilities of academic life and their potential places in that life. This was certainly true for us, and we ignore the hidden curriculum at our—and our students'— peril.

Most WPAs likely have examples of learning, particularly about institutional politics, in the ways described by Austin. As graduate students, we attended parties, witnessed interactions between our professors, and occasionally overheard gossip we shouldn't have. We participated in institutional politics as we took classes together, taught together, and competed with one another for awards, opportunities, and plum assignments. Those who attended conferences learned a great deal about identity, disciplinary values, and networking that probably wasn't explicitly taught as part of their graduate curriculum. Still others may have served in administrative positions as graduate students, and, there, learned first-hand about being both colleague and not-colleague with peers.[6] More generally, we may have revised or co-edited documents for faculty nominations, taught linked courses in service-learning or co-curricular learning communities, held joint appointments in multiple departments, or navigated split dissertation committees—experiences that can broaden our understanding of disciplinary powers and communication or teach us to assimilate others' disparate desires for us into a coherent pathway forward. All these lessons are valuable because they offer examples of how a WPA functions and negotiates her identity in an academic community, and we should continue to provide opportunities for such *unintentional* learning, opportunities which might emerge through a variety of avenues we discuss in this chapter.

In retrospect, Kate acknowledges the ways the hidden curriculum at UNCG taught her the need to find balance between research, teaching, service, and herself. She observed her different mentors finding ways to plan time for research and make time for walking, yoga, gardening, and enjoying their teaching. She watched two different WPAs administer a busy composition program with grace and integrity and a value of collaboration as a natural part of the endeavor. Because she had a range of mentors, she saw different ways people sought balance and made themselves a life: how one faculty member seemed to have a gift for answering a whole range of questions in an office appointment lasting only a half hour, how another knew when to shut her door and get her work done, and how a third found intellectual stimulation in working with graduate students who reinvigorated her research interests. And how they all forwarded a sense of caring that made even the challenges of graduate school and dissertation writing do-able.

While we cannot and do not want to control the lessons of the hidden curriculum, we can, with some measure of intention, offer extracurricular opportunities through which our students can learn—not always what we intend—but learn nonetheless. Kathryn Valentine describes in "'Acting Out' or Acts of Agency" how she sought to redesign her writing center training opportunities to "focus on supporting consultants to negotiate the meanings of their work in hopes that this will also encourage them to develop identities of participation in regard to that work" (Valentine 150). She writes about her efforts as the writing center director to create "space for agency on the part of consultants" (Valentine 152) rather than trying to over-determine their behaviors. But this requires an environment of openness and trust, one which allows for moments of learning without prescribing what is and isn't open to discussion.

As MA students, Jonikka and Colin had the atypical opportunity to serve on departmental committees tasked with reviewing the faculty's annual evaluation portfolios; the authority granted them in these roles allowed them learning opportunities in which they gained a sense of the range and relative value of faculty work, something most faculty have to learn on the job at a time when the stakes are tremendously high. Faculty in their program were amazingly supportive, investing them with the authority to respond to (and even critique) activities claimed for service, scholarship, and teaching. Reading these portfolios gave Jonikka and Colin not only a sense of what "counted" at that institution and beyond, but also what differences in value sometimes surface in the work of different disciplines, where community service activities, for instance, might be more prevalent and valued in creative writing than they are in literature. Colin remembers one such occasion when a faculty member on the committee struck up a conversation with him about the history of faculty evaluation at the institution and the difficulties he experienced in equally evaluating the work of two of his colleagues who engaged in significantly different types of service. The conversation wasn't planned or expected, but it emerged from a relationship of trust, interest, and curiosity, and presented itself as an opportunity for that faculty member to mentor a potential future colleague, and to share his institutional knowledge and ideas about what matters in faculty work. And, while it was not an intended outcome, when Colin and Jonikka began their first faculty positions, several of their senior colleagues noted how well they represented their work in their own annual evaluation folders, an ability they trace to their early work on these committees as graduate students. Because they had a rich understanding of how systems of value work and how to represent their own contributions in a language which was recognizable in those systems of value, Jonikka and Colin were better able to read their new institution's tenure and merit evaluation policies and weren't as anxious as other junior faculty in their early years as assistant professors.

While we, as faculty, do not have a great deal of control over what our students learn from the hidden curriculum, we are well-served by an awareness of its operation and should take every opportunity to make the lessons learned an explicit part of our conversations with our students, whether through classroom discussions or as part of our mentoring relationships.

Mentoring

The anxieties surrounding professionalization that we mention earlier could resonate with anxieties about mentoring in general, and we recognize that in some university, programmatic, or departmental cultures, mentoring raises contention and concern. How can we propose a mentoring model when there is suspended belief in some humanities disciplines about whether it is the role of faculty to mentor their graduate students and/or the role of faculty to mentor one another? This question may not simply reflect a rejection of the value of mentoring, but may stem from a longer tradition of institutional or material factors that render mentoring improbable in a particular campus culture. On the other hand, it may reflect ways that academic mentoring *models* themselves have fallen short of their fullest potential, i.e., by placing too much pressure on a single mentoring individual, by creating unreasonable demands for mechanistic rubrics, by raising unreasonable expectations in terms of what mentees should gain, by purporting that mentoring can stand in for other essential coursework or instruction, by relying overly much on nurturing or affective characteristics that have most often been attributed to women or junior faculty, or by remaining unquantifiable and/or off-grid and informal and, hence, invisible.

In their own work, "Conceptualizing the Academic Life: Graduate Students' Perspectives," Jeffrey Bieber and Linda Worley propose a socialization "schema" over a mentoring "model" to help graduate students imagine a mentoring relationship where they might not have had one before; to conceptualize their future careers as theoretical, contingent, and reflective; to note institutional "politics" (1025); and to heighten their levels of commitment to a faculty career by seeing "also . . . the 'good' things that are part of faculty life" (1026). Bieber and Worley rely on Wilkes's definition of schema—"'symbolic representations that serve to encode our generic knowledge concerning objects, scenes, and action sequences'"—in order to "avoid the possible confusion attendant on the large semantic field surrounding the words 'model' and 'pattern'" (1011). In short, Bieber and Worley suggest that staid mentoring models themselves are insufficient for helping students to feel "intimately connected to their academic life" (1026) because they do not remove distance or provide insider perspectives, but rather perpetuate unsupported hierarchies.

Although Bieber and Worley justify using Wilkes's schema theory because of revealed trends regarding students' largely material motivations for attending graduate school, its complexity serves even those mentoring situations that are characterized by unbridled intellectual interest in the discipline (of rhetoric and composition and/or of WPA). Schema theory carries weight for GenAdmin inasmuch as it reminds us of the need to "augment what we have learned about graduate education from socialization theory as well as from other conceptual perspectives" (Bieber and Worley 1011)—that is, GenAdmin looks beyond and outside of our discipline for imagining ways of preparing practitioners for the multiplicinarity of the work, and we seek to iterate schema that can then be realistically employed beyond just our programs. Graduate students' intellectual interest in WPA can be quite complex, and may encompass material desires, i.e., their intellectual interest may well exist alongside the desire for aspects of "flexibility" and "personal autonomy" (Bieber and Worley 1020). Thus, Bieber and Worley's appropriation of Wilkes marks one way to capture that knowledge, not only by recognizing in our own education what can and has acted as "mentoring," but also by finding achievable ways to do it even in contexts where formal mentoring structures do not exist or in places where motivations for doing the work diverge.

By design, writing program administration as a field is committed to frequent and good mentoring. Even when our institutions, our colleagues, or our faculty members are not (or cannot be) there for us, other WPAs are. Those networks we discussed above are a testament to that. In the 1990s, when few WPAs claimed to have much preparation for WPA work, mentoring was an important component of a WPA's education, especially on the job. In 1992, Sally Barr Ebest found that 74.3% of her WPA survey respondents claimed an administrative assistantship was "the most essential to the training of future WPAs with mentoring and tutoring ranked second and third" ("The Next" 75). In an article focused on the gender breakdown of her survey results, Ebest noted that "men were twice as likely as women to have received guidance from mentors; they attributed 60% of their positive on-the-job learning to mentors" ("Gender" 54). More than fifteen years later, Rose and Charlton reported at the 2007 WPA conference that 46% of CWPA members credit mentoring as graduate students and mentoring from other administrative colleagues while on-the-job as part of their preparation for WPA work, suggesting that mentoring still plays an important role in the professional lives of WPAs. The current CWPA Executive Board and presidential team are clearly committed to focusing the field's attention on mentoring; they have dedicated a strand of the more recent WPA conferences (since 2009) to workshops and panels which directly provide one-stop mentoring, and they have begun a WPA Mentoring Project, complete with a national survey to try to pinpoint ways in which its increasingly diverse membership can benefit from more organized and explicit attempts to build mentoring relationships, not just early on, but throughout one's WPA career. GenAdmin pushes us to become more aware of the variety of WPA roles and the complexity of WPA subjectivities, and, as we do, we recognize the need for a range of mentoring opportunities and relationships that address the diversity of our needs and desires.

Many graduate programs now place a strong emphasis on developing mentoring relationships with students. gWPAs are often in the most enviable positions as they usually have more access than most to WPA mentors. While some would (often rightly) argue that "Graduate student administrators only see 'part' of the job, being offered rare glimpses of the dirty, behind-the-scenes work of writing program administration" (Edgington and Taylor 163), the benefits of such relationships are easily identifiable. As gWPAs with a range of roles and responsibilities, one of the most important things we all got from our experiences was the opportunity to watch a WPA negotiate rhetorical and institutional challenges and the opportunity to mentor our peers as teachers. Jonikka and Tarez were active in these positions when their WPA mentor was in the midst of developing and garnering support for a major curricular revision. Jonikka was given access, as part of a directed self-study on professionalization, to the previous WPA's notes from meetings across campus in which he had to negotiate and argue for the value of this curricular change that affected every college's degree requirements. She talked with her WPA mentor about the rhetorical strategies being employed to sell the change within the department as it was taking place, and she was there as the WPA worked through ideas for implementing policies which would both track the changes and monitor whether and how they were being made at the individual instructor level. Tarez was given access to the same information in the context of her seminar on empirical research methods, and later worked with another WPA on a collaborative mentoring initiative, specifically on developing models for engaging non-WPA (and non-rhetoric and composition students) in the types of program work they thought had pedagogical value beyond the first-year mentoring experience.

Colin had a very different mentoring relationship, one in which he was both mentee and co-mentor. Early on, an organic mentoring relationship developed between Colin and one of the rhetoric and composition faculty members in his program. His mentor showed him drafts of his writing as he turned his dissertation into a book, and, in doing so, he taught Colin that you have to write about what you're doing, that you can make connections between your teaching, your service, and your scholarship. Colin applied those lessons to his own dissertation, which focused on what he was doing at the time—mentoring—and his philosophical/theoretical interests. He was also able to team-teach with his mentor, in effect becoming a co-mentor for the large group of new graduate students who were assigned to them. As they worked to mentor a mixed group of graduate students (MA, MFA, and PhD, from different disciplines, with varying experiences as teachers), Colin learned a great deal not only from his own struggles of trying to teach others to teach, but also from his mentor's struggles doing the same. His mentor was philosophically opposed to telling others how to teach, which was difficult for him since most of his mentees wanted him to do exactly that. Colin learned a lot that semester about the difficulties WPAs can have as TA mentors, and he learned it because he was coping with life as a student, an instructor, a mentor, and a mentee. In a way, Colin's situation reflects his concern about building a pedagogical culture while surviving in the existing one—a situation that each of us has experienced more than once, but one that puts us on our way to considering mentoring as a *gravity*, rather than a hierarchy. This gravity—not unlike Strenski's use of Bourdieu's "force-field" to describe the negotiating that occurs for her while "re-training" experienced teachers (82)—causes us to attend to ways that mentoring can and does occur reciprocally and can create a project that exercises its pull on all participants. While we recognize that not everyone will have had similar opportunities and experiences as ours, it becomes incredibly important for all of us to make spaces for those opportunities more readily available—both for those on WPA "tracks" and those who may never aspire to hold formal WPA positions.

In addition to the mentoring relations that exist for us in graduate school, we want to highlight the value of mentoring relationships we all have in the early stages of our careers as faculty. Jonikka's WPA mentor in graduate school became her writing/research partner; what began as a teacher-student mentoring relationship transformed into a mutually enriching collegial relationship based on shared interest in WPA preparation and identity. They now Skype weekly, talking not just about their current collaborative projects, but also sharing their questions, excitement, and challenges as faculty and WPAs. Kate still benefits from the mentoring and co-mentoring relationships she developed at the WPA workshop, where senior colleagues gave her advice about her career path and other colleagues became conversational partners in thinking through WPA issues that cross campuses.

We all owe more than we can say to our mentors, many of whom were/are WPAs. From some, we took key parts of our administrative philosophy, from others we talked through career decisions and research interests. We have all experienced a range of mentoring experiences, some helpful, even enlightening, others less so, even damaging. We know that some of our mentoring relationships are destined to be one-sided; in our lives for a brief time, mentors pass on valuable strategies and philosophical tidbits we carry with us long after the relationship dissolves. Some, though, continue to grow over many years; if we're lucky, these mentoring relationships deepen into friendships that are sustaining and mutually beneficial. We would encourage WPAs of all levels of experience to broaden their understanding of mentoring beyond the common expert-apprentice models, wherein the senior WPA holds the knowledge and the junior WPA or new TA is its recipient.

This sense that the newer colleague merely receives knowledge replicates Freire's banking system of education, creating a one-way model of mentoring in which the expert's knowledge is deposited in and reproduced by the newcomer, leaving little space for the creation of new knowledge that could emerge by listening to the experiences and ideas of the mentee. For the WPA to be effectively trained to do the work required of her, she needs to be listened to by her mentors in a way that recognizes the reciprocal nature of these mentoring relationships and seeks to explore the richness of all WPA experience and expertise, as GenAdmin does. WPAs have much to offer one another, much that is not grounded in a language and ideology of leveling, assimilation, or expertise, but one, perhaps, of mutual curiosity and commitment to effective writing instruction and program administration. We see the possibilities for such co-mentoring models through experiences like Colin's and through the co-mentoring we do with and for one another where giving and receiving is mutual and reciprocal. While hierarchical models of mentoring can be successful, GenAdmin values dialogic models that recognize the fluid roles of mentor/mentee and recognize that a newcomer to the field can offer different experiences and ways of thinking that can lead to new strategies and knowledge for newcomers and senior colleagues alike.

Extra-Institutional Networks

We would also like to pay brief, but special, attention to the extra-institutional networks that are particularly important in the continuing education of WPAs, especially since faculty are both more mobile and more willing to establish extra-institutional mentoring relationships and build knowledge collaboratively. Examples of these networks are the WPA listservs (WPA-L, gWPA-L, jWPA-L); the WPA Summer Workshop, Conference, and Institutes; and the recent formation of WPA special interest groups (jWPA, WPA-GO) that meet at our annual conferences. These networks serve in both explicit and implicit capacities to "teach" WPAs in an ongoing professional development "curriculum" which is both fluid and adaptive. Each of these networks was created in response to a group identity and a group need: a need to share information and stories, a need to ask questions and find answers, a need to keep learning from one another. The CWPA Executive Board understood there was a need for members to learn about assessment, not a focus of most members' graduate education, and they began to offer a one-day institute to address specific issues in the area. Other institutes have spoken directly to a changing WPA identity in which research and scholarship play central roles in the WPA's life. At the 2009 CWPA conference, Nancy Sommers led an institute designed to provide much-needed time and an audience for WPAs to plan and write towards WPA-focused projects. And, for the first time, CWPA offered a WPA Renewal Institute for mid-career

WPAs (WPAs with five or more years of experience) who wanted to "investigate the joys and challenges of sustaining administrative leadership and professional development" ("WPA 2009"). These institutes bear witness to our field's commitment to continued learning, not only about disciplinary issues, but also about ways to sustain a WPA life in the face of many demands.

WPA affiliates like the Philadelphia, Australian, Small Colleges, and High Mountain Affiliates (HMA) also create opportunities for WPAs in particular regions or situations to meet and collaborate on interests of special, local concern. The HMA, which includes colleges and universities in Idaho, Montana, Eastern Oregon, and Eastern Washington, has a particular interest in dialogue and resource sharing in the rural west. The WPA affiliates are likely to diversify the WPA organization even as affiliates find a sense of community and belonging through their affiliation.

The gWPA listserv and SIG are also of special importance, particularly to our ideas about GenAdmin and the role of WPA professionalization in identity formation. The idea for the gWPA listserv and the gWPA SIG came out of discussions in the WPA seminar which Tarez and Amy took. Seminar participants wanted to carve out a space for gWPAs across the country to talk to one another about their work because they recognized that gWPAs represent a distinct WPA identity. In the "Graduate Student WPA Identity and Position Statement" Tarez drafted with eight other gWPAs based on the SIG discussions at the 2005 CWPA conference, we see some of the early indicators of GenAdmin as participants synthesized their various subject positions and experiences. They wrote:

> We identify ourselves as first-time attendants at the WPA conference and fairly new entrants into the discipline (with less than two years' experience in our current roles as student-administrator, or having served as administrators-only without prior disciplinary or scholarly support). Our experiences include directing writing programs, assistant-directing writing programs, assistant-directing WAC/WID programs, assistant-directing portfolio programs and large-scale assessment projects, directing writing or learning centers, mentoring in TA training programs, overseeing empirical research in cross-institutional instruction between FYC and secondary school,

> holding leadership roles on the governing committees of first-year writing programs, and completing formal study in writing program administration theory or practice. . . . We bring WPA issues/discussions into our fellowship work, coursework, and writing. It informs everything we do professionally, in and out of the classroom. We . . . act as another venue for the CWPA's progressive work in areas such as community literacy and civic action. Our voluntary interest in it lends the field legitimacy. (Breland et al.)

Each of these networks lends our field legitimacy, and even better, provides avenues for WPAs to keep learning and redefining what it means to do WPA at different points in our careers, in different regions, and through different modalities.

CREATING SPACES FOR LEARNING

> *[W]here writing program administrators differ—or should differ—from most other college administrators is that the most important part of their job is not managerial but directly educational. Writing program administrators in their administrative capacity are writing teachers. . . . [B]oth of us are actively undertaking to create conditions in which learning can occur.*
>
> —Kenneth Bruffee

"WPA" is no longer simply a marker for a set of tasks or a particular position with a recognized job title; WPA identity is much more complex than that, informed as it is by experiences both in and outside of the academy. Our professionalization as a field and a discipline has led us to an exciting and challenging place in WPA history. We have developed a legitimacy borne of our expertise, a profession built on a growing body of stories and theory and research. On the one hand, the legitimacy of (the) WPA could create in us a desire to replicate ourselves, to create a set of "best practices" that are rarely interrogated or challenged or a sense of safety and privilege that we use as a shelter from productive critique and the potential for change (Dobrin). On the other hand, we see before us an opportunity to consider new ways of doing WPA work with new generations of WPAs, teaching assistants, and students, a chance to consider the repercussions of leaving "best practices" unchallenged. We remain, as GenAdmin, committed to the idea that we must attend not only to our own lifelong learning and professional development as WPAs, but to the education of future WPA generations and to the integration of their knowledge and experiences into our own.

For almost twenty years, WPAs have been making wish lists, dreaming of what we could do to ensure that the next generation doesn't have to begin learning about WPA work on the job. Our mentors, and now we, are committed to fulfilling that promise. We recognize others' skepticism at the notion that WPA can or should be taught or learned, but we believe, if we create spaces in which we let ourselves learn from one another—in graduate school and beyond—then our identities and understanding of ourselves as WPAs will continue to develop over the course of our professional lifetimes. In his editorial for the inaugural issue of *WPA*, Kenneth Bruffee attempted to explain to a skeptical writing teacher audience why there was a need for a WPA organization. He argued, in the quote that begins this section, that WPAs have a special educational mission—to create conditions in which learning can occur. As GenAdmin, we are committed to doing that, not just for our students, but also for ourselves, for our colleagues, and for those who are yet to hear the call of WPA work. If we can do that, we will flourish.

Interlude

ON EXPERTISE

To start getting at connections between writing program administration and ideas of expertise, I want to draw from a project I developed for the end of a first-semester first year writing course titled English 1301-Rhetoric and Composition I. Why this site? For our writing program, this class is both threshold and springboard—it sets a tone for writing/writers at our university, and it establishes that writing, like the writing program, is much more complex and ongoing than student distaste for required classes suggests.

It is a site where the concept of expertise, and all the connotations of skills and arrival that go with it, can be productively questioned.

In this culminating project, I ask students to take their cumulative ideas, research, and writing (about writing, reading, and/or learning) for the semester and design a public project that enacts one or more of their findings. The project handout is more like a book chapter, and there are moments of potential in it that are more about opportunity than direction: (1) dissonant epigraphs that include a quote from Heidegger on teaching, an image and description of an automatic bathroom door handle sanitizing gadget, and lyrics from The Killers' "When You Were Young"; (2) a section subtitled "Models, Hybrids, and Finding *Your* Way"; and (3) an image with twelve steps that show how to fold a paper box. And I add a little text to the image (*It's not about thinking inside or outside of the box*) with a thirteenth instruction (*it's about redrawing the lines*).

At some point in my first class discussion of this project, I noticed some furrowed brows and heard shuffling papers. By the end of class and our discussion of how to take a traditional "essay" and go public with it, people were hanging around, talking to each other, and trying to figure out collaboratively how to make a box out of their quickly torn paper squares.

An impromptu lesson in origami was never my intention.

I simply thought the image would provide a springboard for me to talk about how formulas and designs can create wonderful things, but they can also disguise adaptation and hybridity if we are more concerned with expert directions than less-experienced undertakings. I thought students would have questions about why I included the epigraphs and how they were connected. Instead, many found a set of instructions they could follow, maybe an intriguing set in an assignment struggling to displace direction with open-ended possibility. This example of unsolicited box-making helps makes several points relevant to this Interlude:

- Without much prompting, many students will follow a set of directions. That means teachers and writing program administrators should be very strategic about how curricula and projects direct students towards *openings* (like the epigraphs I mentioned) as well as necessities.
- Organic collaboration is just as useful a site for learning as staged group work. That means we can, without solely depending on spontaneity, create opportunities in which learning together makes sense to students (rather than it making efficient or effective sense to the authorities in the room).
- My pedagogical plans can be revised for the better by my students' involvement, even when it leads to a variety of paper boxes littering the classroom followed by un-orchestrated discussions with me about the nitty gritty of the project.
- "Familiarity" is a complicated concept that can inform a pedagogy and contribute to short-term student confidence, but we can and should deploy it in a rich class context that emphasizes long-term student confidence goals. Such long-term goals would be better if grounded in understandings of unexpectedness, hybridity, and in-expert attempts.

So the concept at issue here for me, and for us as GenAdmin, is how to balance two things: (1) the desire for expertise (for teachers and students) that can prompt us to learn, cause us to stress, lead to community certification as a member of a discipline, and contribute to dangerous assumptions, and (2) our pedagogical and theoretical need (as teachers and students) to work on our abilities to interpret, evaluate, adapt, and create knowledge. This is not a case of clear opposition. We can have both in interesting combinations. But I think the conversation about expertise needs to be front and center in writing programs, between writing teachers and students, not as a way to put off engagement but as a way to prompt, invest in, and increase it.

If we shut this avenue of thinking down as writing program administrators, I think we get into a dangerous territory that makes it easy for us to think of our jobs/actions as binary, as intellectual *or* managerial. For us, as we developed GenAdmin as an administrative philosophy, we defined it is a generative art that does not assume any or all administrative or managerial practices are pre-determined or lesser in moral meaningfulness than other academic or service work. We aren't archetypal, and we aren't interested in academic martyrdom. I don't think the five of us are ready to write a book called *Zen and the Art of Writing Program Administration*, but D. T. Suzuki has something to offer us when we are considering how ideas of expertise, if rooted in western notions of discipline, are neither natural nor necessarily desirable:

> People often imagine that the discipline of Zen is to produce a state of self-suggestion through meditation. This entirely misses the mark. . . . Satori does not consist in producing a certain premeditated condition by intensely thinking of it. It is acquiring a new point of view for looking at things. Ever since the unfoldment of consciousness we have been led to respond to the inner and outer conditions in a certain conceptual and analytical manner. The discipline of Zen consists in upsetting this groundwork once for all and reconstructing the old frame on an entirely new basis. It is evident, therefore, that meditating on metaphysical and symbolic statements, which are products of the relative consciousness, play no part in Zen. (95)

The foundation, in Suzuki's understanding of Zen meditation, is upset so that a person can rebuild the old on the new. In a GenAdmin sense, the materials (of an idea, a writing form, a program philosophy, and an administrative style) are reworked and put into a new relationship. The idea of expertise, then, is not a villain to be vanquished in higher education. Our arts as teachers, writers, philosophers, administrators, etc. are symbiotically tangled up in systems of assessment, certification, and accountability. Simply put, we can't, nor do we want to, remove hierarchy from a system that grants "degrees." But we can affect perceptions, language use, and the cultural capital we use to exchange ideas in our *writing* classrooms.

In a writing program, in a writing class, in an email exchange between a teacher and student, we can take the disciple of our *disciplines* out of our thinking and language and replace it with potential—to focus potential towards action, but not towards a defining action, to foster a culture of learning that does not depend only on programs of study that are inorganic, culturally overproduced, or naturalized. A telling example is the first email exchange between a writing student and teacher. Whether a student is asking for feedback on a particular piece of writing, trying to explain an absence, or just touching base, the student email may not look like it "belongs." Maybe the informality of his language is strange. It might look more like an abbreviated text message. It may not even be possible to tell who is emailing because of an unfamiliar alias and a lack of identifying information. Regardless of how well it fits a particular model for e-communication, the message is a point of contact. A connection is waiting there with potential. A relationship is waiting to be written with a reply click and a few keystrokes. We often talk of student engagement, but what about re-theorizing teacher engagement? Not every interchange deserves a disciplinary action about form, content, or appropriateness that wants expertise. To engage with what a student actually writes in an email is an act of listening to the moment, perhaps, in a suspension of expertise. In such suspensions, a place for new knowledge occurs. It is a simplicity of reaction, a reaction that is performative, and I would suggest that the performance does not have to only involve a student speaking teacher-ese or vice versa. What we should try for in resistance to our assumptions about mimetic tendencies is to establish a discourse with another human being who, like me, is literally unfolding in his articulation. Engagement, in this example, becomes a two-way street. I learn about the email language of a student, and he learns about mine.

If we want to re-think how we frame expertise in writing classrooms and programs and the consequences of this framing, a culture of exchange makes sense as an alternative. What composition and rhetoric (as a discipline) does best is engage in acts of begging, borrowing, stealing, blending, and unfolding ideas (Lauer, "Composition Studies"; Sirc, "Box-Logic"). Linguistics, psychology, psychoanalysis, space as a cultural phenomenon, cultural anthropology, visual representation—from Sophistic philosophy to massive multiplayer gaming, the tent we reside in is large and fluctuating, maybe more than other disciplines with more limited definitions of domain. Always wanting authority and recognition, what a perceived discipline or field of composition and rhetoric can also do, unfortunately, is create classroom environments and programmatic scenes that promote over-specialization while fostering apologies for multiplicinarity. Perhaps, on a smaller scale, the struggle to assume and displace the idea of expertise in a writing program is parallel to the history of models for writing in higher education. If we can take the process out of process, inventiveness out of heuristics, then we as teachers and program designers need to be careful about the degree to which a philosophy of the expert *programs* our curricular choices.

4 Becoming WPAs

> *Some who live on the edge claim a certain craziness; for others it's very much nose to the grindstone, running in place to keep the wolves at bay.*
>
> *The wild ones say they're wide open and they spend their lives suffering the consequences. It's like they never learn; it's like they use themselves as testing grounds for the forces at play in the world.*
>
> *They build their identities out of impacts and escapes. They push things to see where they'll go.*
>
> —Kathleen Stewart

> *The simplest answer is to act.*
>
> —Fortune cookie, received at lunch, 04/10/2010

At this point in our project of theorizing what we would like to call the gravity, or the pull, of a GenAdmin WPA identity, we have looked back at the WPA histories we inherited, how they made a space for us, and how we experienced the definition of that space (Chapter 2). Next, we considered WPA preparation—where to begin, what to study, how to position oneself programmatically and disciplinarily, what activities to engage in, what potentials to tap, and the consequences of such choices (Chapter 3). It might make sense, then, in what seems quite the chronological identification story of progress, to continue by sketching a narrative of identity arrival: To be a GenAdmin WPA is to be X. If looking at X is like looking at a reflection, you are here.

This is not, we believe, where the significance of GenAdmin should lie—for us, for people who see pieces of themselves in our emerging portrait, for those who will primarily see this project as an opportunity for critique and a sign that something significant in our writing pedagogies and program theorizations is being lost under the wheels of administrative practice, or for those who may see our ideas as still subject to a subjectivity they do not claim, desire, or seek to enact.

Like the curious ones "who live on the edge" in the opening passage from Kathleen Stewart, we build/experience/adapt our identities "out of impacts and escapes" (117), though we differ from Stewart's wild ones in that our primary goal *is* to learn—even if, by pushing ourselves, our colleagues, our students, our programs, and our contexts, we live the life of a testing ground. This is a will to *act* with an awareness that the power allotted a WPA has value precisely because it is so practically small and so potentially great. In this chapter, then, we want to account for the values that inform who GenAdmin is; we want to theorize how our particular approach to administrative identity works; we want to suggest how WPAs can benefit from seeing themselves as rhetorical agents of hybridity, more than *either* agents of change or tools of maintenance.

Rhetorical Knowledge and Emptiness in a Becoming Identity

While working on this book, and trying to delineate our ideas about assuming a non-assuming WPA identity, we were lucky enough to find our concerns already emerging in Donna Strickland and Jeanne Gunner's collection, *The Writing Program Interrupted* (2009). In particular, Joe Marshall Hardin attempts to establish a "terrain" for WPA identity that does not depend on "antagonism between the corporatization of the academy and composition's idealistic vision of itself" (138). Hardin's vision of the WPA as an empty signifier acting as rhetorical agent is not a liberal heroism of either/or. It is not dependent on a both/and synthesis of value that is aware of its corporatized values while continuing the talk and walk of emancipation. It is an attempt to move towards an unresolvable position, to change the terms of WPA possibility by not assuming our options are to overcome or be overcome.

To understand our philosophy of this positioning is to understand our relationship to a WPA's *becoming*, not *being*.[1] It's a simple but fundamental distinction, and as with understanding all things simple, we must push through complex context—in this case, of the competing subject positions available to a WPA. We do not think that we assumed the position or that the position assumed (consumed) us. Rather, we can't remember a time when we didn't assume we would be doing the kind of work we do because we think programmatically, even when we're not necessarily thinking about the health of a writing program and its various stakeholders. While we understand the history of WPA identities in terms of indebtedness, embeddedness, and emergence, we have productively resistant ways of reading the past and crafting the future of WPA identity that work in light of our philosophies, positions, and choices. One dominant characteristic of WPA identity for GenAdmin, then, is a pervasive feeling that we are always in the process of becoming—not in the sense of our arriving at a particular WPA identity or becoming *the* WPA, but becoming in the sense that we aren't asking to arrive or survive. We are seeking to rhetorically thrive and continually change, and we have learned from other generations of WPAs—those who happened upon the position, those who struggled to be heard, those who promoted coherence to create action, those who are looking in the mirror now to determine who they were, are, and will be—how deliberately we must choose this philosophy of change as our goal, how systemically we must live it out, and how necessary it is that we re-imagine the production of knowledge as rhetorical in the administrative positions we inherit, adapt, create, and work through with such a philosophy.

Before we look ahead to the actions of becoming WPAs, this line of thought on becoming can benefit from a look back at rhetoric, knowledge production, and Janet Atwill's teachings about deploying techne. Atwill's interpretation of techne speaks to the fluidity, creativity and generativity we associate with theorizing writing program administration. Aristotle theorized that productive knowledge is one of three knowledge domains: theoretical (*episteme*), practical (*praxis*), and productive (*poesis*). Each domain is related to a kind of inquiry, and all three are specifically tied to causality, first principles, and ends. In this theoretical system, the principles of universality and certainty characterize theoretical knowledge. Theoretical or scientific knowledge, which includes the study of philosophy, physics, and math, is "a mode of conception dealing with universals and things that are of necessity; and demonstrated truths and all scientific knowledge (since this involves reasoning) are derived from first principles" (*Nicomachean Ethics* VI.vi.1). Theoretical knowledge seeks knowledge for its own sake (*Metaphysics* I.ii.3). Traditional, western epistemology extends from this sense of theoretical knowledge. Alternatively, productive knowledge is more akin to concepts of crafting and making located in the realm of human production, and thus in the realm of probabilities and contexts. It is the "state of capacity to make, involving a true course of reasoning" (*Nicomachean Ethics* 1140.a.9-10) and concerned "with contriving and considering how something may come into being which is capable of either being or not being" (*Nicomachean Ethics* 1140.a.12-13). Examples of productive knowledge include medicine, architecture, military strategy, and navigation.

Practical knowledge or prudence, the third branch of knowledge, includes politics and ethics and is marked by action and human happiness (*eudaimonia*). It is "a reasoned and true state or capacity to act with regard to human good" (*Nicomachean Ethics* 1040.b.12). Alternatives to western epistemology that value experience and so-called common sense are often allied with practical knowledge. For Aristotle, these three kinds of knowledge were all important as different approaches to knowledge, though later interpretations locate these knowledges in a hierarchy, privileging one or another kind of knowledge in different contexts.

Over the years, different scholars have staked out claims for why rhetoric is one or the other kind of knowledge in order to both describe and esteem its study. Edward M. Cope's nineteenth-century studies of Aristotle's *Rhetoric* argue that rhetoric is practical knowledge while William Grimaldi's 1972 text, *Studies in the Philosophy of Aristotle's* Rhetoric, argues that rhetoric is theoretical knowledge. More recently, Janet Atwill has argued that Cope and Grimaldi each sought to achieve disciplinary status for rhetoric by aligning it with these two kinds of knowledge; she believes that this status seeking turned rhetoric into something it is not and also created an undesirable theory and practice split. In *Rhetoric Reclaimed*, Atwill recovers an ancient definition of *techne* as productive knowledge to argue that rhetoric is productive knowledge. What is at stake for Atwill is not rhetoric's disciplinary status but interpretations of the history of rhetoric and *techne*, and the potential for rhetoric as an art of intervention and invention.

Atwill's comments about Cope, Grimaldi, and desires for disciplinarity offer an interesting counterpoint to our efforts here. Atwill's discussion of productive knowledge and institutional lines is thus of general interest for the questions of disciplinarity she raises and of immediate concern for the more complex ways she encourages us to consider the relationships between theoretical, productive, and practical knowledges. For Atwill, productive knowledge offers a flexible, context-dependent way for people to intervene in the world by making something to be used by the self or by others that changes peoples' interactions with the world. In his foreword to Atwill's book, Wayne A. Rebhorn writes, "Atwill shows how Aristotle's concept of productive knowledge is in turn derived from a centuries-old tradition in ancient Greece and is an equivalent for the key term *techne*" (x). Subsequently, the definition of *techne* Atwill culls from an examination of works from the seventh-century BCE through the fourth-century BCE becomes synonymous with her interpretation of Aristotelian productive knowledge. Atwill writes that "Productive knowledge is defined by three characteristics: its concern with the contingent, its implication in social and economic exchange, and its resistance to determinate ends" (172). These characteristics map onto the three main features of Atwill's interpretation of *techne*: (1) that it is "never a static, normative body of knowledge," (2) that it "resists identification with a normative subject," and (3) that *techne* marks a domain of human intervention and invention" (7).

Contingency, the first characteristic of productive knowledge, reinforces the first feature of Atwill's interpretation of *techne*—that *techne* is not an unchanging, normative body of knowledge. The second and third characteristics, exchange and indeterminacy, follow suit, corresponding with the second and third aspects of *techne*, so the discussion of the non-normative subject aligns with exchange and indeterminacy aligns with the notion of productive knowledge as a "domain of human intervention" (Atwill 7). Different Prometheus narratives help Atwill develop her argument and offer a good example of *techne*. Prometheus's wit and skill in stealing fire from the gods to give to humans is an exchange of power from one group to another that promotes a change in the social order, including the rise of other arts, like smithing. According to Atwill, this argument about techne, productive knowledge, and *techne* achieves an understanding "of the art of rhetoric as a valued mode of intervention into existing conditions and a means for the invention of new possibilities" (189). Atwill describes this kind of knowledge as an inventional model of knowledge, focused on construction and making rather than description and definition. Atwill helps us re-see knowledge production as invention and intervention and helps us recognize our agentive potential. Moreover, we recognize that while Atwill draws renewed attention to productive knowledge, we also find ourselves compelled to privilege rhetoric as practical knowledge—as doing oriented towards *eudaimonia*—because of our investment in pragmatism. GenAdmin does not, we must emphasize, seek the ease of promoting one kind of knowledge over another or even two side by side, but recognizes that in a complex all-at-onceness (Berthoff), we bridge the inventiveness of rhetoric as making with our pragmatist activity of doing through our oscillating positioning and movement between places and spaces.

SPACE, PLACE, AND INTERSTITIALITY

We offer one example that stems from our GenAdmin belief that the best portraits cannot hang statically on walls but can hang together. They can in-*form* (bring into being) a gallery, but they cannot fill one. The Assemblage Project is just such a portrait in flux. We send cameras out to people with WPA interests, we ask questions, we ask responders to review other taped clips, the footage comes back to us eventually, and we archive it and begin to index it—by concept, by value, by principle, by assumption, by position or rank, by geographical area, and even by name. Our idea is that, in an area like WPA where identity seems to be a key location for theoretical struggle, we do not have enough portraits in motion to help us understand identity as fluid.[2] We want to push through that struggle to a critical mass of stories that is both readable and un-manageable so that no one narrative sticks—so that we keep on investigating who, where, and why we are WPA.

While it is important to think through the written histories and portraits of WPA-ness that circulate to know ourselves better in relation to the work we do in the present, we want to use our identification-in-process as GenAdmin to promote an awareness of, and provide a theoretical challenge to, the narrative binaries of loss/survival or administrator/intellectual that we may implicitly or explicitly circulate. To foster an open-ended sense of becoming for WPA identity that works in our day-to-day activities is more suited to the complexities of a writing program and to the needs of thinkers who can be administrators in complex conjunction with other identities.

We are not the first to recognize the potential consequences of privileging narratives that posit victims and/or anti-intellectuals. Building out of a critical distinction between place (representing stability) and space (representing freedom), Sidney I. Dobrin has attempted to unpack the emerging "administrative empire" of writing program administrators. In "Freedom and Safety, Space and Place," he writes,

> Writing program administrators have come to identify the wpa position as a position of power, and have defined the wpa place as holding the possibility of power, albeit questionable and questioned. Such a depiction is necessary in order to allow the power of the wpa to operate safely within the WPA [organization] narrative of oppression. (64)

In thinking alongside Dobrin's understanding of how an *individual* can influence a *program* of cultural capital, we recognize the danger of investing too much energy in resisting the materiality and mythos of an oppressive weight. Dobrin warns that standardization is an undesirable negative outcome of such a relationship with our administrative and organizational identity. But, even in the disciplinary context we inherited, we don't seek a pre-conceived identity from the "mothership" of WPA. Members of GenAdmin do not seek a space of freedom embedded in an administrative and concretized-obsessive hierarchy, nor do they seek an identity, complete with a logo and T-shirt, that can lose reflective sight of its criteria for "good" works and "best" practices as professionals underneath recognition and acceptance. For us, Bill Readings's theory of dissensus in *The University in Ruins* better illustrates an identity that is neither wholly complicit with nor wholly unique to whatever master narrative circulates through our actions. Dissensus is not limited to an outcomes-based existence in actions familiar to WPAs like designing and leading professional development meetings with colleagues, distributing assessment results, being available for crisis management between a frustrated teacher and a struggling student, networking with extra-university student service organizations, etc. A dissensual position cannot be completely defined by problem-solving actions, and this is incredibly important to a GenAdmin outlook because management and problem-solving narratives depend on the destination of wholeness. The desire for wholeness, especially an administrative wholeness, positions WPAs as reactionaries trying to perfect a ceaselessly modulating system.

One limit to Dobrin's view of the WPA organization/wpa individual may be this dependence on perceptions or metaphors of emptiness and fullness in order to critique the past and imagine a future. We might heed his warning of the resulting relationship between our practices and the value we place on our narratives of development, but we also choose to focus our ideas of identity in terms (possibly new and unfamiliar terms) of the plane between place and space, the juncture where identity is in a productive and inventive flux, what anthropologists and others recognize as liminality.

We believe it possible to be comfortable with not belonging, that WPAs invent, assume, or discover identities that are always under investigation, because we do not believe that theories (of identity) can actually exist apart from any practical application or enactment. WPAs have always occupied a place of liminal tension, lived the life of the membrane between two seemingly distinctive environments. But such a membrane, in order to survive as such, is porous to a certain extent, is capable of bringing balance or serving as a bridge. GenAdmin is both traffic and trafficked, and we are interested in understanding the patterns of value that emerge and play out more than policing either our criteria for what a writing program should produce in student writers or what an organization should promote.

There is something in this idea of liminal tension akin to the "value of plasticity" that Christopher Burnham and Susanne Green argue for, building out of Hephizibah Roskelly and Kate Ronald's conception of an outcomes-driven pragmatic disciplinary identity, in "WPAs and Identity: Sounding the Depths" (179). In the end, though, Burnham and Green gravitate towards an identity that progresses through sedimentation (owing to Susan Speer's "full-bodied notion of identity" (184)) and sum up with this process picture of teacher identity in a writing class: "If we remember and teach that identity is a journey, the outcome of a process, then students and teachers are prepared to consider who they are in a writing classroom and what that means" (184). Our idea of a GenAdmin positioning values collection but not necessarily sedimentation or a kind of lock step progress narrative. Nor do we think we come close to being aware of all the permutations and consequences of our identity choices (see our interlude "On Strategizing"), though cementing these choices would certainly better allow us to occupy the place of the reflective expert.

Instead, we posit the WPA as a post-administrator, "post" in that her discipline is intellectual, theoretical, and seeks an understanding of the relationship between knowing and doing, a potential set in motion by Rose and Weiser's *The WPA as Theorist*. Knowing and doing are institutionally bound. It isn't that the practice merely tests and extends the theory, or that the theory serves the practice, but that they are inextricably emergent and developing as they are in play. This understanding of praxis views post-administration as a site for reflection, negotiation, and action—including the committee table, the e-mails and hallway conversations, the program documents, and the TA training program. In a sense, these become sites for enacting and dealing with resistance productively, and we weave together several epistemological concepts in order to arrive at this thinking: Burke's critical reflective pedagogy; Porter et al.'s rhetorical action; and Aronowitz and Giroux's transformative intellectual. We draw on these voices, along with Gilles Deleuze who reframed one conception of becoming with ties back to Plato's conceptual framework of rhetoric, to rethink "rhetorical performance" as humane, akin to Burke's desires for his own post-Cold war educational theory of critical reflection (one in which he desired that students would think meditatively on language and its uses and effects, rather than use it merely to be assertive or competitive).

We are, in part, calling for WPAs to experiment with withholding the stability that Dobrin fears. What does it mean to withhold a stable—or fixed—identification? For some WPAs, as for many academics, identity is a stable goal. They want to reach a plateau of professional comfort and familiarity, even if it is defined primarily by tenure or contract, to be able to apply a formula for understanding the world when a familiar situation presents itself. But what it means to be a WPA is contextual and changing. That doesn't mean that people who are responsible for the design, revision, and maintenance of a writing program are not WPAs; it just means what they do as a WPA today is a bit different than what they might have done last year or what they may still do at a different institution. We see this instability as a Burkean attitude—a posturing, a leaning towards. It might also be an attitude suffused with Deleuze's understanding of the relationship between a concept, like an imposed identity, and a process or a becoming that cannot be paused in the sense of a snapshot, but materially and psychically continues to fluctuate.

Our book is not necessarily a Deleuzian project, but we see great value in drawing on Deleuze and Guattari's idea of creating concepts on planes of immanence: "philosophy is a constructivism, and constructivism has two qualitatively different aspects: the creation of concepts and the laying out of a plane" (*What is Philosophy* 35-36). Understanding what a concept is and what a plane is will allow us to understand what it is to do philosophy, and how it is that philosophy embraces the interesting, the remarkable, and the important. In addition, it will allow us to return to the concept of becoming with the appropriate background, having in hand both what it is for something to be a Deleuzian concept and what it is he is trying to do by creating them (May 141).

We are further drawn to May's discussion of "planes of immanence" as a way of describing how we have composed our work in the spaces left by past narratives, including some that we haven't liked and some that we think have been nonproductive or damaging to the field:

> Concepts are not formed and do not exist on their own. They are part of a system, and in two senses. First, new concepts are molded from already existing ones. One does not create a concept out of nothing, but out of a context of concepts which (a) forms the soil from which a new concept emerges and (b) is the foil with and against which the new concept takes its significance. Second, in the formation of a philosophical perspective, the concepts of that perspective form their own system of interconceptual relatedness. This latter system occurs on the plane of immanence. (141-42)

Our emerging idea of GenAdmin as a placeholder from which we can engage professionalization and retain inventive potential is, in a sense, possible because of the persistence of a number of tenacious binaries, like victim/hero narratives and junior/senior hierarchies. But our book is by and large an attempt to delineate a new plane of immanence through which we can create a philosophical perspective that is not merely bound by past relationships or aggregated professional knowledge.

Our comfort with a *becoming* identity stems from the fact that our notion of "choice" leads us (1) to choose our responses and approaches to a particular WPA job rather than letting the job choose them for us, (2) to choose them in large part because we cannot "turn off" that WPA-ness, and (3) to acknowledge that multiplicinarity requires a regular resituating of "expertise." With this understanding, we can offer ideas about how our philosophy functions when put into play, and how others with similar values might re-think (writing program) administration because of it.

This hermeneutic of understanding challenges us to thoughtfully, that is, humanely, persuade teachers to engage our programs, including helping others to perform well as teachers because of our own commitments and desires as WPAs. WPA work is a rhetorical performance, public persona in all different sites. As rhetors, we enact and embody—rather than just prepare for—the ideals of the university (Slevin). Somewhat reminiscent of the ways that Porter et al. offer up institutional critique as "a methodology" for rethinking classroom practice (617) and institutional advising as spaces for reflection that can lead to a rethinking of the discipline, we offer a revised, understanding of how feminist pragmatic writing program administration can embody humane and productive aims, beyond the de/recentering of absolute power. In the program and philosophy that we envision, certain program participants still hold varying levels of power, but more importantly, power holders (e.g., administrative assistants, assistant directors, and mentors) collaborate to find ways of modeling a horizontal empowerment. Such an empowerment may mean committing to meeting often and purposefully, publicly upholding one another, or making their intellectual conversations, debates, and deliberate points of dissonance public. In this program, participants may vie towards a nascent resolve—towards strengthening a program's goals and aims—very much a *do in the spirit of what we have theoretically agreed to try*, not a *do as I say* rhetorical performance. Mastery by similarity is not the best model for us and neither is negative positioning. We would rather imagine and draw from more contingent histories of development by establishing a *program* as an idea, keeping its disparate parts in conversation as much as possible to see and pursue what possibly shakes out of such discourse. Thus, in our argument to lose the damaging metaphors that construct histories and portraits of WPA-ness (and that seem to only re-articulate narratives of loss or survival or the binary struggle between being an administrator and being an intellectual), we find it more advantageous for WPAs to adopt an alternative, open-ended sense of becoming.

Here is one example of how a becoming attitude can inform what we could call a multiplicinary moment, one that will likely become more common within departments and across campus units. For several years, Colin taught a special topics sophomore-level introduction to literature class. He built more of an interdisciplinary curriculum designed to help students identify characteristics of fictional works, from anime to short stories, and asked them to read theoretical works in philosophy, fine arts, and science. The course was quite popular, especially since it filled a core requirement that didn't force non-majors to "appreciate" literature. However, the popularity of the class and Colin's position as a Rhetoric and Composition professor (with a Master's in English Literature), rubbed some faculty the wrong way. A senior faculty member acting as chair of a newly formed literature committee politely asked what was going on in the class, and Colin saw the writing on the wall for his class, which met established student learning outcomes but did so on the fringe of the value system functioning for literature faculty. If he was determined and determinate in his rhetoric and composition identity, he would have closed up and moved back to a place of much narrower pedagogical and philosophical safety, but he didn't. He made the course an even more complicated upper-level special topics class investigating convergences among science, science fiction, rhetoric, and art. The evolution of the course was not all that enjoyable because political pressure isn't enjoyable even in the guise of a senior mentor nudging a junior grasshopper. Yet, the move towards multiplicinarity found a space and place somewhere between an old designation and an ingenious potential.

While this example is about one person and one class, it exemplifies administration, in the form of curricular design, as invention. It is an object lesson in how becoming pushes through to complexity rather than allowing the rubber band to snap back and collapse back into binary assumptions. As a WPA, Colin also coordinates a developmental program consisting of two classes. And he does not perceive that he's designing one set of courses for developmentally-tagged students and one for upper-level students who are looking for an alternative to their perceptions of literature. He's doing both for people as an extension of his ethical concern for delineating a writing program that can extend through and affect the total undergraduate curriculum, and so he moves away from disciplinary terrain as a challenge to an idea of expertise that privileges belonging (epistemologically predetermined in, for instance, the types of language recognized for a literature or rhetoric class) over becoming (epistemologically undetermined in, for instance, how a unique teacher and a group of students can build a language out of the moment).

In our experience, the best WPA mentors, whether advising us on a one-to-one basis or as writers and thinkers who have a long-distance impact on us, are visionaries who do not expect or promote the idea that they are stable, predictable, one-dimensional, or linearly progressive. To promote such ideas is to lose our potential for theorizing a new type of intelligence for the WPA without settling for an either/or narrative of loss and gain. If we can promote fluctuating (or oscillating) WPA identities that do not settle into fixed metaphoric proximities, we can better support the energy and inventiveness that WPAs need.

Breaking the Waves

Eliding stable identities is important to us as a group of people who do our best work when we face positive resistance that encourages connectability and novelty. We welcome a certain instability in our WPA-ness as a Deleuzian becoming, a philosophical perspective aimed not at finding a Platonic Truth or affirming the tradition of analytic philosophy, but helping us "to see and to live in a fresh way," and helping us to understand philosophy as a discipline "through which the world takes on a new significance" (May 142). Those of us who identify as feminist pragmatists find compelling resonance between Deleuzian becoming and pragmatism's orientation towards change and innovation, since neither one is wholly descriptive or prescriptive but rather both are enabling.

If we think of disciplinary development as a movement, the WPA story is ostensibly consistent with other fields, especially sub-fields in English studies. The first wave in this movement is of self-awareness and naming: people with certain responsibilities, not specifically related to their educational background, recognize a lack of helpful theories and human support. Networks begin to emerge—like-minded scholars practice common research methods, attend specific scholarly conferences, publish monographs, and join specific professional organizations (Goggin 28). The second wave is of outer recognition: other people and groups recognize the group as cohesive and value-project-ing. Vertical power, evident in the distribution of a particular value-set and the active promotion of those values by people at different levels of a university hierarchy, is still a ways off, but horizontal recognition becomes more of a reality. In essence, the emergent language of WPA finds articulation and becomes more available to those who know where to look, but it hasn't worked its way into a larger vernacular context.

We see this fissure in the ways that composition is mis-characterized as merely service and the teaching of writing at any level is figured as catching students up with writing behaviors, often related to correctness, that they "should" have already learned. Ross Winterowd and Vincent Gillespie remind us that the limited view of composition's potential disciplinarity is also spatially recognizable: "the historian can wander into the departmental coffee room and find someone who is interested in his or her work, who reads the same journals, and who attends the same conventions. There is no such coffee room for the compositionist" (qtd. in Goggin 28). In other words, this second wave of disciplinary formation for compositionists, and arguably even more so for WPAs,[3] is both fraught with and reliant upon the tension between how WPAs view their work and how others regard it.

In the third wave of identity negotiation, and this is incredibly important considering how so-called sub-disciplines in English studies emerge, the group has enough critical, generative mass to see how they view themselves, see how others view them, and attempt to re-negotiate a third identity that can exist in an overlapping space between others' demands and their personal desires. We see evidence of this kind of generative identity formation in journal articles and publications on writing program administration, on the WPA-L, and at the annual summer WPA conference.

We suggest here that we are living in and experiencing an intellectual and pragmatic fourth wave of *conscious identity resentment*, in the Nietzschean sense of *ressentiment,* or a re-sentimenting in which we are frustrated and attacking that which we are a part of, generating a reactive value system. This means two things. First, that enough in-roads have been made into an established identity that an unfamiliar value-system can emerge and have room to breathe as an alternative identity, in part, because it isn't perceived as threatening the established way of being WPA. Second, that alternative identities, though uncertain, are indeed viable. When this wave metaphorically began, there was an undercurrent of frustration. In a time and space when the domain of "writing" is expanding, especially in terms of "new media," we think it is fitting that we begin to let go of the term "administration" as a titling authority that connects us back to these frustrating origins of WPA identity, to other administrators who are always blamed for decisions that do not take into account the "right" information and are increasingly economically driven. Our interactions with upper administrators, such as deans and provosts, tell us that they do not view us as administrators in the way that they are since they have access to power structures that we do not. To wit: when she was newly hired, one of Kate's provosts told her she was lucky not to "be an administrator" because it's harder to make friends. Kate was more worried that someone in the provost's office didn't seem to recognize her administrative role as she did. For us, the baggage of administration is not worth its perks and assumed influence, particularly when "administration" is read as "manager" by colleagues and recognized within our discipline as "institutionally sanctioned responsibility without accompanying institutionally sanctioned credentials to act with authority" (Anderson and Romano 5).

We believe it is time to begin negotiating and re-conceptualizing our definitions of and metaphors about "administrators" so that blame, reaction politics, and an intrinsic dislike of these roles are replaced by productive invention of curricula, employment, responsibility, and assessment. One example of this kind of effort is Linda Adler-Kassner and Susanmarie Harrington's reclamation of "responsibility" and "visibility," and their rejection of "accountability" as ways to identify the work of writing program administrators ("Reframing"). We're endeavoring to assert a holistic, philosophical approach to reclaim "administrator" as a positive WPA signifier, even as it remains in flux. Just as in Chapter 1 we discuss the challenges and possibilities of theorizing identity in the spaces left by other theorizations of WPA, in this chapter our philosophical approach relies on achieving more pragmatic understandings of identity, materiality, and expertise. We view these understandings as constituents of a rhetorically productive perspective, rather than simply indicative of "the way things are."

Circulating and Circumventing WPA Narratives

Even still, we are well aware of the hegemonic and normative force of commonplaces operating for and within WPA, and that so many of them circulate as "war stories" or "cautionary tales." In one sense, the heuristic potential of these commonplaces arises from our desire to recognize them for what they are: commonplaces and thus ideologies that can be revisited, disrupted, and revised. Jacqueline Jones Royster's three inter-related activities of story-telling, history-telling, and theory-making as processes related to a "re-cast" view of knowledge-making as a rhetorical process have the potential to challenge not only the current landscape of rhetorical history but the landscape of writing program administration. We see the transformative potential in these three processes to more broadly help WPAs rethink normative beliefs and practices in order to be "adventurous in our thinking to take a different path, to find a different viewpoint, and to critique the terms of engagement so that a different sense of the landscape can be made visible, can be deemed valuable, and can become instructive in the re-envisioning of what constitutes knowledge" (Royster, "Disciplinary" 161). What we suggest in this book, and especially in this chapter, is that WPAs are ready to begin new directions in storytelling, empirical interpretation, and metaphoric reflecting.

We want to address several WPA stories in order to talk about what kind of WPA identities GenAdmin live out and how they come to be in juxtaposition to, for instance, a published history of WPA identity that has aggregated narratives of loss, survival, disappointment, and bifurcation. Edward White opens the preface to *Untenured Faculty as Writing Program Administrators* with this comment: "the most interesting professional books are those that take a fresh look at what 'everyone' knows to be true" (vii); in other words, texts that rethink commonplaces, including whether or not people should avoid WPA positions until they are post-tenure. We appreciate the ways editors Debra Frank Dew and Alice Horning and their contributors explore the tension between this adage that pre-tenure WPAs are doomed and the fact that many WPAs are in fact junior faculty members. In addition, whereas *Kitchen Cooks, Plate Twirlers, and Troubadours* tells the stories, in large part, of "reluctant administrators" "becoming WPAs," we find ourselves in a different place, generationally and ethically as scholars who may choose administration even pre-tenure. We hope to further consider such tensions as those caused by the understanding that, while the work is not often easy, it's intellectual, creative, satisfying, and productive. Thinking again about these WPA commonplaces is important for all of us who are connected to and affected by writing programs because it is through them that we come to understand how we are mentored and how we will mentor, how we are constructed and how we construct, how we become human (and humane) in our actions and how our actions can become who we are.

Not Only Corporatized Material. Material conditions do not have to be the initial impetus for an administrative act. A WPA can make a choice based on an aesthetic desire, or a philosophical desire, or a curricular desire, or, yes, a material desire. But it is a trap to think that material conditions rule the "work" place of a WPA, a work that should include play, creativity, etc. To fear boundaries—the limits of materiality—before they are met can create defensive moves that may not be necessary.

When we use a recognized identity strategically—for putting historical knowledge to work, for identifying program-sized problems, for innovating without ostracizing—we can't avoid the creation of a container. We imagine a shape that takes on weight and texture, a person who is a collection of best practices, similar to the ideal student who stands off in the distance as we develop student learning outcomes. Writing teachers face this tension constantly when evaluating a piece of student writing in light of, but also in resistance to, a satisfactory or ideal response. The destination of the model, the ideal, or even the satisfactory just doesn't seem to work for us. We hope that, by this point, our curiosity for the unexpected, for possibilities, helps make sense of why we instead turn our attention to how a person who identifies him/herself as a WPA can maintain (and use to her/his advantage) a fluctuating or undetermined identity, not only for programmatic gain but also for re-inventing expertise.

To keep identity at play, in oscillation, and viewed and reacted to as in process is also an important way of re-seeing WPA disciplinary identity, which we believe cannot thrive if defined (whether good or bad) as a single "thing" or as an identity always defined by the "perils" of such a life. In life, but particularly in administration in its most limited sense, the primary responsibility is to administer and control, to see a pattern and subsequently imprint it so that there is a degree of certainty about how a writing program decision will affect students and teachers. Our guesses get better the more we can repeat the pattern and imprint it on our colleagues and students alike. A good example of this would be how, after years of research and publication in composition and rhetoric on the plagiarizing phenomena, you can still find yourself in an English department where an emergent phenomena of expertise with authority, synthesis, and format is read simply as the imprint of apathetic students refusing to do what the teacher says. We redirect this kind of hermeneutic gap via re-seeing administrative identity as uncertain, in flux.[4]

Rethinking Maintenance and Change

Beyond defending theoretical studies of WPA identity, beyond arguing anew for the intellectual grounding of this discipline, and beyond rethinking commonplaces in the development of WPA histories, we also find ourselves defending "administration" as a site for creating new conditions, and nowhere is this as evident as in the way we understand maintenance and change as two dimensions of the same activity. In his preface to *Untenured Faculty as Writing Program Administrators*, White also suggests that a junior faculty member "has less stake in tradition, in keeping things running as they have been. . . . The jWPA may be more interested in challenging than maintaining the way things are done" (x). We do not necessarily embrace this assumed either/or choice that White suggests WPAs make between maintenance and change, although we note that perhaps this attitude towards change does preclude a generational positioning for WPA hires, like Kate, who were hired to replace WPAs who have been in the job for twenty years and where the rhetoric of such hirings emphasizes the need to change static programs. Certainly, the reality of the desire for such change may range for different stakeholders along a continuum from enthusiastic acceptance to resentment that the new WPA has in fact made good on the promise of change. In addition, change is often a *motive* for hiring WPAs as Susan McLeod makes clear in her discussion of WAC directors as change agents and a *desire* of activist WPAs who seek to do the kind of "story-changing work" Linda Adler-Kassner advocates for in *The Activist WPA*. We thus join in rewriting assumptions that WPAs in general and jWPAs in particular are interested in change simply for the sake of change with an argument that GenAdmin is interested in keeping the tension between maintenance and change in productive flux with the aim of making better programs. Quite simply, for the WPA, change and maintenance are intertwined. Suggesting that WPAs like GenAdmin are interested in change just for the sake of change positions us as upstarts rather than individuals comfortable with programmatic and curricular change.

Changing curriculum isn't just about getting a program up to speed; it also supports collaboration and dialogue among stakeholders, emphasizing if not highlighting the mediation that is always going on in programs. For example, E. Shelley Reid writes, "If we define *changing* as an expectation rather than only as an imposition, and we approach it as a multifaceted process, we can provide teachers and administrators with opportunities for productive leadership . . . and for authentic collaboration" (12). In reflecting on the program work undertaken for Introductory Composition at Purdue when she was a graduate student there, Tarez also found opportunities for collaboration and reflection a meaningful part of curricular reform related to participants' ongoing understanding of the idea that programs and their interpretations are always in flux. After a five-year planning period, the program as a whole mapped out another five-year development period in which to assess specific aspects of the curriculum. This consisted of several work groups building syllabus approaches from the ground up based on a set of common goals, means, and outcomes; an initial approval process and then ongoing renewal process for these syllabus approaches; an initial and then ongoing showcasing of student projects, where the venue and outcome might change from year to year; and reconstruction of all the internal and external program documents that articulated parts of the course. It also initiated research projects—everything from surveying instructor attitudes and perceptions in the conferencing center to learning how classroom spaces were being used under the new design. And because several of the university's supporting technologies changed every year, sometimes within the year, instructors often were learning new platforms, new programs, or exploring new ways of mediating their courses.

The tensions between maintenance and change underlay all phases of the course, leading to focus groups of new instructors who needed a space to talk about what they still didn't understand or why they felt it difficult to enact the curriculum and encouraging revisions of mentoring curricula, and requiring the articulation of new policies as needs arose (i.e., guidelines for making course websites accessible via ADS standards). As a mentor in the program, Tarez recalls understanding the challenge of mentoring, teaching, and carrying on in the face of nascent and temporary understandings, and saw the WPA's role as one of promoting inquiry about teaching and encouraging teachers to gain knowledge about what they were doing via inductive reasoning—not to change commonplaces or overturn ideologies, but to make a space for them to be discussed, since she knew they were going to always be challenged.

This belief that we can create better programs through an orientation towards programs and curricula as ever-changing, even in their interpretation by new stakeholders, is one of the guiding forces at work in Tarez and Kate's article "From 'What Is' to 'What Is Possible': Theorizing Curricular Document Revision as In(ter)vention and Reform." They resituate curricular guides as active genre systems in writing program systems, thus emphasizing the dynamism of programs and their texts. The heuristic they offer for practicing guide revision as an art of intervention and invention goes on to highlight the inventive, collaborative, and reflective work that being oriented towards change entails in the context of curricular revision. While their research focuses on programs in the midst of change, the heuristic and philosophy that informs it also positions maintenance as more change-able and in flux than typically expected. Certainly, maintenance of any program's goals and outcomes means regular involvement with many acts of change as teaching staff turns over or student bodies shift in number and interest.

What "Administration" Are We Choosing?

In spite of our efforts to rethink, recast, or elide metaphors, we cannot shake George Lakoff and Mark Johnson's insight about metaphorical dependency, especially when it comes to theorizing the organization and administration of university programs or units. Take an extended example from Robert Barnetson's 2001 article," Performance Indicators and Chaos Theory," in which he helps organizational theory try on a new set of terms:

> How we conceptualize the nature of the world affects the organizational metaphors we use to guide our actions in it.

> Traditional scientific thinking is now giving way to more complex models of the world. For example, chaos theory suggests order is an inherent aspect of systems as they shape and reshape themselves in order to facilitate their primary purpose. The patterns and boundaries of these systems are caused by attractors. *Attractors* are elements in a system with drawing or organizational power. (148)

As attractive as it may be to re-think our WPA-selves as part of a system that locates power in attractors and reflects a complexity beyond our local understanding, we would only be replacing one set of patterns or forms with another—displacing a set of overcoming narratives with narratives of emergence, for example. Maybe that's the best we can do when it comes to understanding our lives and our work. It may be time to stop living by and through the metaphors we inherit and perpetuate, and time to start recasting our collective lot both symbolically and practically so that we can understand our lives and our work in fresh ways.

The five of us say this with the knowledge, gained from Lakoff and Johnson, that

> our ordinary conceptual system, in terms of which we both think and act, is fundamentally metaphoric in nature. . . . Our concepts structure what we perceive, how we get around in the world, and how we relate to other people. Our conceptual system thus plays a central role in defining our every day realities. (3)

Because the frame of metaphor "is so ubiquitous in the language and in thinking that most people don't recognize it as a strategy that allows them to name and control reality" (qtd. in Dunn 80), it's critical for WPAs to re-consider the metaphors and stories that have shaped how we're viewed and how we view ourselves. For GenAdmin, the old metaphors—whether of wife or circus performer or the myriad others we encounter in WPA literature—fail us, as much as we depend on them to organize our lives (Lakoff and Johnson) or organize our organizations (Cutright). Building out of the old sets of blocks results in identities that tried to make, for instance, victim narratives fit our experience. For Gertrude Buck, metaphors were "radical manifestations of an early stage in perceptual development" (Vivian 99); if we recognize metaphors in this way as well, they might evolve as we continue to explore what we want our WPA identities to mean and what metaphors we want to cast off, including then the plethora of problematic WPA metaphors, from the domestic, to the managerial, to war metaphors.

Familial or domestic metaphors, from Doug Hesse's WPA as father to WPA as ideal wife (Grimm 15) or divorced parent (Lamonica 150) are not only uncomfortable evocations of family dynamics that may be unhealthy, infantilizing, or patriarchal, but also reassert the feminization of composition that Susan Miller first articulated. Circus or variety show metaphors like the plate twirlers, Song and Dance Men, and Troubadours (George xi, xiii) set WPAs aside as freaks of nature. Yet we do not wish to occupy the role of the side show academic, or to be defined by an "otherness" read negatively because of our inclinations towards nascent positioning. While we recognize the use value of defining ourselves by saying what we aren't, we also want to shift away from the idea that difference should always be defined in the negative, positioned as *not X*. For this reason, we appreciate Deleuze's understanding of difference, which is not set up as otherness: "For Deleuze, difference—difference in itself—is not to be defined in terms of the same. We characteristically define difference negatively, as the not-sameness of two or more entities. . . . What Deleuze wants is not a derivative difference" (May 144). Rather than stable being where difference is defined negatively, we have instead becoming, or the "unfolding of difference in time" (May 146), which appeals to us because of it doesn't constantly frame us as outcasts.

Managerial metaphors, crafted perhaps because writing program administration is often viewed as a service, are among those that so often distance us from our colleagues, even from within our discipline. Lynn Worsham's view of writing program administration aligns it with service and opposes it to the intellectual work of theory. Scott McLemee's 2003 interview with her published in *The Chronicle of Higher Education* asserts Worsham's disdain for writing program administration:

> Because I'm in rhetoric and composition, people have regularly assumed that I'm a candidate for writing-program administrator," she says. "Well, I know nothing about it. And I have no interest in knowing anything about it. For the past 30 years, people in the field have tried to define [composition

studies] as an intellectual discipline, not a service component of the university. But now it seems like people are embracing it as a service component. (McLemee)

While service doesn't need to have such a negative connotation—witness Linda Adler-Kassner's positioning of the WPA as activist in the Jewish tradition of *tikkun olam* (10)—WPAs are often seen by those who don't understand our work as intellectual as simply work anyone can do without special knowledge or abilities. M.L. Tiernan, for instance, writes about her frustration at being called "Xerox Queen" by a male colleague (168). The tension between the authority WPAs might exercise versus the responsibilities we have points to the low status accorded the WPA as manager. Of course, this metaphor is problematized by the corporatization of academe that is the site of many struggles on our campuses. Darla Twale and Barbara De Luca argue that one of the reasons for the increasing climate of incivility on our campuses is the shift to a more corporate culture. As such, it's not surprising that WPAs, when figured as managers of a cash cow business, are seen as antithetical to the high-minded intellectualism of academe. Faculty who feel this way "may choose to bully others to regain the old values" (Twale and De Luca 139). Because entrepreneurial colleagues, or those perceived that way like WPAs, may find themselves bullied, it is important for WPAs to collectively challenge this metaphor.

Ideas of management may position WPAs—for better or worse—as white collar workers, but other WPAs use more blue collar metaphors to talk about our work. In the opening paragraph of "Notes from a New WPA," Megan Fulwiler offers a whole slew of work-related metaphors ending with "I feel like a plumber sent to fix a broken dam with a roll of Scotch tape" (92). Stuart Brown's comparison of WPAs to first responders or firefighters, based on his personal experiences, reinforces the service image (if not the hero image) of the WPA (132). We're not sure what we think of these comparisons, but we do know we must interrogate them for what they mean about writing program administration. For one thing, we'd like not to operate on a regular basis in the crisis mode that the emergency plumber or firefighter operates under. War metaphors, the use of which is quite popular among WPAs, continue this sense of crisis and affront our commitment to peace. In *The Promise and Perils of Writing Program Administration*, Randall McClure refers to himself as an "army of one" (104), Edward

White refers to jWPA "troopers" (129), and finally, Lauren Ingraham speaks of WPA "war stories" (290). One of Kate's job descriptions included the word "ambassador" to describe assigned tasks related to committee work and work with academic services and other departments across campus. As Susan McLeod points out, "there are certain difficulties associated with this role" ("The Foreigner" 110). Diplomats "have no power of their own; they merely represent their government;" the WPA as diplomat might be at best a figurehead, at worst a spy ("The Foreigner" 110).

Like Tom Fox, we often find that "the depth of the conflict between my institution's definition of me and the view of composition that I share with my colleagues in the field is sometimes astonishing," so like Fox, we seek ways to "function both ethically and politically within institutions and to find ways to change them" (92). These metaphors that permeate our discipline are unsatisfying to us. We want to counter WPA narratives as "war stories" and "cautionary tales" with something more productive. We would like to actively work with stories as becoming moments for invention rather than as benchmarks in a war against the oppressors. We might even say that we have become tired of the Big Bad and defining ourselves against it. It may or may not be a materially real Big Bad, but if it serves as our point of departure for forming an identity, we are already overcome as victims. Because we believe with Gertrude Buck that metaphor is not compounded like a prescription with intent to produce a certain effect upon the person who swallows it; but it springs spontaneously out of a genuine thought-process and represents with exactness a certain stage of a growing perception. It is no artificial, manufactured product, but a real organism, living, growing and dying" (Buck 44), we do not offer here new metaphors for readers' consumption.

We would rather see ourselves as overcome with potential rather than people who can or are overcome. But we forget the distance that meta- (above) forms suggest between experience and perspective. And so, we find ourselves trying on metaphoric identities that cannot oscillate because they don't give off vibrations; they cannot fluctuate because they do not move in physical space; they cannot move as an ocean tide because they aren't made of water. Re-thinking our WPA-selves as part of a system that locates power in attractors and reflects a complexity beyond our local understanding is intriguing and challenging and displaces a set of overcoming narratives with emergence narratives. And this is where we are comfortable in our discomforting positions, suspended and in active oscillation among disciplinary identities with organized weight, local contexts of material limits, and our philosophical understanding of writing programs as experimental, rhetorical terrains that should challenge and be challenged by a desirable lack of stable identification.

Interlude

ON STRATEGIZING

Read collectively, the narratives of WPAs at work could suggest that the successful WPA is the strategic WPA. She considers what she wants for the program she leads, who she has to convince in order to get it, and how she can best position herself in relationship to those in power to achieve her goals. The strategic WPA is one who can be the hero of her own program, advocating for those with limited power (first-year writing students, graduate TAs, adjunct faculty) while carefully considering the hills she's willing to die on and those she can ride by. She is one who finds success by tapping in to her skills as a rhetorician, knowing that the different stakeholders she must convince are motivated by different values and concerns—the dean cares about money and negotiating competing departments' needs and desires for those funds; the chair worries about how the program fits with the rest of the curriculum, national rankings, and consensus building within the department; the instructors care about how programmatic policies fit into their classroom on a daily basis and whether or not they'll make their lives easier. By being strategic, by carefully considering her audience and framing her argument to reach that audience, the strategic WPA is one who plans, manages, and controls her discourse with colleagues in a measured, intentional way.

When I first began my tenure at my current institution, several of my colleagues encouraged me to enact the strategic WPA role. Because I was new to the program, its students and teachers, and the institution as a whole, my colleagues were keen to give me the lay of the land. Before my first university curriculum meeting, in which I was responsible for presenting a revised curriculum for our first-year writing sequence, a colleague kindly prepped me with an overview of the different characters I would have to contend with there, identifying who would most certainly raise questions about technology, who would question students' general preparedness for college writing, and so on. He was right—our colleagues said the things he predicted they would say, and because I had that information before I went into the meeting, I was prepared. I was strategic.

That first meeting was a success from a programmatic perspective—I carefully crafted my argument about how this curricular shift was based in disciplinary principles of good writing pedagogy that would benefit our students, and members of the curriculum were positive in their review of our plan. My strategy worked, and the program benefited from the committee's support.

Despite this success, however, I felt cut off from the success I experienced that day. I felt that I had cheated: I had a crib sheet that gave me inside knowledge on the personalities and perspectives of the people in that room, and while that allowed me to carefully craft my presentation, it didn't allow me to get to know these colleagues on my own. As Technology Colleague spoke, I thought, "Ok . . . I'm ready for this. I know what he's going to say, and I know how I'm going to respond." I didn't actually listen to what he said, and when I realized this after the meeting was over, I was disappointed in myself. I work hard to be a good listener, attending to not just what people say, but why and how people say what they do, because doing so helps me hear—really hear—the questions and worries and values and beliefs that shape a person's perspective. This allows me to see them as a whole person with priorities, concerns, and interests that are as varied and seemingly disconnected as my own.

For me, the act of rhetorical listening that Krista Ratcliffe has explored is an ethical and personal stance I strive for in my day-to-day life as a WPA. It makes me better at my job when I can hear and attend to the whole person. I could immediately chastise the adjunct who has been shirking his office hours, but because I have listened to him and know that he is stretched thin by caring for an ill, aging parent, we are able to devise a solution so that he could hold virtual office hours from home. I could become frustrated by a colleague's resistance to a curricular change, but because I listen for the underlying concerns, I'm able to talk with her about her larger frustrations about the politics of the change and explain how our curriculum is in the best interest of the students, even if the process by which we got there was flawed. I wouldn't be able to communicate effectively with my colleagues if I didn't understand that there is more to their comments or actions than what would appear on the surface, but when I strategize instead of listen, I cut myself off from the relationship-building that is an important part of the WPA job as I see it.

I've been on the receiving end of this strategizing, too, and I know what it feels like to not be heard. During my first year on the job, I participated in open faculty discussions with administrators in the university. When I attended one of these sessions and introduced myself as the writing program director, one administrator said, "I bet you're going to tell me how much we need a writing center." He was right—I did want to talk to him about our need for a writing center, along with computer lab space and ways for faculty to become more involved with student life concerns—but I felt silenced by his assumption that because of my position as WPA, he already knew what I was going to say. It somehow seemed to indicate that I didn't need to say it at all, that I didn't have a perspective or argument that he hadn't already heard. I felt deflated and discouraged.

Because I know intuitively that I am more complex than the title of WPA would suggest, I have become skeptical of administrative strategizing (both for myself and others), because it limits our understanding of a person to a disciplinary subject position that doesn't reflect the multipliscinarity many of us embody. Certainly there are philosophers or biologists or nurses who have a particular disciplinary point of view that they advocate for in meetings, discussions, and university-wide votes, and administrators do well to take those allegiances into consideration. However, assuming that those philosophers, biologists, and nurses only make decisions based on those concerns and static disciplinary perspectives enacts the same kind of limiting stance that we are trying to complicate by exploring GenAdmin as a more complex identity and perspective.

Administrative strategizing, like athletic, military, or political strategizing, is designed to prepare the WPA to "win." If she is prepared well enough—if she knows what someone will say before he opens his mouth—then she can craft her message to dissuade someone from speaking at all, or at least be ready with a powerful counter-argument. But what if "winning" isn't the goal? What if the goal is consensus, or relationship building, or a genuinely collaborative writing program? Those goals require us to focus not on winning, but on listening. Sure, we may get scraped up in the process. We may not achieve all we want to achieve for our programs. But I think a stance of careful, active, rhetorical listening will do more for our programs, our colleagues, and ourselves as WPAs than strategizing for the win does.

I know we can't be WPAs without strategizing, but we would do well to think more about what strategizing to listen (rather than strategizing for the win) would look like. For me, it means taking into consideration the subject positions of various stakeholders without letting those be my only view of them. It creates space for others to speak—and be heard—and it allows for my WPA perspective to be shaped by those who also care about the program but have different responsibilities to it. And while I may strategize and plan before a big meeting, I'll also listen and reflect, discerning what is in the best interest for the program, its faculty, and the students it aims to teach. It's a different way of thinking, to be sure, this strategizing to listen rather than strategizing to win. But I think it has the potential to move writing programs and those who labor in them to a more humane stance, one that recognizes, listens to, and respects the whole person.

5 Enacting GenAdmin Discourse

If you do not change direction, you may end up where you are heading.

—Lao Tzu

For as long as there is conversation—not just hierarchical or adversarial exchanges—between different forces, there is openness and the possibility of change.

—Joseph Janangelo

[D]iscourse *(without community)* lacks the heuristic power of discourse community.

—M. Jimmie Killingsworth

Part of putting forward a theory and model of GenAdmin discourse means stepping back and reiterating our understanding of writing programs as complex activity systems—not only because they represent "collectives" (Russell 81) and emphasize "collaborative interaction and dynamism" among these collectives (Engeström 78), but because they are categorically inter-relational and marked by kairotic acts of exchange (Graban and Ryan 90). These acts of exchange help us realize the hermeneutic as an oft-forgotten element in our negotiations with others, especially if others see themselves as very firmly positioned when they speak. In the same way that we argue for GenAdmin as more than—or other than—a stable identifier for writing program work, we offer GenAdmin discourse as a set of principles that can be used or employed by WPAs, even in the absence of the kinds of fixed identifications we describe in Chapter 4. We do this not to discount or dissociate ourselves from the principled identifiers that drive such documents as the WPA position statement on "Evaluating Intellectual

Work," but rather to better use such statements within and among contexts where our rhetoric and composition peers are unwilling or unable to support what we do as enacting or advancing disciplinary knowledge.

What drives GenAdmin discourse for the five of us is the reality that we must always interpret where we are and in whom or with what we are in relationship. Location is key, and considering who we are and what we are supposed to be doing takes place as we dwell in or move between different places and spaces, and as we engage with discursive partners in those places and spaces. Our particular notion of discursive engagement as *topos* rather than *chronos*, or even *kairos*, is most affected by the various successes and failures each of us has experienced while drawing from existing WPA statements in order to argue for our curricula, our program goals, or our roles across the institution (including their visibility, their credibility, and their remuneration). The sorts of categories we need to reinvent relationships among ourselves, our students, our teachers, and our colleagues, require an ongoing and articulated commitment to conversation, negotiation, and empathy, given that the institutional definitions of our work, not to mention the contexts in and expectations under which we work, remain in flux.[1]

Thus, we write this chapter with three aims in mind: (1) to articulate the discursive potential of understanding identity as location; (2) to introduce rhetorical agility as a kind of self-positioning without othering (i.e., without assuming others' agonism towards us or concretizing ourselves in their perceptions of us); and (3) to understand how we do employ (and can employ) this rhetorical agility within GenAdmin discourse towards the creation of new knowledge. While much of WPA discourse can be understood as offering responses to resistance, we see in it greater possibilities for knowledge making and identity construction. Rhetorical agility affords us the agency to recognize that potential in our responses to others, in turn positioning our discourse as epistemic. This process of becoming more rhetorically agile underscores how the five of us understand each communicative interaction as one to be negotiated and mediated—that is, as a hybridization of speaking and listening moves, where our interpretive powers are as sharpened as are our powers to respond.

The Discursive Potential of Identity as Location

The resistant WPA in Chapter 2, who challenges the familiarity of the hero/victim binaries that have perpetuated in our field in favor of "changing things for the better," helps further unpack this notion of discursive identity. Much of our theorizing about GenAdmin discourse and how to enact it stems from the fact that, although WPAs rarely work in isolation of material circumstances or institutional paradigms, their success still seems to be marked by how (well) they respond to resistance. While resistance is and has been an integral strategy in our past, present, and future work with designing, deploying, and developing writing programs, we don't wish our responses to always be read as reactionary or to be defined through resistance, in spite of—perhaps because of—the importance of resistance to the development of WPA scholarship.

We want instead to further distinguish between reactive resistance and resistance that is productive. The way in which Linda Adler-Kassner reframes and restories writing and writers in *The Activist WPA* appeals to us because resistance is neither passive nor reactive. Christy Desmet helpfully provides us with intricate ways of understanding and classifying resistance's role within writing programs according to political attitude and ideological process (41). In discussions of resistance, Christine Farris sees the potential for "reflection and change in both individual and program praxis" (100), while Rebecca Rickly and Susanmarie Harrington call resistance "generative" (113). Even in our writing of this book, we came to perceive our resistance to each others' ideas as a necessary, inventive way of allowing our collaboration to retain its complexity. While we add our voices to this ongoing work, we hope to position GenAdmin discourse as more than a response *to* resistance, largely because resistance is coded negatively when it is situated in traditional power dynamics and contexts. By understanding identification as more than a fixed set of ideologies—in fact, as both contingent *and* locatable—we can understand rhetorical identity as an evolving understanding between two dynamic parties, in turn redefining the power relationships that impel and guide our discourse, emphasizing our agency as actors and WPAs.

We are particularly motivated to consider WPA discourse and related issues of power and identity because of what we have come to call the *gravity of disappointment*—that legacy of WPA disappointment Laura Micciche charts in "More than a Feeling" when she acknowledges that "it is not only common to experience disappointment in academia or to witness the disappointments experienced by those around us, but also to become *accustomed* to, even to *expect*, disappointment so that intervening in the positions that create it often becomes unthinkable" (47). We find it circulating in our departments, our programs, and even in our professional literature. We hear it in the talk that circulates about how many meetings we have to attend, in the negative connotations aggregating around the archetypical concept of accountability, in the number of memos from administrative university units that react to crises compared to the number that celebrate accomplishments—most compellingly, in the recurrent, woeful comments that what we create at the program level must go "all the way through system," requiring often uninformed approval from disconnected or decontextualized departmental or larger units. Yet even as we are surrounded by this disappointing academic culture, we find ourselves becoming something else through our philosophy of adaptation and invention. As writers, writing teachers, and writing program administrators, we are constantly immersed in, and quite conscious of, rhetorical negotiations and choices. How we characterize and enact this immersion makes all the difference.

One way of characterizing this immersion is to recognize the historical moment that GenAdmin occupies, which we have tried to articulate in earlier chapters. As part of a generation of WPAs who seek out and explore explicit scholarly preparation for this pedagogical, philosophical, and epistemological work, we are faced with the fact that our authority is, as David Blakesley and others describe, *ethos-*versus discipline-driven, urging us to flesh out the benefits and complications of this reality. Jeanne Gunner, citing Blakesley, writes, "If our disciplinary authority is tied to ethos . . . what we see as reasonable and supported claims only serve to give us credibility as speakers, not agents with disciplinary authority"; in other words, "[o]ur authority is based on the community's consideration of us" ("Cold Pastoral" 36). Although neither Gunner nor Blakesley argues specifically about the untenured WPA, as untenured faculty and WPAs at institutions ranging from private teaching-focused to public research-extensive while writing this book, none of us has the institutional, departmental, or even programmatic *ethos* deemed necessary for the work, yet each of us has been doing program work since the first day of our present jobs.

Though we were all hired to some degree for our perceived expertise in writing program administration, our expertise isn't fully trusted for a myriad of reasons—either because there is no space made for the role of WPA where we work (thereby creating a void or an absence of subjectivity), or because as newcomers to our campuses we lack an immediate sense of local perspective and history, or because as incumbents we inherit the prerequisite powerlessness of newcomers to the faculty hierarchy, or because some aspect of the activity system in which we work discredits our discipline. While the interlude to Chapter 3 considers the benefits of disrupting nonproductive bifurcations between novice/expert, teacher/student, analysis/production, and participant/observer in the classroom, we want to point out that "expertise" in itself need not be void of any productive capacity for writing program work, particularly since one of GenAdmin's challenges has been, and will continue to be, redefining the nature or source of others' beliefs in our capacity to do the work.[4] In any case, the current construction of who we are as junior faculty and writing program administrators on campus constructs a meager identity for us to fit into, informed as it is by a hierarchal definition of power and dualistic sense of value. Something else must fill these identity gaps, perhaps some paradigmatic realization similar to the claim that Anderson makes in the closing of *Identity's Strategy*, reminding us that the banality of identity

> may itself be the very key to its consequentiality. To be so basic, so assumed as to be taken for granted is a rhetorical status with a powerful rhetorical warrant. For no rhetorical enterprise materializes ex nihilo: rhetors construct persuasive discourse out of what they find available, and what they labor to build with these available means must stand upon something. (162-63)

Anderson's reliance on the substantive complexities of character—its intrinsic engagement in and its duality between what *is* and what can *come to be* (168)—resonates with our understanding that identity is rhetorical. Subjectivity, then, need not be something for which we should apologize, feel inadequate, or feel pressured to overcome in order to participate more fully and more powerfully in the academy— at least, there is no epistemic reason why this should be the case.

Wherever our way of thinking doesn't coincide with the context or conditions in which we work, new discourses can arise. We are thus compelled to reexamine GenAdmin discourse as one component of our intellectual identity with potential for dialectical disruption. We see in identity's situatedness (Dana Anderson), instability (Ratcliffe), and hybridity (Desmet) a discursive potential that is largely untapped, perhaps because most WPA narratives still alternate between seemingly fixed identifications (i.e., gWPA, jWPA, director, coordinator, assistant, etc.) and experiential labels (i.e., "I am a WPA because I do, did, have done, or will not do") rather than rhetorical or intersubjective identifications. GenAdmin might be more productively defined by its commitment to discourse, particularly if we accept that identity stands for "a person's ability to articulate a sense of self or self-understanding" (Anderson 6). Anderson's notion of identity elides stable or finite experiences that two parties have in common and relies instead on evolving understandings that two parties can commit to. Such notions of identity seem, to the five of us, dialectical and transformative for GenAdmin.

From here, it is only one step further in our theorizing to ascribe GenAdmin discourse with enough agency to promote understanding, and to realize GenAdmin participants as "*in medias res*" (Desmet 58), or on their way to becoming—able to temporarily surrender or exchange some autonomy and personal ideology with other members of the program, whether that exchange occurs between WPA and TA, TA and student, or WPA and other faculty member. Whereas Gunner calls for a dialectical replacement of the kind of moral authority that is perceived to be underlying all writing program change ("Cold Pastoral" 36),[3] we offer one small step in theorizing a discourse that is not wholly based in the community's perception of the authority we lack or in whether that community feels we have earned or ceded our moral right to lead. In other words, GenAdmin discourse relies on an identity that is neither wholly consumptive of nor defiant toward the "moral order," or ruling ideologies that dictate a university's use of its own writing program. This discourse relies on an identity that is more pragmatic in its vision and enables us to participate more fully (with more agency) in the present moment, resulting in what we call a kind of "rhetorical agility," or a discursive potential untapped in becoming.

Rhetorical Agility and Pragmatic Activism

This agility has three aspects, which we define here before suggesting a set of heuristic principles for enacting it. By "rhetorical agility," we first mean the ability of a program participant to self-position without the need for discrediting others or othering, not unlike Melanie Kill's employment of "uptake" in first-year writing classrooms as a way of moving her students beyond their reliance on positioning themselves the way they think others expect them to be positioned (223), and not unlike Dylan Dryer's employment of "genre uptake" in observing how many writing programs enact the social and material re/constitutions caused by recurrent and revised documents or texts (32). For Kill, a more authentic positioning occurs when students (and teachers) rely more on their present interactions and less on memories of past ones, and when they understand each interaction as an exigent situation to be negotiated. For Dryer, the various abilities or inabilities of WPAs to recognize and more effectively take up certain genre systems are not only contextually determined but can be detrimental by causing us to miss out on opportunities to narrate the arguments we value (46). Even as we write with a consciousness of how many levels of an activity system we want to penetrate through our discourse, we realize that those actors whom we perceive to be challenges or barriers (whether they are students, colleagues, or circumstantial entities) are themselves heavily contextualized. Some days our particular communicative philosophies are best directed at them; other days, they are best directed at other actors within their contexts. Most days, we do well to remember that others' responses are informed more by past rather than present location, and are informed by flexible roles. For example, we might be easily frustrated at how our hard-earned decisions about textbooks, curriculum, staffing, or training regularly get usurped by more senior faculty with presumably less explicit preparation in, desire for, or motivation towards the kinds of work that we do, before realizing the categorical differences between how we both understand preparation, desire, and motivation. GenAdmin—as a philosophy and a discourse—leaves no room for a simplistic rendering of heroes and villains, but rather makes room for the requisite complexity of the multiple systems in which we work and, in fact, requires that we cultivate empathy in a range of ways that do not rely merely on two-way identification, i.e., on the identification *of* rather than identification *with* one another.

The second aspect of agility is in its fluidity, i.e., its interest in raising discord by providing a "path for identity formation" (resulting from self-reflection) and "an outwardly directed political framework, oriented . . . at creating social change" (Satterfield and Antczak 149). In other words, pragmatic outcomes of GenAdmin discourse are tied more to nascent goals, or "commitments," leading us to other points of mediation where we *temporarily* dwell, causing us to occupy a space somewhere in between self-commitment and commitment to selves-in-a-community. Like Jay Satterfield and Frederick Antczak, we find that neither Richard Rorty's utopian revolutionary who "abandons the public realm" for incremental change (151) nor Cornel West's charismatic leader who inspires communal action (152) is sufficient for our discourse because neither goes far enough to promote the dialogic communication between the WPA and his/her community that we seek.

The third aspect of rhetorical agility is its commitment to humanistic outcomes, and we draw on Kate and Tarez's prior use of Steven Yarbrough's "discursive power" in re-theorizing WPA/TA communication to make this point. A traditional definition of power remains a fairly static relationship where one interlocutor has "access to the threat of actual or deferred force" and thus power over another (Ryan and Graban 257); many accepted academic practices related to reinforcing hierarchies, like those between pre-tenure faculty and their tenured colleagues, find traction through this definition of power. Discursive power, on the other hand, is a relational and provisional activity that doesn't assert the status quo; instead, it is a means to mediate differences charitably with the goal of facilitating dialogue and productive engagement and action. Discursive power begins with an acknowledgement that we speak out of our own conditions and differences and relies on the initial belief that others mean well as a means to work towards understanding and communicating with them—towards mediation.

Discourse, then, doesn't work *through* a medium like language or culture; it is its own kind of competence (Yarbrough, *After Rhetoric* 242), enabling us to credit those we interact with for meaning what they say—for speaking and enacting what they know to be true—and helping us to assume that the conditions informing what they say are unlike our own, creating a kind of "middle ground" tied to situational, suasory goals that enable us to communicate humanely, even with conflicts unresolved. Whereas a compromise involves sacrificing part of what we want in order to gain another part of what we want (usually an ideal), a middle ground occurs wherever contradiction and conflict make a "mediate" position possible or desired (Yarbrough, *After Rhetoric* 158). To illustrate, Yarbrough introduces the situation of two people arguing about who between them is the least racist, and claims they are both right. Without their shared belief in the existence of culture, they cannot argue with one another. Paradoxically, for that same reason, they cannot reach agreement. Their shared belief—the belief that one *has* to share a complex set of linguistic and cultural beliefs in order to communicate them—is what prevents them from sharing other beliefs in the exchange (Yarbrough, *After Rhetoric* 2-4). Thus, for Yarbrough, being fully human means being in conflict, but it need not mean an end to productive communication, as statements from any language, culture, or discipline can always be brought within the problematics of any other language, culture, or discipline. What it does mean—for Yarbrough, and for GenAdmin—is that our communicative goals turn to mediation, to the middle ground that he calls "humanism" (Yarbrough, *After Rhetoric* 5).

Rather than valorizing "administrative" (or managerial for that matter), we see administrative identity as capable of creating new intellectual conditions through an activism that occurs on the level of rhetorical and communicative ideology. As such, it follows that our discourse must work actively as well, allowing us to participate in ideological conversations where our colleagues and institutions will see or feel them the most quickly and urgently, and requiring us to find—in traditional points of tension and conflict—opportunities for making new language to describe what we do, justify why it is doable, and explain how it is productive, not merely symbolic of our professional hopes.

Sites of Invention: A Heuristic for Discursive Identification

To offer a heuristic for GenAdmin discourse, we begin with Kate and Tarez's prior scholarship on feminist pragmatic rhetoric and WPA/

TA discourse. Drawing on the work of such scholars as Kate Ronald and Hephzibah Roskelly, Yarbrough, and Janet Atwill, they define feminist pragmatic rhetoric from an epistemic/rhetorical perspective to guide better mentoring practices. The discourse model they offer for WPAs and TAs reflects this perspective as it seeks to move beyond the kinds of unproductive resistance that often bog down composition practica and may lead to undervaluing of the program. We see in their WPA/TA discourse model a helpful discussion of power and identity that is located intersubjectively. In their model and in our own model for GenAdmin discourse, we privilege dialogic mediation as a way of better negotiating diverse perspectives to move towards action. But we find that this mediation and discursive power have often been under-theorized or oversimplified, usually described as push-pull or either/or interactions between stable positionings.

This notion is too limited for the work that characterizes GenAdmin. While each of us occupies some WPA role, we are not always *the* WPA, nor do we carry titles that ascribe us with visible power. We all engage in the hard work of outreach; that is, reaching out, making space for productive talk, engaging in difficult and uncomfortable ideological discussion, and getting seemingly nowhere, and we understand that something creative can come out of our choosing how to respond and in the subsequent construction of spaces *for* response that might otherwise be denied us because of superficial power structures. Our notion of a pragmatic discourse is one that remains temporal, contextual, and shifting, even in light of the fairly static and very material conditions that writing programs are often believed to operate under.

While Gunner helps us understand that resistance travels and resituates itself differently in each institution according to a host of factors ("Cold Pastoral" 36)—thus implying that a set of strategies cannot necessarily empower one WPA to be the same WPA in a different context—we do not give into the truism she notes within some WPA theorizing that "general rules apply only weakly to varying local conditions" (29). Instead, general principles of pragmatic, feminist administration can be enacted across institutional contexts because, by their very nature, these principles are shaped by the people, material conditions, and institutions that create such kairotic moments. That is to say, systems—and the people and communicative patterns in them—often prove themselves to be far more fluid than we tend to (or allow ourselves to) imagine. The kind of discursive identification we outline above helps us see that a heuristic for creating these conditions can be and has already been located in the collective wisdom of writing program administration, demonstrating writing programs as "meaningful social structures and sites of meaning making" (Gunner, "Ideology" 7). We present this heuristic in several phases, hoping to identify creative sites for writing program change.

Positioning Ourselves as Mediators of Institutional Memory

The first phase of our heuristic follows Gunner's notion of intervening in the re/formation of a program's ideological context so that the program itself doesn't become a fixed genre ("Ideology" 9). In response to Terry Eagleton's definition of ideology as "practices mediated by political power," Gunner urges WPAs and other program participants to "tak[e] advantage of our potential for material agency" ("Ideology" 9), thereby disallowing extant ideologies to shut out or shut down our theorizing—our acts of describing, predicting, and/or explaining phenomena ("Ideology" 8). We have seen in our own experiences the wisdom in producing public documents as one enactment of this productive theorizing, as one way of materializing the program and bearing witness to the breadth of the activity system it represents—past, present, and future.[4] Jonikka has seen the power of this strategy in designing inclusive professional development workshops, a *Soup's On!* series that combines food with discussion and revision of program goals and outcomes, so that invention and collaboration occur in small group discussion, evaluative feedback, and a sharing of documents in development. What made this more inventive than other of Jonikka's collaborations was not simply this combination (although Jonikka notes that her willingness to prepare food for the group reversed several negative expectations), but how she forged space for instructors' voices in her particular context. The workshops disrupted and extended what had historically been an evaluative, single-day orientation for contingent faculty (mainly long-term lecturers whom Jonikka worried would doubt her role and her authority as the new WPA on campus) before classes began, and maybe be supplemented by a workshop or two throughout the year. This extension/disruption in turn sparked an egalitarian effort to "start from scratch" with the composition curriculum, buoyed by her instructors' sense of buy-in after meeting together each week for a year, and after taking it on themselves to conduct classroom observations.

In two different programmatic contexts and two curricula revisions, Tarez has also used curricular document construction—and its ensuing stages, demands, and exigencies—as a site not just for more publicly articulating some information that was unavailable or held close to the program before, but also for drawing (sometimes unwilling) parties into conversation about the goals or aims of a course that may not have been understood by all of its constituents before. To constitute a true act of *mediation* (specifically, a mediation of institutional memory and commitments) this work should not dissuade or disallow those constituents (including advisors, instructors, and other administrators) from remaining involved in the tasks of defining, understanding, or questioning the ways that general education courses are described, particularly when they involve high-stakes, high-need, or non-traditional populations of students. By and large, this mediation need not threaten our programmatic roles when we can define it and our need to know the historical contexts we are stepping into as ends in themselves, while accepting the construction of the documents or of program archives as a residual activity, and the documents and archives as temporal themselves.

The socially productive nature of writing programmatic documents has already been well established in the work of Anne Ruggles Gere, who suggests that a close reading of the discourses of our writing programs—departmental memos, curriculum reports, committee minutes, and course descriptions—creates a space for conducting important research in composition studies and asking questions that are valuable to the field as a whole, especially to get at the contradictions and conflicts (131). Likewise, we build from the work of Christopher Burnham, who believes that broader reaching documents such as the *WPA Outcomes Statement* can help to distill, balance, and demonstrate the values and rhetorical motivations underlying assessment (313), which requires a reciprocal engagement between the audiences and conversationalists who validate the findings and the reconciliation and application of the findings themselves (304). Furthermore, the usefulness of curricular documents in promoting pedagogical reflection and enabling systemic change (Reid 14) helps position their very act of construction as located knowledge-making and rhetorical reform (Graban and Ryan). Finally, document construction challenges the singularity of the author-audience metaphor, as WPA work on documents conjoins what M. Jimmie Killingsworth calls "local and global discourse communities" (112), demonstrating the diverse range of rhetorical concerns a single document must accommodate, and positioning readers as both senders and receivers of information (110). Killingsworth uses "local and global" to refer to the various community models and social pressures that affect the practices of individual writers, and we argue that re/constructing writing program documents necessarily conjoins these local and global communities because it requires a meta-rhetorical awareness. That is, writers of curricular documents must negotiate their goals for articulation with their audience concerns, and must envision an audience large and complex enough to include all current and future users of the documents, even themselves.

But the heart of this heuristic phase is not in the value of these documents as speech acts, rhetorical performances, or even dynamic activity systems; rather, it is in the way such public articulation allows us to co-own and responsibly co-opt institutional, departmental, and in some cases programmatic histories for making new knowledge and for constructing genealogies for future program participants. Following Anis Bawarshi's argument for genre theory as a rhetorical methodology, Gunner describes the epistemological function of writing programs (as productive genres) in helping WPAs to

> structure a relation of language and culture. They help establish the cultural rules for language use, what its cultural work is: how we are to form categories of language users; how we are to hierarchize discourses; how we are to correlate specific discourses with ability and social worth; how we are to validate the differences produced. ("Ideology" 11)

Where Gunner allows for disrupting stagnant ideological structures through the language and discourse conflict that can come from writing them, we further argue for program documents as proactive in that they provide opportunities for understanding writing programs as emergent, cyclical, developing, and contextualized—even during those times in the program history where there was *no* WPA, or only *a* WPA. In other words, researching and writing program documents for various purposes causes us to position the program and our roles within it as situated not only in the present, but in an "ongoing past," and as part of a developing writing program vision.

Like Debora Cameron et al., we do not advocate viewing program documents as mere knowledge objects (145), but as representations of the nascent methodologies that drive our research and historicization of the field. The writing of these documents may also offer a unique site for inquiry into the language dependence of social reality, i.e., into the ways we have used them to position ourselves and our values, and it may complicate relations between the researcher and the researched, as various stakeholder conversations become enacted and then examined in future revisions (Cameron et al. 149). Examining the evolution of any document makes the process of revising it more pragmatic, and more productive in terms of fulfilling its original goals, not to mention revealing language politics that may embroil us unwittingly in past conflicts.[5] Furthermore, an archivist's mindset helps WPAs view these records and documents as interdependent with research (Rose and Weiser, *WPA as Researcher* 279) and helps the WPA to develop a "long view" towards the writing program's future ("*WPA as Researcher*" 276). But even beyond the document or the archive (beyond the technology of rhetorical memory, so to speak), we see practical value in being agents of remembering in our programs, and of playing the role of mediator of sometimes historically entrenched and difficult conversations that preceded us, a sentiment that is echoed in Donald Hall's impetus for writing, which we will address in Chapter 6. In short, as agents of memory, we often shape our past to help us in the present as we imagine the future. But more importantly, re-covering and re-mediating documents in this fashion may help to re-situate the history (of the course or program) less in some*one*'s idiosyncratic memory and more in claims or circumstances that are tangible, debatable, and concrete.

Practicing Charitable Interpretation as Active and Pragmatic

For each of us in our programmatic and institutional contexts, "doing the work of WPA" varies widely, from offering Pierre Bourdieu's "cultural capital" as justification for a first-year composition course that emphasizes writing in multicultural and multilingual contexts, to serving on institutional subcommittees charged with restructuring general education curricula, to conducting faculty roundtables on the use of emerging digital technologies. What we have learned, and what WPA scholarship has already taught us, is that we can expect to be thrust into the role of cultural interpreter, not only where we are positioned as on the "outside" of others' ideas, but also where we are positioned as immersed in the same humanities-vision others around us believe themselves to also be following, or as co-creators in the humanities-vision that others around us truly desire to build, or even as conspirators in a program where the views of our rhetoric and composition colleagues diverge widely from our own. The biggest mistake we could make is in assuming that our rhetoric and composition colleagues do not also need to be helped to understand the long and rich history of our assertions and our intellectual positioning, and that they do not deserve or need the time and effort that understanding takes.

The wide range of these experiences teaches us that the ability to place ourselves in other subjectivities and the willingness to believe others' subject positions carries heuristic value. Yarbrough's dialogic model that we mention above, suitable in one-on-one conversations as well as larger group contexts, draws on Donald Davidson's concept of "interpretive charity" to help us understand those "with whom we speak" and to know "what caused them to speak as they did" (qtd. in Yarbrough, *After Rhetoric* 6). We understand charitable interpretation to be like Augustinian *caritas*—charity—but we offer another way of understanding its relevance in the context of GenAdmin. In *On Christian Doctrine*, Augustine contrasts this concept with the less charitable *cupiditas* (III.X.16), a term he uses to refer to the kind of self-aggrandizing enjoyment of others or of objects (including victories) we desire to possess. As a culture of WPA, *caritas* is a useful concept in our consideration of how we define and understand the *gains* of our work. This attitude promotes listening and working towards understanding, not by claiming a Burkean identification and being content to disagree but by recognizing difference as a window into epistemological limitations and possibilities that helps us hear others even if they do not ultimately agree with us.

As humanists, we find this aspect of the heuristic necessary for establishing a productive intellectual presence, and, though we recognize its difficulty to establish, it is central to establishing an *admin* identity. We find this aspect necessary for making ourselves indefatigable in current conversations regarding the future of our courses, our programs, and even our instructional paradigms when they occur, since each of us has, in our previous or current positions, experienced the powerlessness that comes with not being ready to participate, not recognizing the unfamiliar contexts in which these conversations occur, or not being able to empathize with the ideological stance from with other interlocutors speak.

Perhaps the most pragmatic way to view this aspect of the heuristic—and to imagine how to be charitable—is in being willing to traverse identity "fault-lines," or what we consider to be active "contact zones" in the formation of key beliefs, ideas, and hopes that shape acceptance of or resistance to our work.[6] But to traverse them, we must first note and embrace them as possible sites of contention. In our own experiences, we identify the following fault-lines or zones where charitable interpretation is carried out or can be carried out more systematically. In our collective experience it has been the case that most conversations surrounding our programs that we perceive as threats to the positive gains made by the CWPA in the past two decades stem from differences in thinking about one or mores of these zones:

1. *Nature of the collective.* A number of our most difficult struggles have boiled down to unspoken conflicts regarding the different paradigms participants may take as starting points. We do not mean to naively state that paradigm discussions are the panacea for convincing institutional structures far removed from writing programs that we need to do things a certain way. However, we do take seriously that these disagreements and discussions need to be had more often, and that we often lack a safe space in which to have them within our departments and programs; we also lack the forcefulness of a collective vocabulary empowering us to speak up for our courses or our programs when unexpected opportunities arise for us to do so. Obviously, this involves training in what we might call the *sensus communis* of WPA dialogic negotiation (Vico 1709), but we argue that that knowledge—that set of beliefs—is multilayered and complex, part disciplinary but mostly geospatial, and that it fluctuates, recycles, and evolves in creative ways. For this reason, we not only count on the willingness of those in our local contexts to engage us in epistemological or generative discussion, we rely on it, even if they view these discussions as culminating in little more than an immediate decision to raise course caps, reduce or enlarge an instructional staff, or eliminate a course.

2. *Nature of the inter-disciplinary person.* Other struggles stem from our interest in the people with whom we work as representatives of different disciplinary thinking. At times, this interest may lead to unpopular choices, choices that seem narrowly focused, self-interested, myopic, or secondary (rather than primary or astute) to the material pressures regarding enrollment, staffing, and funding courses on our campuses. These may range anywhere from renovating a curriculum so as to better position the multilingual learner as an agentive participant in a writing course, to foregoing (or devising alternatives to) assessment in order to give students some choice in their own course placement, to going out of our way to liaise with language or library programs who have disciplinary ties to our courses. More often than not, this interest and our desire to make others feel valued in their interactions with us leads us to take the hard and more time-consuming road, or leaves us open to criticism, especially since the results of these cross-disciplinary interactions are not often immediately deliverable, and by some arguments may seem detrimental to the emergence of rhetoric and writing studies as its own discipline. We do deploy disciplinary notions quite often, for example, in reaching out to the information technology group or the literature faculty or the honors college or the librarians and letting their own locations help to inform how they understand what we do (or where we are). Thus, if we are deploying disciplinarity as an act of locating, then empathy necessarily operates differently from disciplinary essentialism, because these locations can be (or should be) disruptive and question-raising, helping us to note the contradictions in our locations, rather than making us feel like we have to be more firmly defined by or entrenched in them.

3. *Nature of human flourishing.* Some struggles have boiled down to perceptions of good or bad behavior—whether directed or incidental—and these will range anywhere from a perceived overlooking of the psychic condition of our teaching staff, to a lack of commitment to productive and vision-oriented discussion among members of a faculty. As we discuss in Chapter 6, "flourishing" conditions and behaviors are tied to a number of

orientations—ethical, rhetorical, and pragmatic—and are not simply or concretely obtained devoid of established consensus. One consequent outcome of the geospatial (and temporal) contexts in which "GenAdmin" emerged as an identifier may well be an orientation towards considering our responsibilities via others. This is not to say that "GenAdmin" is uniquely linked to caring while other subjectivities are not, but rather that our professionalization has consisted principally of a critical filtering of most other rhetorical processes via questions of how our choices and subjectivities reflect onto others with whom we worked. This in turn places added pressure on our ability to occupy the discursive position of someone (or ones) willing to understand.

4. *Possibilities and means to knowledge.* Since any one of these fault-lines can be recentered as an impetus for more difficult systemic change and productive conversation—without naïveté, without forgetting that in the changing economic landscape, we may be in less control of our programs and our courses than before—the first step in doing this is helping one another identify these fault-lines across programs (and possibly departments and disciplines), helping one another recognize how they are developed and shaped in these various sites, and helping one other recognize which ones should be overturned (because they are damaging) and which ones should be encouraged and rehabilitated over time. These fault-lines involve interdisciplinary engagement and discovery of how we and others make sense of the world, of writing programs, and of conflicting perceptions of how we see what we do for students, for colleagues, and for universities or other agents of delivery. As we articulate in earlier chapters, for GenAdmin, few programmatic decisions can be or are construed separately from the knowledge-making processes that we value and have worked hard (alongside others) to make central to our discipline.

Rather than an imperative, we offer charitable interpretation as evidence of several recent scholarly directions that have come from WPA seminars and point to an intellectual (and disciplinary) interest in theorizing power structures for scholarly collaboration and decision-making. Margaret Morris, in her presentation for the 2008 CWPA conference, empirically devised what she calls a "Consociational Model for Collaboration." This model understands all collaboration as exigency-based and illustrates complex factors that coalesce or cluster around a single collaborative event, favoring "consociation" rather than "association" for the way it allows the cluster to be reconfigured several ways.[7] At that same conference, a panel of graduate students presented an interactive board game they had developed called "Praxis and Allies," which allowed each player to imagine how they would navigate the activity system of their campus or institution. Designed for the WPA seminar, this game was intended to give students experiential practice in two areas: (1) "using knowledge, ethos, and resources"; and (2) "finding and making allies." Players have to make decisions that are motivated by material needs and circumstances, that consider the subject positions of others, and take into account imaginative allocations of the resources at hand by allowing themselves to investigate and be put into the role of other subjects.[8]

The roles and experiential dilemmas made possible by this game echo, to some degree, the kind of classroom-based Situated Performance Activities that Shirley Rose and Margaret Finders developed for the TA training course ("Thinking Together"), although they also represent a unique attempt to describe the actual, intellectual emphasis of WPA as serving as a lens for or perspective on inquiry (Rose and Weiser, "Beyond" 172). But where they reflect the active and epistemic potential of our heuristic the most is in the opportunities they create for what Kelly Kinney posits as "situated leadership" (40), a relevant model for critical administration even in today's corporate downturn because of the institutional demand it creates for WPAs to use their training as rhetoric and composition scholars and perhaps be called on to rethink the ethics of service and to reimagine a labor and pay structure in programs where needs are most dire. Perhaps what these directions imply for our heuristic is that if we can learn to identify, build on, and build away from all the complex factors that coalesce around an event or that lead us to unexpected points of decision, we are one step further in being able to enact pragmatic discourse.

Speaking With and To

In our own experiences with colleagues, teachers, students and mentors—and in the interstitial tensions between the WPA narratives we inherit and our attempts to dissociate them—we notice that the default position for supporting untenured or junior WPAs reflects what Linda Martín-Alcoff calls "speaking for" others, rather than equipping us for speaking (and listening). More often than not, this discursive responsibility that others bear on our behalf has predisposed us to fixed subjectivities and is based in arguments that we find disempowering and nonproductive. We recognize the risks that we take in presuming to speak for a generation of WPAs while writing this book; although we know the impetus for our book is rather to describe what generational aspects arise from the contingencies in which we all work, even still we would prefer that our colleagues might note the risks they take in speaking for us and look more honestly at the protective measures that may be weakening us in specific contexts. Alice Horning's adamant argument that "jWPA positions should be abolished" (40), which she frames via her experiences as a full professor and WPA, is one we find philosophically frustrating. Our own discursive positioning prevents us from fully crediting Horning's arguments or intentions, however well intentioned, because we have the feeling she's speaking *for* us without fully crediting the desires or perspectives we bring to the work. She also inadvertently argues against (the need for or viability of) seeking out what other support measures might be required in institution-specific contexts.

Martín-Alcoff acknowledges that never speaking for anyone but oneself is not viable, and that well-meaning scholars do try to speak for others in order to advocate for them. But her articulation of the challenges of speaking for others makes two significant points we want to draw attention to. First, which we have already discussed in earlier chapters, location affects meaning and truth claims and is therefore "epistemically salient." In other words, what we understand and believe is shaped by our social, historical, and affective positioning. Second, and consequently, when more privileged people "speak for" less privileged people, the result may "increase[e] or reinforc[e] the oppression of the group spoken for" (99). In other words, when WPAs recommend graduate students and junior faculty avoid WPA jobs, they might exercise caution when speaking for us about the problem of gWPA and jWPA positions.

As an alternative, Martín-Alcoff recommends "speaking to" and "with" others to create dialogue—a hermeneutic exchange that is complementary to our model of discourse—and cautions that when speaking for others, such as when speaking out against oppression, speakers must pay close attention to how they represent others needs and desires and how "the *listener's* social location will affect the meaning of my words" (105). By speaking "to" others, we advocate imagining the other's perspective and getting a sense of how their words will be received by the listener to help the speaker initiate dialogue. And this imagining would be reciprocal—as are all other aspects of GenAdmin discourse—in that we do not prevent ourselves from hearing what others advise, even as we explicitly articulate the ways in which their advice disallows us from fulfilling our own goals of knowing and understanding the other better. Our own response might be to note their advice as temporal and contextualized, to acknowledge its usefulness alongside its limits, to set parameters in which we can reasonably give and receive advice, to embrace the possibility that others' motives may be better or worse than we expect them to be, and to selectively resist or willingly apply their advice where salient. Each of us knows better than to say that all advice works in isolation of all other, or than to assume that we might not repurpose what others tell us to help us fulfill more salient goals.

We would love for our colleagues—senior WPAs, members of our departments, and members of our institutions—to (keep) speaking *with* junior faculty members and graduate students who hold WPA positions, to imagine how we hear what they say, to imagine *what difference it would make* if we worked to redefine or explore the tensions of being junior faculty WPAs, and reconsider the range of possible, successful jWPA identities, including those for women. Speaking *with* and *to* can spur dialogue about situations, positions, and possibilities tied to epistemic responsibility that resist slipping unreflectively into simple statements or perpetuating uncomplicated roles.

Demonstrating Rhetorical Power as "Rhetorical Listening"

This phase of the heuristic deals with how we translate listening into action and why we embrace the idea that limits of discourse are fluid and can change. We share Irwin Mallin and Karrin Anderson's interest in understanding theories of discourse and communication as embodiments of something beyond argumentation—their constructive argument is an embodiment of a hope for better things, better conditions in which to argue, mainly because they commit to adaptation as a discursive goal: "Understanding is a prerequisite to adaptation. . . . Instead of always treating understanding another as a mere means to refutation of that other, a constructive arguer may also see the value in understanding another as central to achieving mutually satisfying outcomes" (125).

Like Mallin and Anderson, we also commit to adaptation and recognize the critical benefit of attending to both the emotional and rational dimensions of argument. In fact, we extend that to treating both the hopeful and the hopeless aspects in the discourse. It's "hopeless" if you cannot see beyond the limits of agreement. We aim for not the agreement, but for the process of transcending epistemological boundaries.

They note invitational impulses, *vis-a-vis* Sonya Foss and Cindy Griffin's "Beyond Persuasion," in Kenneth Burke, Richard Johannesen, Donald Bryant, and Richard Fulkerson—but where they locate their theorizing at the convergence of feminist criticism, social science, rhetorical criticism, and conflict theories,[10] we find these same productive possibilities in a convergence of rhetorical invention, feminist pragmatism, and discourse theory, perhaps because of our expectation that rhetorical participation should redistribute power. While their argumentation model functions according to how all participants' desires are integrated, our heuristic strives to make spaces for modeling institutional critique and ideological disruption as ethical. This may be because its other aspects necessitate that we live and work (well) with disagreement.

While Kenneth Burke names such metaphysical moves "identification" (to differentiate them from division), we might better describe them as empathetic listening for their multiple transformative dimensions. That is, there is as much hermeneutic potential in our powers to respond as there is transformative potential in our powers to listen. Beyond the paradoxical consubstantiality or "acting together" that Burke says can ambiguate demarcated units that seem to act singly which also sharing other positions (21), our heuristic calls for an ethic of listening, much like Krista Ratcliffe's "rhetorical listening," which we also see as a trope for interpretive invention: "a stance of openness that a person may choose to assume in relation to any [other] person, text, or culture; its purpose is to cultivate conscious identifications in ways that promote productive communication, especially but not solely cross-culturally" (25). Like Ratcliffe, we see the need for a space "wherein listeners may employ their agency (which Stanford drama theorist Alice Rayner defines as both 'capacity' and 'willingness' [7]) to foster conscious identifications" (26).

Three things compel us about Ratcliffe's description of the four "moves" that comprise rhetorical listening for the way they help us to re/define power. First, it resonates with how we differentiate between pragmatic resistance and pragmatic refusal, especially in helping us to determine what conversations and situations we can reasonably participate in and how to continue in our work even when others no longer wish to engage. Secondly, her second and fourth moves—"proceeding within an *accountability* logic," and "analyzing *claims* as well as the *cultural logics* within which these claims function" (Ratcliffe 26)—afford WPAs the agency to be good rhetorical theorists in motivating, modeling, and maintaining productive argumentation. Finally, her notion of "understanding" as "standing under" represents what we see as a more worthwhile goal for persuasion than simply receiving, appropriating, or agreeing to truth claims, all of which are limited to the listener's orientation and desire to protect a self-centered reality and a desire to be heard, rather than to "le[t] discourses wash over, through, and around us . . . then liste[n] to hear and imagine how these discourses might affect . . . others" (Ratcliffe 28).

In practice, this listening is realized in any number of strategies that represent what Ratcliffe calls "listening metonymically": "assum[ing] that a text or person is associated with—but not necessarily representative of—an entire cultural group" (78) so as to resist gendered, racialized, or other cultured silences that often end the discourse (79). It might be realized in ways that GenAdmin encourage others to question resistance, attend to their own process of definitions, and get them to take accountability for their own discourse and assumptions underlying what they say, think, or believe (Belanger and Grogan). In an ethnographic sketch of her life offered at Feminisms and Rhetorics (2009), Kelly Belanger and Brian Grogan pinpoint these as principal strategies that Olympian Nell C. Jackson used to neutralize a harmful (in many cases racist) discourse she often encountered as an NAWCA

Administrator and athletic coach in a racially dominated higher education.

In more mundane ways, we see rhetorical listening in the sometimes complex turn of discussion threads on the WPA-L listserv, where listers work hard to imagine representative responses to their posts, and in fact mention explicitly what they expect the response will be and where they expect it to originate. We see this move in critical WPA collections (most recently in Strickland and Gunner's call to "make space for critical discourse" (xi)), inviting essays that confront the origins of static ideologies that WPAs find themselves working against. We may even recognize it in the way we willingly model uncertainty and irresolution for our graduate students and faculty colleagues, because we believe that irresolution (or relinquishing our own right to culturally associate) will lead to genuine and rigorous efforts to make consensus where logics at first diverge.

For example, as Amy spearheaded her department's efforts to revise the first-year writing course to meet changing general education requirements, throughout the year, she met with resistance to the proposed revision, and while it would have been tempting to categorize these resistances as unwillingness or refusals, it became clear to Amy after repeated discussions that these resistances were not about the curriculum or even first-year writing; instead, they were borne of concerns about the revision of the general education curriculum at large. With the General Education wheels already in motion, there was no space or exigency for Amy's colleagues to express those specific concerns, and they instead translated into objections to the first-year writing course at the department level. It was only in putting aside her own frustrations at what she perceived as their unwillingness, and in being willing to suspend her own disbelief in these objections, that Amy could neutralize what had before been a threatening lack of agency, and could listen to and hear the underlying concerns. Only in this way did Amy nudge rhetorical listening towards actually "replacing subjectivities."

For the five of us, this kind of listening signifies much more than simply "doing more listening"—which Joe Janangelo cites as a principal component in negotiating "differends" in writing programs to keep them dialogic and evolving (18), and which we do value as activity in itself. This kind of hearing is more than simply a description of our tendency to see, critique, and tropologically refuse—tropes that, as John Schilb demonstrates, represent acts of participation by "seek[ing] the audience's assent to another principle" and "cast as a higher priority" (3). This kind of hearing represents for us a reciprocal dwelling, a willing suspension of what could be seen as teleological "ends" or "wins" for another kind of "win" that promotes the kinds of behaviors we desire in ourselves, our students, and our colleagues.

Modeling Dialogic Negotiation Even When Deliverable Outcomes Are Unclear

As we have established in prior chapters, a Deleuzian becoming recognizes that identity isn't a monolithic, non-changing entity; rather, it elides stable identity in favor of a flexibility and fluidity that embrace the possibilities of change, choice and invention. This doesn't mean neglecting material conditions that shape our social and historical locations and affiliations, but it does mean recognizing that our identities oscillate among these multiple positionings as we move about and communicate with others. It may also mean acting deliberately without an extant goal in mind, i.e., without being provoked or nudged by an extant need.

In Chapter 4 we posit becoming as something other than a difference that is grounded in identity. In other words, like Deleuze, we start with becoming—with difference itself—not as a defining characteristic of identity, but as what we call the gravity of a multiplicinary identity. Who we are becomes more a question of *when* we are (May 144). In order to shift our focus from chronological time to virtual time, then, it is necessary for us to realize that in trying to locate stable identities within each moment we are really only recognizing that each moment contains connections to other past moments. What we know of as the momentary stable emerges from all the differences of the past. For Deleuze, virtuality is more real than stability; and while we recognize the institutional and disciplinary forces that privilege stability in the midst of (perhaps because of) major upheaval, we also recognize that most decisions, paradigms, and working philosophies are constructed in only snapshots of understanding the complexities of large and vibrant programs. They carry with them a history and an inertia that can be reused or reformulated to build collective and discursive understanding out of moments of necessary conflict.

For the five of us, multiplicinarity serves as one part of a critical orientation that is native to GenAdmin, i.e., as one of our foundational pieces, as one of the topics or issues that stumps us and troubles us and inspires us to keep working it through. We—like most readers of this book—are quite deeply contextualized by geospatial concerns, whether these concerns are constructed by an institutional ethos or a regional locale. Each of us has been oriented toward public articulation, consensus building, and programmatic disruption as necessities, knowing full well that our notions of what it means to "build consensus" would themselves be disrupted, and that the ways we have been taught to talk to those outside of our programs are locally derived. In fact, we work not for the *uni*versity (*universitas*), but for the *loci*versity, a useful paradox given that there are communal assumptions underlying our identification as a group of rhetoric and composition scholars or WPA practitioners, even as our discursive needs are institutionally determined. What this means, practically, is that our GenAdmin discourse must usefully account for and make visible precisely what identifications are being negotiated between, across, and within disciplines. It is often the case that such negotiation does not result in a single, agreed-upon outcome (e.g., how to meet the needs of developmental writers on a large college campus by offering a single course) but rather results in illuminating the particular stasis or stases in which such conversations have gotten stymied in the past (e.g., What should be the role of the FYC course on this campus? Whose notions of academic writing in the disciplines hold sway? How do we measure and assess "developmental" writing among this population of students? What should be the role of assessment in FYC administration, if at all?).

Working through disagreements over terms and concepts, whether it is how rhetoric and composition scholars view rhetorical response as a wholly different phenomenon than reader response or literary criticism, requires three things of us: (1) most obviously and most simply, that we understand what we are trying to say from our own disciplinary perspective, but also from the perspective of others who are already trying to situate our theoretical orientations in terms that make sense to them; (2) that we be aware of how others think and build epistemic knowledge; (3) that rather than feeling bent out of shape when we realize how much these conversations highlight our differences (and represent the ways our disciplinary perspectives can often be mis/portrayed as lesser, inferior, or subsequent to others), we let them re-direct our interactions with colleagues away from the fear of standing out or being different towards the revisionist potential that our successful dialogues with colleagues can have on the productive potential of difference.

In a way, our concept of modeling dialogic negotiation represents one goal of what we call feminist pragmatic rhetoric—rather than achieving clear-cut resolution and/or winning, our goal is in fact to promote dialogic negotiation, which presumes a deeper commitment to philosophical underpinnings and which, we have seen, has far greater and longer-lasting impacts in campus writing programs. Thinking long term and thereby pressing for the kinds of long-term changes we wish to see in writing programs does not mean we are ill equipped to attend to daily crises or that we think a long-term decision we make today is guaranteed or promised to be true several years from now. Rather, thinking long-term means deliberately viewing everything as a small step towards building ideological bridges in spite of the pressure to deliver goods on a daily basis. As we articulate in the interlude on "Empathy," for GenAdmin, the bridge is not often in the "goods" but in the transformed ways of talking, thinking, or acting—those, ultimately, equip us to historically mediate, discursively participate, and act with more agency.

Positioning Ourselves between *Sophia* **and** *Phronêsis*

As we discursively participate, we often find ourselves negotiating our own actions with our colleagues' perceptions of what we should do, how we should do it, and what attitudes we should hold while doing it, and more often than not, this can result in our simply enacting parts of the role as a way of responding to daily challenges and critical needs of the program. Yet the public optimism and theoretical disruption provided by other scholars of WPA (especially those we discuss in Chapter 1) remind us that in anything we do we are in fact modeling not only isolated decisions, but also ways of making them. We see much of our discourse, then, as imagining alternative ways of responding—and in fact, as imagining new ways of *imagining* this response. In short, we see our discourse as carrying epistemological potential in contexts both large and small.

We are compelled to theorize GenAdmin discourse because we see in it the potential for making new language to describe what we do, why we do it, and why it is important. But in making new language, we realize the production of new "means to knowledge," placing us as theorists and mediators somewhere between what have traditionally been identified as separate branches of wisdom, but that our own disciplinary positioning causes us to recognize as merged. It is an uncomfortable positioning at best. It is often in the enactment of discourse as a hermeneutic and argumentative principle that the space between these two dimensions of wisdom is recognized as a space. Here, we try to articulate the relationship between them as a pragmatic principle.

As intellectual virtues, *sophia* and *phronêsis* are not always easily distinguished, though the former implies a kind of discernment while the latter implies a kind of prudence. We could look towards philosophy and differentiate them according to how they acts as lenses onto teleological or epistemic deliberation, i.e., where *sophia* describes the virtue of being able to discern (perhaps empirically or scientifically) the nature of the world, and *phronêsis* considers the principles through which change is delivered in the world. Even still, both branches would be prone to action and reflection, so one need not be understood as more or less practical than the other.[9] None of our attempts at explaining possible distinctions will seem anything less than reductive, because both branches can be rationalized as ongoing and rhetorical arts. Both are understood to be linked to the processes of life—although we recognize that one might be more equated to epistemic and ontological activity than another—yet they are not the same. What this difficulty in distinctions tells us is that much of the criticism that GenAdmin contends with may result from the fact that our critics expect or assume us to operate from an epistemic orientation that is far less complex, less rich, or more bifurcated than the one that defines how we have been brought up in or intellectually oriented towards the work.

Noting and having a disciplinary history helps us understand practical wisdom as one way of transforming arts into ethical actions, ultimately positioning the *sophist* or *phronimos* as "fundamentally a person of action" (Rowland and Womack 20). In this sense, GenAdmin discourse is not only pragmatic but inventive—that is, it can affect more than just the writing program and can make gains towards communal dialogic negotiation by improving the working conditions of teaching staff, re-defining graduate student mentoring, promoting dialogue about pedagogical shifts, raising awareness of linguistic diversity, or demonstrating our willingness to participate more broadly in the digital humanities, interdisciplinary studies, or general education reform. It seeks to arrive at the indeterminate, is concerned with what "is possible" over "what is practical," and aims towards transgressing epistemological boundaries. It seeks, in other words, to enact *différance* (Derrida 18; Janangelo 6).

But to understand its potential for inventing new conditions, we first embrace it as doxastic, contingent, and outward reaching. In between Rorty's "ideal space" and West's "public philosophy," Satterfield and Antczak offer an inventive pragmatism that relies in part on West's prerequisites for prophetic thought (156), and in part on the ability of a philosophy to create "new thought that is workable, but also sharable" (158), i.e., organizations or doxastic commitments that are separate from the singular values of an individual or a leader. For us, a critical point of convergence between invention and pragmatism is in pragmatism's emphasis on instantiated human knowledge and feminism's emphasis on subjectivity as a valid knowledge-making practice. In other words, we recognize the importance of contingencies and subjectivities for informing knowledge making and doing. While our communicative arts may not be coercive, neither are they value-neutral and they need not always elide truth-principles or values that are answerable to all members of a program.

This dual groundedness leads us to position ourselves in between knowledge paradigms. Ultimately, this means we have come to understand that GenAdmin discourse offers a dynamic model for action through dialogic negotiation—one that takes into account positioning as something that principally informs dialogue towards understanding *both* as an act of knowing *and* as a guide to living in the world. In Donna Qualley's words, GenAdmin discourse includes "a commitment to both attending to what we believe and examining how we came to hold those beliefs while we are engaged in trying to make sense of an other" (5). It also recognizes revisionist practices in rhetoric and philosophy as significant means to create new and evolving alternatives for communication. In being dually grounded, GenAdmin discourse becomes a kind of activism in the sense that revising traditional, unsatisfying, and not so successful methods of communication is a significant effort to reform beliefs and practices about power, identity, and communicative goals and means.

Rhetorica utens + *Rhetorica docens*: The WPA as Symbol-User and Symbol-Maker

Ultimately, GenAdmin discourse underscores a commitment to Stanley Aronowitz's and Henry Giroux's "transformative intellectual"—the teacher-scholar who is nurtured within educational discourses focusing on "the immediacy of school problems" and substituting "the discourse of management and efficiency for a critical analysis of the underlying conditions that structure school life" (37). It urges us to move beyond the empty measures of "excellence" that Bill Readings posits as a result of the post-historical university in *University in Ruins*, and that Aronowitz and Giroux claim haunts American public education (33). What makes those measures empty is that they masquerade as equitable opportunities, rewards for good behavior, but in reality deprive program participants of occasions (mandated or not) to become critically reflective. They fill in the void left by institutional culture/identity and prevent program participants from having to periodically reinvent their *raison d'etre*. Yet this reason for being won't emerge on its own—it must be modeled, committed to, and performed. It must be enacted not towards an "unresolved" stance, but towards a nascent resolve that can be achieved at the fusion of knowledge resources with the deployment of knowledge about how to use them well.

While consensus-building is unstable, temporary, and shifting, we fully realize and accept that WPAs must regularly act while they can without waiting for resolution. If we can learn to break apart all the complex factors that coalesce around any communication event, we are a step further in promoting real understanding. This means that as fast and as much as we open spaces for program participants to doubt, we need to be good mediators of those discussions rather than hands-off observers. This means neither shying away from the conflicts nor allowing each conflict to draw essential programmatic principles into question, but using them as sites for modeling the behaviors we desire. Thus, our discourse doesn't offer power as "something that either works through" circumstances in unquestioned ways, or as "a negative instance of social control that repress[es] the possibilities for struggle and resistance" (Aronowitz and Giroux 136), but rather with a "dialectical quality" (Aronowitz and Giroux 136) by being organized and developed around "the languages of possibility and critique" (Aronowitz and Giroux 137).

In their introduction to *Culture Shock and the Practice of the Profession*, Virginia Anderson and Susan Romano describe the tensions of "reinvention and representation" expressed by their writers in a way that echoes the same tensions leading us to write this book—"speak[ing] of the ways in which they embody these conflicts, striving to be the 'new' and the 'other' while becoming, at once, 'in' and the 'same'" (6), and negotiating the "indeterminacy of what rhetoric and composition graduates must be ready to do" while fulfilling the need to cultivate a relational, rhetorical education with all of the other plays in our activity systems (7). We are familiar with this tension inasmuch as it is caused by the way we privilege relationships as a kind of *telos* themselves (an intellectual positioning that we cultivated through our professionalization experiences in graduate school) over what may seem like more concrete goals. To synthesize, GenAdmin discourse offers the following opportunities for thinking transformatively about our discipline:

> Allows us to accept the rhetorical possibilities of resistance, and to differentiate between types, kinds, and motives of resistance, further helping us to differentiate between productive *resistance* and nonproductive *refusal*.

> Encourages us to engage in what might be considered "hopeless" arguments by transcending the limits of agreement, further helping us to understand theories of discourse and communication as embodiments of something beyond the argumentation—embodiments of better conditions in which to argue.

> Contributes a new discursive setting for our work, resulting in programmatic and curricular "mediation" as something beyond compromise.

> Encourages more tolerance for contingencies within our practice by enabling us to ask different questions about the nature of our work, further helping us to understand which territories are endowed by which contingencies and to demonstrate

> possibilities for how those contingencies can be refigured (Royster, "Disciplinary" 149).
>
> Enables us to position WPA as the site for broader university reform, not just being activist and humane in responding to extant conditions, but in imagining and creating new conditions.

Like Gunner and others, we do not wish to underestimate the deeply rooted nature of issues and ideologies that affix themselves to almost all of our daily tasks and "minor victories" ("Cold Pastoral" 29). We have found ourselves beginning with broader understandings of our goals and ending up confused or lost while being pressured to "settle" for mostly cosmetic or non-dialectical change. Thus, we require a discourse model that helps us either turn those victories towards more systemic change, or that allows us to trade them for better indicators of dialectical disruption. We require a model that relies on identification, positioning, and listening neither as agentive and hermeneutic activities simultaneously.

We are all in situations where it is daily necessary for us to choose how we respond to others' choices for us. Rather than (or alongside) asking ourselves how to make the program space "better" or more "practical," it becomes more acceptable to consider "what *can* be done with this space?" This question is one commonality of what we posit as GenAdmin, and it is the reason why we value this discourse. Both pragmatic and artistic, both contextually aware and unsettled, we hope to move through our lives as WPAs allowing this question to expand the discursive spaces we can map out with ourselves, our students, our colleagues, and our universities.

Interlude

ON ADVOCACY

One of the hardest parts of the job for me, especially in my first few years, was the recurring moments I did not anticipate in graduate school that exposed significant gaps between my disciplinary affiliation as a WPA, my assumptions about the position of composition director, and the beliefs about writing held by many of my colleagues across campus. Loosely, these gaps manifested as tensions arising among colleagues reflecting different assumptions, beliefs, and expectations about what it means to teach writing, direct a composition program, and enact professionalism. In other words, instances (a euphemism for all sorts of small and large experiences) arose that highlighted, without unpacking or resolving, these differences, these gaps in beliefs and experiences. Sites of these occurrences ranged from hallway chats to private conversations that sometimes found their way into greater gossip circles or even the content of meetings and projects. The repercussions of these encounters can persist in the ways they impact careers, collegial department life, and certainly student experience in writing classes. As such, it is ideal to strategize how to rewrite gaps as reasons and motives to communicate rather than reasons to stop communicating.[1]

Identifying the unavoidable point that WPAs and their colleagues are often operating out of distinct paradigms and different disciplinary affiliations better positions us to remake such gaps into "places of possibility, sites of action" (Roskelly and Ryan 43). By narrating and reflecting on the prospects of remaking two gaps, the value of the discourse model we outline in Chapter 5 emerges, as does the importance of preparing future WPAs to respond to unexpected beliefs and their associated challenges. In addition, this project has the benefit of shifting the possible characterization of WPAs, like me, as negative gadflies or iconoclasts to an alternative recognition that such WPAs are operating out of a different set of beliefs, practices, and codes with the potential for positive, energizing contributions (rather than an atrocious lack of tact). To be a gadfly then might be, to reference the AAUP statement on collegiality, a legitimate stance and a compliment, not a condemnation.[2]

A fairly typical gap within English departments is related to hiring part-timers; WPAs committed to hiring the most qualified adjuncts for the job, based on their past successes and promise as writing teachers, might find themselves in opposition to their colleagues' desire to reward a former graduate student with a job or keep a well-liked but not terribly qualified adjunct in a job. Here, two paradigms bump up against each other. The first paradigm is one I see as a programmatic, disciplinary perspective that entails the belief that not all part-timers bring the same backgrounds, skills, and abilities to teaching writing, and that composition and writing programs should and can expect to hire writing teachers, including part-timers, based on their experience and promise as writing teachers. This stance is well-articulated by Joseph Harris in the closing to "Déjà vu All Over Again," in which he reflects on the debate over where writing belongs:

> What I object to is the sort of triage that many composition directors are routinely required to engage in. So it's become clear that several of the graduate students placed under your charge are either unready to teach writing or cynically indifferent to the work? Too bad, you're stuck with them for the remaining years of their fellowships. Those part-timers still xeroxing course materials composed on manual typewriters? Or the perpetual ABDs? Well, they've all been around so long they've accrued a kind of de facto tenure, so there's not much you can do about them, either. And the same goes for the spouse of that powerful faculty member, and the really good local poet who needs health insurance, and the technical writer who's an awfully nice person and really not such a bad teacher, and of course all those recent PhDs produced by the graduate program who didn't find jobs in their fields but who are willing to take on a couple of sections of comp while they work on their manuscripts and look for something better. Any time a writing director is asked to hire someone for such reasons—that is, for any reason other than that she or he is a

> good teacher—then she or he is being urged to set some other set of interests above those of undergraduates. (Harris 541)

When I first read this article, I immediately said, "Right on!" and taped this passage critiquing "triage" hiring to the inside of my office door—where only I could see it (and where it shares space with resonating texts). From a disciplinary, programmatic perspective, the prospect of hiring anyone "for any reason other than that she or he is a good teacher" is anathema because it diminishes disciplinary values, it disrupts qualification-related hiring protocols, and it doesn't serve students well.

The second paradigm of this gap related to hiring is one I describe as individual-based, where the department privileges "taking care of" adjuncts who have worked for the department in other capacities or are well-liked by keeping them employed as long as they are doing a good enough job rather than a good or even a great job. One of my non-composition colleagues once described this approach as a system of patronage serving as a response to the unethical and unsustainable practice of hiring part-timers with low wages, no health insurance, and no prospect of long-term employment. In other words, it's an attempt to care for people who have a history with the department. Recognizing that this paradigm intends to be one focused on caretaking rather than on condoning inadequate teaching is a step towards bridging the gap.

One way to further mediate this gap between caring for a program's integrity on behalf of students and caring for individual teachers is to rewrite it as something other than programs versus individuals by uncovering attendant beliefs that can improve the possibility for mediation. I suggest that at the heart of this gap is the question of who can teach writing. Those of us in composition and rhetoric are fully aware of the disciplinary knowledge that informs our principled stance about the qualifications of potential writing teachers. However, we also know adjuncts are regularly hired across the country at the last minute to teach composition through English departments. In areas without a ready population of prospective, qualified applicants, these hires may have no experience taking or teaching the course, while other places may in fact have a competitive group of composition teachers available. At worst, these last-minute hires are handed a book and left to their own devices or, at best, folded into a program with high expectations of writing teachers and robust composition teaching communities. In other words, departments, composition programs, and campuses regularly participate in this hiring scene. It's important for WPAs to recognize that one way our complicity with this system of inappropriate hiring writ large manifests locally is that it communicates to colleagues the message that anyone can teach composition. Naturally, then, when we argue with chairs and colleagues on adjunct hiring committees about principled hiring practices, this call may in fact seem confusing and misleading given the long history and practice of a larger system of unprincipled hiring at many institutions, including mine.

I find myself, then, in the context of a highly flawed system of adjunct hiring needing to first make the case for shifting the frame of how we see and conduct hiring as it pertains to qualifications while simultaneously working with others in the discipline and institution to transform these unethical hiring practices at the point of issues like pay and insurance. We may be able to differentiate between our beliefs and goals for our programs and historical practices to effect changes that show caring for teachers and students in part by outlining qualifications for teachers based on completed composition and rhetoric coursework, past experience teaching composition, and potential for success and commitment to the enterprise. We might be able to recognize our colleagues' desires to care for others and suggest how this care doesn't serve adjuncts long-term (it doesn't target the problems of poor pay, conditions, etc.) or necessarily extend such care to students.

Moreover, we might recognize the assumption that anyone can teach writing has been perpetuated by the sheer number not only of part-timers with non-composition degrees who teach writing with little to no preparation or support, but also by the numbers of MA candidates in unrelated fields who teach composition without preparation or interest in the enterprise beyond graduate school funding. A WPA making arguments for reasonable hiring expectations of adjuncts appears to be undercut by the TA enterprise s/he seems to embrace. However, it's important to recognize that the comparison of part-time hiring practices to TA appointments is a false analogy. The TA appointment scene is a different system (albeit one with its own flaws) that rewards academic promise and/or teaching potential with a teaching appointment in composition. In particular, TAs more regularly have opportunities for teacher development through practica, mentoring programs, and meetings; they essentially receive "on-the-job training," whereas adjuncts are expected to be hired able to do the job and still grow in it. WPAs can work to shift this hiring gap within their departments by listening to other perspectives and trying to untangle the different arguments and beliefs involved to rewrite the assumption that anyone can teach writing even as many of us are also utterly implicated in its construction and need to work collectively on the far slower process of reforming hiring processes.

A second gap relates to discussions on campus-wide writing committees about issues like the rising junior exam on my campus originally intended to test student preparation for success in writing courses in their majors. From a disciplinary perspective, it's quite clear that this kind of high stakes, one-shot writing assessment can at best test students' abilities to do a certain kind of timed writing. Plenty of research in composition and rhetoric indicates that this test will not meet its intended goal; however, faculty regularly complain that "students can't write" and want "something" in place to ensure that such students do not turn up in their courses. While it is fairly easy to get mired down in discussions and disputes about the problems with the test—from logistical problems of making sure students take the test when they are supposed to, to discussions about ideal test prompts or ways to improve validity in scoring—these conversations only mask the gap that is present, at least on my campus.

By and large, those of us in the discipline of rhetoric and composition define writing as a complex, situated rhetorical process while colleagues across our campuses often expect writing to be an ability students should have mastered in their first year writing class, if not before. They expect students should be able (in any situation) to write a thesis and perfectly edited prose, and they may see a single sentence fragment as the difference between a passing and failing grade. These colleagues want such an exam to ensure students enter their courses as "good writers." While in graduate school we typically learn that the current traditional paradigm is over from a historicized disciplinary perspective, it is in fact alive and well on our campuses, as this situation attests. A WPA might have difficulty responding to this perspective as anything other than an outmoded way of thinking, and needs to work hard to resee this gap about assessment as less about the specific assessment and more about different beliefs about writing. Fighting about the test vehicle itself doesn't even help resolve people's actual desire to have students come to class "prepared."

Bridging this perceived gap about writing and testing requires rewriting the conversation to consider contrasting beliefs about writing. From a WPA perspective this requires recognizing this conversation about writing as a living discussion not a historical one, not even one that should necessarily be over. Even articulating the gap in this new way can help all interlocutors focus on the real gap and challenge them to consider how to address it.

The campus-wide writing committee I serve on is just getting to this kind of understanding, after, at least in this iteration, five years of discussion—sharing perspectives, writing experiences, researching disciplinary questions, and studying reports about the test. To get to this point, we have had to engage in the kind of dialogic negotiation described in Chapter 5. And to continue to get somewhere, we may have to engage in new conversations about the differences between individual assessment and program assessment, formative and summative evaluation, and means of gating and guiding students. For my part, I see that it's worthwhile to talk about, first, how the desire for perfect prose won't be met by the test and, second, how a desire for perfect prose is unlikely to be met even if that desire is in fact desirable. Rather, I might be able to draw on the kinds of complexities about writing that colleagues in other disciplines do in fact recognize via their own experiences as writers and from their experiences teaching students to write in their disciplines. Recognizing that challenging course content makes it harder for students to compose a successful thesis or clean prose in an advanced course might help faculty feel less frustrated by student writing and resee the worth of this test. Considering the distinctions between higher and lower order issues and the relationship of form to content, as my institution's new focus on writing to learn in lower level writing courses does, demonstrates the benefit of these conversations. As does treating non-composition faculty as partners in this endeavor, so we might collectively see that all our involvement matters, that we all have a responsibility for writing instruction on our campus.

In this way, redefining gaps serves as an impetus for discussion and collaboration. Instead of practicing what Hall calls "shrill advocacy" (115) as a kind of disciplinary defensiveness,[3] we instead "have to be able to choose the best strategy for explaining our views, while allowing others in the conversation to have their say, and with an acknowledgment of the deeply felt nature of their beliefs" (Hall 115). Practicing Hall's interpretation of Foucauldian genealogy by listening and asking questions, reading available minutes and committee documents closely, using Burke's practice of symbolic tracking as described in Jessica Enoch's article "Becoming Symbol-Wise," and trying to communicate effectively to our audiences, can help us recognize some of these surprises and either engage them productively or avoid them. Likewise, Janangelo's discussion of the ways writing programs differ from other academic units in "Theorizing Difference and Negotiating Differends" offers us a way to see disciplinary, departmental, and institutional tensions and differences as potentially productive because they are dialogic. In other words, Janangelo offers an alternative to shrill advocacy that doesn't have to result in supporting the status quo or compromising disciplinary commitments. We advocate and practice a GenAdmin discourse with the belief that by practicing understanding we might get further than we would by holding our ground or turning others into opponents. That way, when we disagree—when we offer our perspectives, identify our disciplinary affiliations, and recognize the positions others hold—we better position ourselves as people with something to offer campus conversations in part because we can imagine other positions. Ultimately, we're hopeful about the prospect of rewriting gaps that WPAs experience regularly on the job and reseeing gadflies and iconoclasts as advocates.

6 Re-Theorizing a GenAdmin Ethics

> *Seeing oneself as part of a larger social fabric of responsibility provides the impetus for people to consider how the exercise of their individual agency affects the world and the people in it. This, in turn, helps ensure that utopian goals act as spurs towards concrete action rather than as unattainable dreams divorced of any connection to the material world within which we live and work.*
>
> —Dale Jacobs (emphasis added)

> *The challenge of Paulo Freire and the pragmatists in North America who preceded him is the challenge to believe in the possibility of changed worlds, changed minds.*
>
> —Kate Ronald and Hephzibah Roskelly

Part of theorizing a GenAdmin identity for WPAs involves replacing stories of reluctance, disappointment, default, or defeat with those of *eudaimonia*,[1] and, to that end, this final chapter articulates a GenAdmin ethics. Our definition of GenAdmin as a generation of WPAs who have been intellectually oriented in a disciplinary landscape in which WPA is (more or less) a legitimate scholarly enterprise, has created a climate in which many of us freely chose WPA work. As such, we want to explore the ethical commitments and rhetorical enactments entailed with this positioning, especially in the ways it brings together our affective, rhetorical, and scholarly roles under a single "administrative" heading. This move is, in part, a natural outgrowth of our pragmatic interest in bridging becoming with being, but it is also a concrete belief we hold—along with Carrie Leverenz, Stuart Brown, Donald Hall, and Paula Mathieu—that theorizing ethics for any self-identified group in academe offers participants a way "to respond productively to what may seem an endless stream of irresolvable dilemmas" (Leverenz 106); "a step in the direction of agitating for institutional change" (Leverenz 106); a heuristic "position[ing] ourselves as actively engaged in the development and reflection upon the moral and ethical assumptions implicit in our roles as agents and arbiters" (S. Brown 157); and an agency via "consciousness and active engagement" (Hall 6) where communities are the venue for, not just the beneficiaries of, change (Hall 7). In other words, a GenAdmin identity helps us construct and enact an ethics that recognizes our potential as change agents and reflects our desires to have a productive impact on our worlds. This "exit," then, is a way of delineating a community ethics for GenAdmin. We also offer this ethics more broadly to WPAs in the twenty-first century because we imagine that an ethics that emphasizes agency, responsibility, and hope likely appeals to colleagues who might name their subjectivities differently yet equally desire to link their scholarly commitment as WPAs to an ethical stance. Finally, one of our hopes in this chapter—and the book as a whole—is to help sWPAs who historically tell their graduate students who might choose WPA positions to avoid them at all costs to resee pre-tenure WPA positions. This new light calls for a different understanding of responsibility and enactment of collegiality on their part, one that is less protectionist and more oriented to being allies who seek to understand and credit GenAdmin perspectives in conversations within professional organizations, departments and writing programs, and on campuses.

In prior chapters we noted GenAdmin benefited from specific academic preparation in WPA work and from a tradition of positioning WPA work as intellectual and activist. Here, we underscore the point that theorizing a GenAdmin ethics depends on positioning WPAs as rhetorical agents (for agency means believing you can have impact on the present and future), and it extends to include our desires to renew alliances between jWPAs, gWPAs, and sWPAs.[2] It also aligns the desirability of WPA professions with current realities and urges our writing programs towards effective instruction in the context of the eradicating multiple forms of oppression (inasmuch as we can orient ourselves towards this substantial goal). To make these claims, we draw on feminist philosophies, rhetorical studies, and professional studies to explain how GenAdmin identity, active hope, and epistemic responsibility might yield *eudaimonia* out of what Cornel West calls a "usable past."

Re/Locating GenAdmin Identity in Active Hope

One important motive for writing this book is to express our commitment to the discipline and to reposition WPAs as agents within it. In offering GenAdmin as a philosophical practice, we describe a particular orientation toward administration and reclaim writing program administration as a positive professional commitment for all j/s/gWPAs. Key markers of GenAdmin include our stance of productive resistance and transformative action, our desire to offer an alternative WPA identity marked by multiplicinarity and *rhetoricity*, and our considerable interest in gendered forms of oppression, though we recognize that gender is not often separate from other social and historical locations. Like Gerda Lerner, the five of us see gender as one thread of a larger matrix of oppression, and we recognize the enabling tendencies of our whiteness, as gender, class, race, and ethnicity privilege and constrain WPAs differently. Like Anderson, we recognize identity as "interplay between the individual and the world" (32), as always intersubjective, and we extend his treatment of individual agency toward theorizing a group identification for jWPAs in this century. In any case, what undergirds GenAdmin is the belief that identity is a complex interrelation of different material positions and their effects, our abilities as knowers, and our commitments as doers. Lorraine Code's description of the dimensions of subjectivity gives us a language for locating GenAdmin in the following:

> (i) historical location; (ii) location within specific social and linguistic contexts, which include racial, ethnic, political, class, age, religious, and other identifications; (iii) creativity in the construction of knowledge, with the freedoms and responsibilities it entails; and (iv) affectivity, commitments, enthusiasms, desires, and interests, in which affectivity contrasts with intellect, or reason in the standard sense. (*What Can She Know?* 46)

This chapter is particularly concerned with the relationship between desire, figured as active hope, and responsibility to re-theorize WPA ethics via GenAdmin.

One vital aspect of GenAdmin not isolated to any single dimension of subjectivity is our commitment to *active hope*, and we make our definition of hope explicit to equip ourselves and others to *practice* it. Like the authors we draw from, we recognize that hope is not wishful thinking—it may be utopian, but it is not naïve (Mathieu 19; Jacobs 791). It is "critical and reflective" (Jacobs 791). In addition, hope is social; it requires working collectively and intersubjectively towards and for the betterment of our discipline, our programs, and our lives. It is, as Jacobs claims, "decidedly not about individual aims, desires, or ambitions; it is not possible as an *I* but only as a *we*—or, more properly, as the articulation or joining together of individuals into what [Gabriel] Marcel refers to as a communion" (785). And it has its realization in situated pedagogies: "for hope to be of use to us as educators, we need to see that it, like education, is rigorous and intellectual" (Jacobs 798). Our hopes are renewed and supported when we solve problems with one another online, participate in listserv discussions, or attend the WPA conference, but they are also invigorated when we hear about the great day an instructor had in her classroom, have an engaging exchange with colleagues, are happily surprised by our own or a student writer's discoveries about the power of invention, or find ourselves able to push through a diplomatically difficult situation with our contributions and personal integrity intact.

These social and communal dimensions of hope impel us to define it more pragmatically for a re-theorized ethic of writing program administration. More specifically, the definition of hope that we embrace reflects an emphasis on praxis, an informed and guided reflection on our experiences and their social and historical locations in order to better act in the future. Relying on the transformative potential of hope allows us to retheorize "admin" in WPA rather than without it. For Jacobs, "hope . . . combines 'a liberating utopia'—a vision of the future toward which we can work—with 'the scientific analysis of reality'—reflection on action" (797). Paula Mathieu turns our attention to Ruth Levitas's work on "educated hope": "It represents the transformation of wishful thinking into wish-full and effective acting, the move from the dream to the dream come true" (qtd. in Mathieu 18-19). For example, we are all aware we do not just dream about better working conditions, better funding, or better understanding on the job; we actively pursue these changes and learn to recognize "success" in sometimes less tangible but often dialogical ways. Lowering face-to-face course caps, particularly in a recession, might be impossible, but negotiating for low caps in new online courses is a valid, albeit small accomplishment. We also saw the fruits of such labors on the WPA-listserv's "Lollapalooza" thread in May 2009—in which a call to celebrate good fortune led to an outpouring of others sharing recent successes—and continue to observe many other threads that celebrate WPAs and their achievements. Likewise, we do not just wish for our discipline or campus colleagues to change their attitudes toward pre-tenure WPAs; we work actively toward that end, trying to push through clashes in institutional and disciplinary subjectivities and affiliations to arrive at a different place from which to survey our progress.

To view what we do as "progress" requires a vision for seeing beyond the "limit-situation," a stance we borrow from Ronald and Roskelly's renewal of Freirean "untested feasibility." Ronald and Roskelly reinterpret American pragmatism through an activist lens so as to keep experiential knowledge-building grounded in mediation and action (625), and we find their stance imperative to our own reconstruction of GenAdmin as philosophical practice. For Freire, this feasibility was "the future which we have yet to create by transforming today, the present reality. It is something not yet here but a potential, something beyond the 'limit-situation' we face now, which must be created by us beyond the limits we discover" (qtd. in Ronald and Roskelly 615). For others and us today, it represents an alternative to giving in to disappointment; rather, limit-situations are "opportunities for action if we regard them as problems rather than givens" (Jacobs 791).

Jacobs further articulates how hope's future and change orientation are inextricably linked in the way that hope "problematizes time by opening it up to our intervention, allowing us a starting point from which we can articulate and move toward a shared vision for the future" (794). And for Mathieu, hope "mediates between the insufficient present and an imagined but better future" (19). It is for these reasons that those who recognize themselves as GenAdmin are interested in change: not simply for the sake of change, but for the vitality and necessity of turning past and present conditions and limitations into future possibilities, in much the same way as our intellectual predecessors have invited and equipped us to do. We seek to recognize how writing program administration in general, and a GenAdmin ethics in particular, needs hope to focus its vision towards the creation of new possibilities without glossing over the situatedness (and sometimes uncomfortable conditions) from which they are born. Thus, the "progress" we allude to above requires that this hope be oriented toward future possibilities, that it embrace the potential of change, and that it always be tied to action or "doing."

"Doing" hope means considering how to enact it in an ongoing way—beyond simple strictures of *chronos* time. While Mathieu reminds us that "hope does not offer a blueprint to follow, but compels a critical function of engagement" (132), she offers the following as part of her tactics of hope: "To hope, then, is to look critically at one's present condition, assess what is missing, and then long for and work for a not-yet reality, a future anticipated" (19). *Doing hope* means working contextually, inventively, and creatively towards change while being equally creative in how we measure change. This activity is difficult because, as Micciche reminds us, even our best reshaping efforts can lead to personal and professional disappointment that, if left unchecked, "may become a 'fixed' stance, eventually hardening into disillusionment, resignation, passivity in the face of new, ever-changing situations" (446). Yet we believe that working with an eye toward hope can mitigate the effects of these disappointments. In an email exchange about the potential for our GenAdmin ethics in action, Tarez used the word "dreamstorming" to describe our inventive work, a term we all responded to with enthusiasm. To dreamstorm focuses our inventive energies on the best-case scenario first, taking into consideration institutional contexts and possible limitations only after we have identified our ultimate goal, and we keep that dream in mind as we conduct the requisite negotiations required by our institutional context. While hope is both a motivation for and means of forming a GenAdmin ethics, it also is an imperative for enabling WPAs to act responsibly because it impels us to see institutions as powerful but not monolithic, and as "rhetorically constructed human designs (whose power is reinforced by . . . knowledge-making practices)" (Porter et al. 611). In other words, it enables us to understand institutions as not beyond the individual's (or group's) capacity to change (Porter et al. 617). Just because institutions, beliefs, or habits do not change easily doesn't mean they cannot change. Active hope offers GenAdmin one way of enacting what Porter et al. call "an unabashedly rhetorical practice mediating macro-level structures and micro-level actions rooted in a particular space and time" (612), if not by mapping where and how institutional critique operates, then by redefining the spaces in which epistemic responsibility can, does, and should occur at all. We see the need for active hope in contexts seen as "hopeless"; Janangelo "call[s] the writing across the curriculum (WAC) movement a 'frustrated hope' because, outside of writing programs, it is often perceived, largely by default, as a way of teaching students how to replicate traditional paternalistic forms of academic discourse" (9). Like Janangelo, we also work to subvert such forms of oppression.

Defining Epistemic Responsibility

With active hope at the center of our administrative philosophy, even the disempowered WPA is repositioned to be a paradigmatic agent. That the WPA's "local" domain implies a need for *only* local knowledge is utterly false. Like hard scientists, linguists, and litterateurs, the WPA's work may begin within a microcosm of "laboratory," corpus, or primary text (where text is defined broadly, such that a campus is a kind of text). However, her work quickly becomes macrocosmic, as the WPA uses that space to put theory into practice, refine and develop the practice, then rebuild the theory in a relentless cycle of reading (historicizing), writing (reflecting), and revising (articulating), a hermeneutic process that is no less Deweyan or institutionally vital than paradigmatic activity in other disciplines. Richard Bullock describes this activity as the work of "experts and scholars testing and refining their knowledge" rather than "caretakers" of specific tasks (14), while Richard Miller aligns many aspects of composition programs that serve "both students and the entire university community" as affective bargaining power with critical opportunities for self-representation ("From Intellectual" 37-38). Rejecting Sharon Crowley's "narrow" perspective that FYC should be abolished to prevent it from being seen as intellectually stripped servitude, Miller suggests capitalizing upon composition studies' place, especially within the larger research university, as a shaping agent in course offerings, institutional artifacts, and research commodities (33).

It follows, then, that we reconsider the concept of "responsibility" as more than a set of tasks attached to a job description but rather as part of a scholarly, administrative ethic. In particular, we define epistemic responsibility as comprised of responsible knowers enacting social responsibility and ethical responsibility. By enumerating Lorraine Code's concept of epistemic responsibility and augmenting it with Jacqueline Jones Royster's and Donald Hall's thinking, we contribute to conversations among WPAs about GenAdmin identity and theory building that revise limited views of writing program responsibility as a minor set of managerial tasks. In a worldview that sees WPA is a discipline and vital, *chosen* profession, it makes no sense to see WPA responsibility as merely managerial.

In general, epistemic responsibility means being a responsible knower, being responsible for what we know, how we put it to use, and where we stand as knowers. A responsible knower appreciates that "subjectivity matters," that who does the knowing influences the act of knowing. The dimensions of subjectivity we list above are all significant to acts of meaning making. Moreover, Code's model of knowledge, described in *What Can She Know?*, is oriented towards "knowing others" rather than "knowing that": "'Knowing other people' negotiates subjectivity and objectivity, considers the individual in relation to others, and abandons value-neutrality for contextualized values" (Ryan 37). More recently, Code extends this concept to ecological knowing, which considers our "engagement with knowledge, subjectivity, politics, ethics, sciences, citizenship, and agency" (*Ecological Thinking* 5). While positivist epistemology privileges distant, universal, and values-free ways of knowing, this model of knowing recognizes, as Donna Haraway puts it, that claims to knowledge are always partial, always situated and embodied.

Lorraine Code's research in *Epistemic Responsibility*, *What Can She Know?*, and, most recently, *Ecological Thinking*, teaches us that epistemic responsibility is intertwined with social and ethical dimensions not recognized by more mainstream scholarship in epistemology but vital to our ethics and epistemological commitments. "Social responsibility" highlights the *intersubjective* relations entailed in epistemic responsibility and indispensable to our understanding of what it means to be in the world. Social responsibility is significant for its relational capacity and commitment: "Seeing oneself as part of a larger social fabric of responsibility provides the impetus for people to consider how the exercise of their individual agency affects the world and the people in it" (Jacobs 788). Jacqueline Jones Royster's construction of afrafeminist scholarship includes her "commitment to social responsibility" (*Traces* 278). In *Traces of A Stream* she writes,

> A commitment to *social responsibility* (and, I might add, social action) reminds us that knowledge does indeed have the capacity to empower and disempower, to be used for good and for ill. As researchers and scholars, we are responsible for its uses and, therefore, should think consciously about the momentum we create when we produce knowledge or engage in knowledge-making processes. Our intellectual work has consequences. I believe the inevitability of these consequences should bring us pause as we think not just about what others do but about what we are obliged to do or not do. (Royster 281)

Choosing to be socially responsible commits us to making thoughtful decisions about our intellectual actions in light of our communities and contexts. Our needs and desires as WPAs are always situated within larger, social contexts, and Janangelo's suggestion that we see writing programs "as supplements—sources of pedagogical/epistemological surplus within the academy" that can "enrich our institutions by providing a versatility and breadth of knowledge that is not available to other disciplines" motivates us to think carefully about how we might play this role ethically (13). GenAdmin puts what we know and what we care about to work in the construction of humane programs. Such programs respond to the diverse needs of its stakeholders; take as a starting point that students, teachers, and program leaders mean well; welcomes the participation of its members;[3] communicate information through explicit policies; value dialogic communication; reject oppressive or vindictive behaviors; recognize the dynamic interplay of theory and practice and maintenance and change; and thrive on openness and engagement. Discussions of writing programs as activity systems, for example, show this recognition of "writing programs as sites of collaborative activity" for multiple stakeholders (Graban and Ryan 93). Our GenAdmin discourse model assumes a situational dialogism is a given.

Ethical responsibility, a second aspect of epistemic responsibility, links closely to our discussion of *eudaimonia*, which translates variously as "'happiness,' 'the good life,' 'living well, 'excellence,' and 'flourishing'" (Cuomo 66). Because *eudaimonia* and ethical responsibility are intertwined concepts, it's difficult to talk about one without the other, though we treat our understanding of *eudaimonia* more fully below. Our general approach is to work towards a better future to transform "'what is' into 'what is possible'" (Atwill 70). Working with other knowers to create a more just world, whether that refers to our programs, universities, or our larger communities, includes redressing inequities and "constructing a reality that is free from oppression and humiliation" (Renegar and Sowards, "Liberal Irony" 336). Donald Hall identifies academics' specific responsibility as academics as "responsible intellectualism," a concept we adopt as a significant dimension of ethical responsibility. He writes:

> I would argue that the responsibility that all of us share is to take the situations that we find ourselves in, add value to them, shape them to the extent that we can to meet our intellectual and pedagogical commitments, leave them if we find them intolerable, but above all, expend our energy *'aiming at the 'good life' with and for others, in just institutions'* to the extent that we can create that good life and those just institutions. (Hall 30)

Hall, like Royster, embraces an ethics of scholarly responsibility for scholars and faculty more broadly.

For Hall, like the hermeneutic philosophers he draws on (Martin Heidegger, Hans-Georg Gadamer, Angela Davis, and Paul Ricoeur), responsible intellectualism means embracing our ties to others, understanding departments and universities and, as he later argues, our undergraduate classes and our graduate student professionalization, as "texts" that solicit responses. Hall even suggests that critically studying our mentors' and colleagues' narratives can provide answers to certain ontological questions (36), and he urges us—when we are called upon to discuss controversial issues in the academy—to cast our work as "genealogy, not shrill advocacy" (115). While Hall puts forth this strategy as one of five ways to reconnect the university with the public, we apply it to reconnect ourselves with other stakeholders within our programs and other members of our activity systems that may or may not reach beyond the department or the university. That way, when we bump up against "entrenched opinions," we "explain our positions with clarity and resolve" rather than "hostile retorts," "inflamed argumentation," or arrogant posturing (Hall 116). Janangelo refers similarly to the need to "[e]xamine our rhetoric for inherent elitism and antagonism. Let's try to resist the danger and lure of ennobling our difference from the academy, and positioning ourselves in opposition to our host institutions" (18). We agree that academics have a significant responsibility for the environments in which we work and teach and the meaning making activities we support and practice. Ethical frameworks like Hall's that draw on philosophical hermeneutics are valuable because they ask us to try to understand others. Hall forwards the hermeneutic circle as a way to identify "how our individual needs and desires as members of a community must always operate in negotiation with the macrolevel concerns of our departments and colleagues" (11).

The discourse model that Kate and Tarez articulate in "Theorizing Feminist Pragmatic Rhetoric as A Communicative Art for the Composition Practicum" relies on such a hermeneutic, crafting dialogic negotiation as a feminist pragmatic response to resistance that could otherwise stop productive conversation between TAs and WPAs. Our extension of this work in Chapter 5 considers more broadly a discursive identity for GenAdmin that focuses on seeking mediation and understanding. Practicing pragmatic activism is a significant expression of our ethical responsibility. In doing so, we enter into discourse with an openness that we believe has transformative potential because it characterizes our engagements as respectful without pandering and resistant without refusal, injudiciousness or "shrill advocacy." We find it far more productive and more satisfying to imagine that our colleagues, our students, and our teachers mean well and speak genuinely out of their contexts and that we can respond in kind. With this perspective, walls can often become doors.

Contemporary discussions of collegiality in the academy pertain to our exploration of epistemic responsibility because of their joint emphasis on treating others with respect and understanding that the goal of communication is negotiation across differences. Because WPAs are often in sensitive dialogues about campus writing issues and anecdotally and historically face program challenges regularly and because pre-tenure WPAs are often seen as lacking status and thus legitimacy, it is important to consider how collegiality bears on a GenAdmin ethics. In other words, we need to reframe typical views on what it means to be a "good" colleague (where that means being nice and not rocking the boat), especially since such views do not serve WPAs, least of all jWPAs, very well. Hall defines collegiality this way:

> Collegiality means responsible citizenship within our institutions, embracing the same qualities that one would hope for in responsible citizens of the nation and globe: thoughtfulness, attentiveness to the needs of others, and a willingness to listen carefully and engage in meaningful communication across and in spite of differences. It means an ability to work collaboratively to solve problems and set priorities, and, finally, it means a commitment to the ethical treatment of others, and especially those in disempowered positions (such as staff members, part-timers, and junior faculty, in an academic context)" (68).

A recognition of intersubjectivity (particularly honoring differences), a commitment to problem solving, and an awareness of power dynamics all figure prominently in our vision of the kinds of colleagues we want to be and have on our campuses and in our organizations.

Collegiality does not have to mean that we are nice for the sake of being nice, avoiding legitimate conflicts and difficult questions or decisions. The American Association of University Professional's (AAUP) policy "On Collegiality as a Criterion for Faculty Evaluation," which speaks *against* using collegiality as a criterion for faculty evaluation, reminds us that "criticism and opposition do not necessarily conflict with collegiality" (par. 4). We appreciate this stance because it tries to avoid turning likes and dislikes of individuals into tenure-bearing decisions. At the same time, we value collegiality as a commitment to being productive agents in our communities. As the AAUP policy goes on to state, "Gadflies, critics of institutional practices or collegial norms, even the occasional malcontent, have all been know to play an invaluable and constructive role in the life of academic departments and institutions. They have sometimes been collegial in the deepest and truest sense" (par. 4). Being a responsible intellectual doesn't mean being sugar and sweetness; it can, and often does, mean making difficult decisions and offering productive critique. For example, when observing TAs and adjuncts teach, we are mindful to frame this work as mentoring as opposed to evaluation to advance critique as a tool for learning within a context that is framed as a dialogic opportunity. In department meetings we pose curious questions with an understanding that others and their answers could persuade us rather than using what Jane Tompkins calls "fighting words." We seek means to practice discursive identification daily whether working with students, staff, or colleagues in the classroom or at the committee table. What we are talking about here is contributing to a culture of administrative hope, one that recognizes a need to re-see current goals and re-cast them so that potential has play. Rather than desiring a level playing field where the needs of first-year writing students and WPAs are equal to those driven by financial resources, we earnestly speak and listen in ways that privilege the open question and its resultant discursive life. While this stance may seem either irksome or naïve (when many of us daily face active resistance, if not refusal, on the job), enacting and advocating for this hoped-for reality is, to GenAdmin, a quite realistic way of practicing and supporting the potential of productive critique.

Ethical responsibility is an important countermand to faculty incivility, what Darla Twale and Barbara De Luca define as "bullying, mobbing, camouflaged aggression, and harassment in the academic workplace" (xii). We're attentive to the reality of academic bullying because it is antithetical to our commitment to a GenAdmin ethics, yet is a lived experience for faculty, including WPAs, on their campuses—as perpetrators and victims. A bully culture develops when incivilities grow over time and take up residence in the interaction of motivating structures and processes (e.g. campus politics or power imbalances), precipitating circumstances (e.g. scarcity of resources or changing face of the professoriate), and enabling structures and processes (e.g. isolation or lack of policies encouraging collegial behavior) (Twale and De Luca 30).[4] Some of the behaviors Twale and De Luca associate with incivility include: "indulging in self-promotion"; "showing intolerance or disrespect to others"; "indulging in professional misconduct such as breaking confidentiality, harboring rumors, and playing favorites"; and "avoiding taking a stand when one is needed to correct a wrong" (19-20). We appreciate how Twale and De Luca encourage incivility victims to utilize the "bully culture" schema to deconstruct the activity system in which they reside, perhaps as a way to formulate empathy towards the victimizers (and hence towards a quicker assessment of how to respond to incivility behaviors), to strategize alternative behaviors, but also to raise awareness of the dysfunction that leads to these behaviors and causes bully cultures to fall short of more "normative" academic expectations (183). In other words, awareness of an academic culture of bullying can better situate all of us as interpreters of our own experiences. We believe however in the need to go beyond individual situations and turn reflection on such experiences into appropriate, collective response and action. Meeting our responsibility as academic citizens entails challenging workplace aggression in particular and enacting epistemic responsibility generally in the context of writing program administration because of the contested nature of our work and, moreover, the added challenges for jWPAs on the job.

Enacting Epistemic Responsibility

> *Of course, as a junior faculty WPA, I am painfully aware of the tension between doing my job and keeping it. After all, in the end, all that well-meaning advice for junior faculty isn't really about the nature of faculty work; it's about how junior faculty earn a more secure faculty status. For the junior faculty WPA, then, the traditional rules of the game seem to present lousy options: I could be a good junior faculty member but a less vigilant WPA, or a good WPA and a rogue junior faculty member. Everyone knows the peril in the latter, and the former means I cotton to the system at the expense of the work I believe in.*
>
> —Stephanie Roach

Defining epistemic responsibility and promoting awareness of this term is incomplete without a discussion of what enacting epistemic responsibility entails in the context of jWPA lives, particularly in light of the difficulty Roach describes. As she describes it, being a junior faculty WPA is, to echo Karlyn Kohrs Campbell's article on women on the public platform in the nineteenth century, an oxymoron. While junior faculty members are often expected to silently defer to more senior colleagues, WPAs often must speak up in meetings on behalf of their programs and interact regularly with upper administrators and faculty (tenured and not) across campus. Being a wallflower would mean not being responsible to a WPA appointment. As such, Roach must characterize what she does as a WPA as *opposed* to typical expectations for junior faculty, and she (like us) chooses to, in her words, "stay the course" because of her commitment to her profession. We want to go further and advocate epistemic responsibility as a kind of "moral agency" compelling and impelling reforms to render jWPA positions less fraught (Cuomo 76). Quite simply, living with the kinds of tensions Roach describes gives us a means and motive for productive critique.

We return to Twale and De Luca's work to contextualize our focus on pre-tenure WPAs and women in enacting epistemic responsibility. They offer an instructive discussion of two conditions that enable bully cultures on campuses: first, the shift from a homogenous culture to one of increased diversity, and, second, the increased corporatization of academe which raises ideological differences. These two conditions aptly point to tensions embedded in the epigraph to this section. Twale and De Luca, citing a number of other studies, describe the tension between faculty who position themselves as entrepreneurial versus mission-oriented as a kind of "cognitive dissonance, which has proven repeatedly to be a fertile ground for bullying, camouflaged aggression, and mobbing" (145). Gender and minority inequities reinforce the fact that perceiving the academy as an ivory tower separate from worldly problems is simply a myth that doesn't (and shouldn't) reflect—or pretend to—realities on our campuses. The perception that writing programs are purely entrepreneurial can pit WPAs and their colleagues against one another. For example, when competing for scarce resources, faculty in an English department may be hesitant to use department money to fund an ostensible service function to the university (namely, composition courses) when doing so might detract from the more lofty purpose of the department: the major. We seek to disrupt such normalizing tendencies and suggest that service may not in fact be entrepreneurial, but may ascribe to similar liberal arts goals as an English major. Simultaneously, we ask what is so wrong with service? Within the context of our ethics, service regains its orientation towards advocacy rather than the obsequiousness or practicality attributed to it in some academic contexts.

Further embedded in both conditions described by Twale and De Luca are the differences that new faculty may represent. New colleagues with new ideas disrupt the status quo, and this may be read variously as threatening or simply unlooked for, so unwelcome by others. The first-time hire of a jWPA with a doctorate in rhetoric and composition, the hire of a person of color into a white department, or the hire of someone whose ideals do not mesh with their new colleagues all may face challenges in their roles simply because the prospect of change is unsettling. Rather than align change with negative resistance, we locate change in terms of its potential. Like Stuart Selber, we believe that change is "possible if people conceptualize institutions as a rhetorical system, pay attention to its contexts and constituent parts (including operating procedures and working conditions), and acknowledge their own involvements and commitments" (13). Thus, it behooves new hires to listen and gain a local perspective and their new colleagues to welcome them and be receptive to their different perspectives and persons.

An unavoidable difference exists between junior and senior faculty, between those who are on the tenure track and those who have tenure. The process of promotion and tenure is often framed as an initiation rite—a kind of pre-tenure hazing—that supports a victim/izer relationship at worst, or an apprentice/master model at best (a limited best to be sure). An undercurrent at conferences and behind office doors is junior faculty sharing experiences in their departments or on their campuses that are paternalistic or infantilizing and seem to ignore the very reasons they were hired, that is, to be expert scholars, teachers and administrators in their disciplines. Junior faculty might feel they are being asked to follow a code of conduct based on silence and obedience. Certainly, we are too familiar with stories of junior faculty being told by senior faculty not to speak in meetings, and that by speaking even about an issue she's an expert on, such a faculty member might be seen as uppity for disrupting the hierarchy. (We hear these stories as well from senior colleagues who acknowledge the difficulties they faced on the tenure track.) Such faculty "are often reprimanded by being shunned, belittled, or dismissed until they learn protocol and that respect is owed more senior colleagues" (Twale and De Luca 83). Yet, what if speaking up isn't intended as disrespect, but is motivated by enjoyment in the job or enthusiasm for the question at hand? What if a senior colleague's caution is thoughtful and well meant? The problematic legacy tied to the apprentice/master model puts new and pre-tenure faculty unnecessarily at risk simply because it limits the ways that new faculty can interpret or receive helpful gestures and new faculty often represent paradigmatic change: "Colleagues who unwittingly buck the system or challenge long-established patterns or values may be likely targets for bullies and mobs" (Twale and De Luca 24-25). Twale and De Luca go on to say "going against the normal flow or rhythm of the department, school, or university culture can have deleterious effects for the challenger" (27). Sites where different ideologies, perspectives, and local conditions meet—from the meeting room to the hallway—can be difficult spaces for new and junior faculty to navigate. Embracing epistemic responsibility better positions us to disrupt the negativity of this hierarchy because we recognize fault lines as sites of discourse, change as potentially exciting, and difference as an impetus to communicate.

More concretely, we are also cognizant of increased demands on pre-tenure faculty, including increased scholarly production, increased service expectations, and academic advancement procedures that lack clarity, like the use of qualifiers in promotion and tenure documents that can be interpreted in multiple ways or are simply vague—all of which makes jWPAs (in fact, all junior faculty) progressing towards tenure unnecessarily vulnerable. In addition to advising jWPAs and future WPAs to choose their jobs well (insofar as it's possible), we advocate, along with other scholars and academic bodies, for reform in this arena. The 2006 Report on the MLA Task Force on Evaluating Scholarship for Tenure and Promotion, and related articles in *Profession 2007*, makes significant recommendations calling for transparency in promotion and tenure processes, recommending mentoring for junior faculty, and questioning the over-reliance on the monograph as the standard publication for tenure. "The Gen X Professor," a 2006 article in *Inside Higher Ed*, shows that the current untenured population privileges "clarity" in tenure and promotion processes and having a balanced life. Scott Jschik writes, "Gen Xers see the process for getting tenure as something like 'archery in the dark,' and want the process opened up" (par. 7). While an informal committee in Kate's department is working toward a more streamlined evaluation process for all faculty members, and while transparency of both the process and criteria for evaluation has emerged as a critical reform, we would like to see information on tenure reform from position statements, research projects and task forces more fully operative on our campuses and in our disciplinary organizations. We value both the Portland Resolution and the Statement on Evaluating the Intellectual Work of Writing Program Administration as related efforts in our discipline. While we recognize the limits of these texts, like the privileging of the sole WPA (see Gunner) in disciplinary conversations, we value the ways we can use such texts for opening conversations and serving as tools for change.

Because of the way tenure systems currently function, the enculturated treatment of pre-tenure faculty, and the often contested content of WPA work, we recognize jWPAs need to be particularly aware of the prospects for faculty incivility on the job and that meeting our responsibility as academic citizens to challenge workplace aggression can be both productive and empowering. The infantilization associated with pre-tenure hazing, problematic in and of itself, is incompatible with writing program administration—giving us more disciplinary incentive to challenge pre-tenure hazing rather than accept that what we do must be in conflict with junior faculty status. While it may seem like we're making a case here for pre-tenure WPAs to avoid administrative roles, particularly for women, feminists, and other minorities, we aren't. The stance of categorically recommending that junior faculty and new hires avoid pre-tenure WPA positions may seem safe, but we see it as unrealistic if not undesirable. We do not believe pre-tenure women, or any other group, must categorically avoid writing program administration. Making such categorical decisions would be anti-rhetorical and anti-pragmatic.

Instead, our response is to advocate redressing limiting expectations for junior faculty, ones that are paternalistic, and ones that disallow or discourage epistemic responsibility. We don't want to see only two choices for graduate students interested in writing program administration: the demoralizing safety of foregoing one's academic training and abilities for seven years until the safety of tenure, or pursuing a career fraught with personal and professional risks that might end in seven years. GenAdmin recognizes that these polarizing views dominate a number of conversations and advocates for more nuanced and responsible stances. In the context of academic civility this means that, because WPAs have visible administrative roles, we need to be educated about the academic bully culture to recognize how we might become targets for bullies on our campus. But we also need to find strategies and tactics for changing this scene, as it extends its tendrils in many directions. We would like to see graduate student WPAs and tenured and untenured WPAs continue to create alliances to work on these significant, systemic reforms together, and we believe a GenAdmin ethics can contribute effectively to related efforts.

Not only does a WPA potentially face considerable challenges due to competing demands related to social status and job configuration, but we also know from observation, research, and direct experience that "a woman in the field of rhetoric and composition has an especially difficult challenge to be taken seriously" (Ballif et al. 86). The well-documented scholarship on the feminization of composition attests to the challenges for women in rhetoric and composition, including the specific challenges for women in leadership roles. Women's leadership comes under fire simply because, whether perceived as more "masculine" or "feminine" in approach, women in authority represents still an uncomfortable, if not unwelcome, pairing in many institutions. Difference from the majority in terms of race, class, sexual orientation, and age further complicate life for women in leadership positions. As Ballif et al. indicate, a "female is required to 'play like a man,' exhibiting assertiveness and confidence; yet, she is also asked to exhibit the typically female behaviors of graciousness and collegiality" (88). Kenji Yoshino effectively names these competing demands. Women are among the groups asked or expected to cover, that is, "tone down a disfavored identity to fit into the mainstream" (ix), or even reverse cover and act like a stereotypical female (Yoshino 144). "If women are not 'masculine' enough to be respected as workers, they will be asked to cover. If they are not 'feminine' enough to be respected as women, they will be asked to reverse cover" (Yoshino 149). In one department, a woman leader is critiqued for crying publicly in frustration, another is criticized for dressing too professionally, and a third for speaking brashly; the first instance demands a woman cover, while the other two are examples of ways women are expected to reverse cover. A single individual may in fact be expected by some audiences to cover and to reverse cover by others—creating an untenable situation.

Women leaders have a difficult balancing act to perform in academia, even more so when they practice feminist leadership strategies. Men who seek to practice a more feminist administrative style also encounter resistance. In addition to the difficulties related to merely the fact of women having leadership positions or leadership styles in tension with others' desires—competing degrees of assertiveness and nurturing—feminist administrative approaches are "at odds with the larger masculinist academic structure" (Miller 79). In forwarding her support of a postmasculinist administrative approach that combines both feminist and masculinist approaches, Hildy Miller offers the following list of feminist administration characteristics: "cooperation, collaboration, shared leadership, and the integration of the cognitive and the affective" (79). Toy Caldwell-Colbert and Judith Albino discuss the strategic work involved in simply conducting meetings that move the focus from reporting (seen as part of a masculinist paradigm) to collaborative decision-making (76). Ester Shapiro and Jennifer Leigh identify systems thinking, "strategic readings of power in context" (90), research, and self-awareness and reflection as tools for practicing feminist leadership in the health care system. GenAdmin values such strategies and characteristics because we believe we can achieve more together, we value affective commitments and reflection, and we appreciate the way feminist thought challenges definitions of power. Traditionally, power is something that is owned and used to dominate; we assert power *over* others or *have* the "stuff" of power. Power is something to own, something finite, and therefore something to hold onto at all costs. For us, power is relational and dynamic; we think of power as "power to" and, as pragmatists, embrace the idealism of using power to transform our world. We agree with Hildy Miller that "to lead, then, is not to dominate but rather to facilitate, to share power, and to enable both self and others to contribute" (81-82).

It is challenging to introduce feminist administrative models into the masculine hierarchies that structure academe both because writing programs aren't closed systems and because a feminist administrative model may be simply too unfamiliar or undesirable to others because it shifts not just power, but understandings of power. Turning our discourse model and GenAdmin stance towards those who often "have" power in the traditional sense is difficult because those stakeholders have to be willing to think and act differently and might feel they are giving something up if they are asked to change. "Giving up" white, male privilege challenges those who see power only as something finite, something that can be won and thus lost. People who profit most from the patriarchal, hierarchical academic system might not be able to imagine what they gain by changing their beliefs and practicing cooperation, collaboration, or listening with the intent to understand and value another's perspective. What is the incentive for privileged faculty members or administrators to change? It requires a commitment to equality and good will or, for GenAdmin, a commitment to epistemic responsibility. A chair who is asked to share decision-making over composition hires may not want to change a simple act of appointing who he or she wants to hire to include the input of a writing program administrator or composition committee because this move might be perceived as a loss of authority or just more work. When they are layered onto the belief that writing program administration is "simply" a kind of managerial, almost secretarial, service, and that composition is merely about remediating writers, such aspirations as participating in hiring decisions likely seem even more radical to chairs, deans, and other faculty. Further layer onto these beliefs the positioning of an untenured writing program administrator who is viewed as an "upstart," and the issue becomes increasingly complex. As Hildy Miller points out, "When boundaries of administrative responsibility blur, cooperative approaches to resolving conflicts may be mistaken for encroachment into territory, thereby turning mild adversarial approaches into pitched battles" (83). A desire to develop a transparent process of adjunct hiring may thus be viewed as an attack rather than a structural attempt to create an equitable, explicit hiring process. For the five of us, Miller's remedy, to advocate a both/and approach drawing on feminist and masculine models, isn't quite satisfying because she seems more interested in notions of "personal power" while we consider the individual intersubjectively. Also, her notion of feminist WPAs "function[ing] in two worlds" isn't compatible with our sense that we live in one world and that our identity is fluid and multiply constructed rather than limited to one that is "bi-epistemological" (H. Miller 87).

While we recognize the challenges of writing program administration for junior faculty, and the ways they are augmented when combined with gender, we are not satisfied by claims made on behalf of our vulnerability as women, as feminists, as junior faculty. Instead of refusing writing program administration for pre-tenure faculty or protecting pre-tenured WPAs, we advocate for reforms. An important reform is trading in protection for action, though we need to qualify what we mean by protection. Junior faculty should not, for example, be responsible for judging senior faculty merit cases, but should serve on faculty review committees as a means to participate in department governance without getting in potentially difficult conversations related to the work of senior faculty. Likewise, an sWPA who tries to protect a jWPA by not involving her in relevant meetings with a dean may well deny the jWPA the chance to interact with a potential ally or simply the chance to be more fully involved in her job responsibilities.

Instead of faculty mentors and colleagues protecting the weak, we'd like to see increased efforts made to undo the WPA as victim mantra and turn refusal of such junior positions into action against the –isms (racism, sexism, classism, and so on) that plague academe.

Baumgardner and Richards speak effectively to the problem of protection: "As Susan Faludi . . . and others have noted, protection starts out polite—women and children first off the sinking ship and so forth—and ends up justifying why women can't be naval captains or firefighters or subjects for medical research" (66). In feminist circles, the end of protection is simply discrimination. If we do not challenge the sexism—really, the whole matrix of oppressions that shape human experiences and interactions—then we simply need to advocate that only white, tenured male professors should be WPAs because it is "too hard" otherwise. While that might seem to be an ungenerous reading of our WPA colleagues' scholarship, it is a natural extension of arguments against pre-tenure WPAs. Really, arguments against pre-tenure WPAs seem to be an easy way of responding to the victim lessons in WPA narratives. GenAdmin prefers to disrupt the beliefs and actions that lead to these stories with the stories and knowledge we have gained from the collectivity of WPA experience and disciplinarity over the years. This approach is more in sync with our goals to end oppression.

A second important reform is to practice speaking *with* us not simply *for* us, part of our discourse heuristic discussed in Chapter 5. Consider Alice Horning's argument that it is unethical for junior faculty to serve as WPAs because of the difficulties they might face in situations like hiring, dealing with dissatisfied students, and taking stands on issues like assessment. There's a similar practical recognition of the challenges of being women and administrators pre-tenure in *Women's Ways of Making It in Rhetoric and Composition*; the authors indicate a number of their survey participants spoke against women taking on writing program administration pre-tenure because of the challenges of advancing one's scholarship in the face of overwhelming administrative duties, as well as the sexism we acknowledge above. We value this very practical advice, and we recognize that being an administrator (pre-tenure or otherwise) may be less important to some than being a teacher or a scholar. But, in those cases where pre-tenure faculty members want to do writing program administration, we'd rather take a pragmatic approach (even as we sometimes recognize the need to be practical). We'd rather unpack and target the whys of such difficulties and seek ways to transform not just the experiences of individual WPAs like ourselves but the enterprise more generally.

As we have already mentioned in Chapter 1 and reiterate here, we do not intend to take up the argument of whether or not junior faculty should take on specific WPA roles, because even the five of us have different experiences that have shaped our views in the topic. Moreover, the question seems moot given the increasing number of untenured positions with explicit or implicit WPA components, regardless of institution type. We are cognizant of the considerable risks associated with taking on WPA work at certain junctures of a rhetoric and composition career, and we see the risks associated with taking on pre-tenure WPA work at certain kinds of institutions where the work may be unaccounted for or uncompensated, or simply not commensurate with the typical faculty profile or where departments may be plagued with interpersonal and/or organizational problems. And as we already mention in Chapters Two and Five, we also recognize these challenges are compounded for individuals who bring diversity—of race, ethnicity, age, gender, etc.—to their campuses. However, rejecting the presence of pre-tenure WPAs out of hand by arguing that their positions are unethical ignores the contributions those WPAs could make to our understanding of WPA work.[5] There is more productive potential in re-theorizing collective responses to these demands, responses that speak *with* and *to* untenured WPAs instead of *for* them so that those who hold such positions are party to the critical theorizing that informs the response.

GenAdmin's Ethics of Flourishing

To secure our discussion of *eudaimonia* requires one last move in our theorizing. Beyond staid models, narratives, or imageries, we're learning that epistemic responsibilities have always and will continue to be best represented in a dynamic system—an ecology, much like Margaret Syverson's "set of interrelated and interdependent complex systems" where *complex system* is "a network of independent agents . . . [that] act and interact in parallel with each other, simultaneously reacting to and co-constructing their own environment" (3). They are adaptive, varied, and self-organizing (Syverson 4). Accepting a WPA ethic as "ecological" means we recognize its interconnectivity among five "analytical dimensions" through which we can view more closely and vitally these interactions at work (Syverson 18): physical-material, social, psychological, spatial, and temporal (Syverson 19-20), all in turn helping us to understand the complexities of our disciplinary histories, research methodologies, composing processes, teaching paradigms, and research paradigms—our ways of becoming WPAs.

But beyond identifying a GenAdmin ethics as appropriately nuanced, self-organizing, interconnected, and dynamic, Chris Cuomo's work in ecological feminism helps us articulate what we mean by GenAdmin *eudaimonia* as flourishing. For Cuomo, flourishing "captures what ecological feminists want to bring about in and through our interactions. But 'flourishing' also captures something about how we want to *be*—as persons, and as moral agents" (Cuomo 79), and likewise depicts what GenAdmin wants to do and become. Cuomo's revisitation of Aristotelian "ethic" as a consideration of good living and right conduct in human interactions enables us to make pragmatic choices: "According to the norms recorded by [Aristotle] and other influential thinkers in the history of ethics, ethical issues involve the exploration of 'the good,' and 'right and wrong,' and their attempted realization in human interactions" (2-3). We appreciate Cuomo's use of scare quotes for disrupting the presumption that "the good" or "right and wrong" are stable rather than contextual and perspectival categories, even as we recognize that there are limits to what counts as right and good in our valuation of selves and others.

With Cuomo, we find it more useful for GenAdmin to understand and uphold those philosophical tenets that lead to "flourishing" rather than those tenets that are affixed to positionings like "good," "right," or "wrong," simply because we find "flourishing" to be more rhetorically and discursively productive towards calling out disruptive notions of programmatic power, behavior, and response. Donald Davidson's reminder that "there is but one world, a world that we can share" asserts our need to commit to flourishing because we recognize we are in one world and really have seen evidence—large scale and local—that we need to keep on supporting and acting for social justice (qtd. in Yarbrough, *Inventive Intercourse* xiii). Supporting an ethics of flourishing is a way of talking about the belief that what we're aiming for is living in the world together harmoniously without disregarding dissonance (Readings). As such, GenAdmin seeks to be an ethical rhetor, a *phronimos*, or "an active leader who tries to change society for the better" (Rowland and Womack 21). Because "individual and communal flourishing contribute to each other dialectically" (Cuomo 74-75), GenAdmin identity thus is a means and ends for promoting GenAdmin flourishing (even WPA flourishing in the twenty-first century more generally) to contribute to global projects to eradicate oppression as well as more "local" projects to support the flourishing of writing program administrators as individuals and a collective organization.

In the interstices of our world, largely focused on writing program administration, we hope to support the flourishing of other WPAs and our profession more generally, regardless of the circumstances of their jobs. We hope to create new alliances, promote new conversations, new actions, *new imaginations* about what writing program administration is and might become. To conclude our case for GenAdmin, particularly a GenAdmin ethics of flourishing, we look briefly at Cuomo's six aspects of what flourishing entails for an ecological feminism as they relate to GenAdmin flourishing: flourishing is embodied, it is a contextual process, it is social, it is dialectical, it is pragmatic and it is enacted by moral agents. We add that flourishing is rhetorical, a point implied in Cuomo's work but not one she names explicitly. First, that flourishing occurs in bodies emphasizes flourishing entails both physical and emotional health. She writes, "Although the concept of 'health' is always relative, and can certainly be misused (as in eugenics), it is possible to develop and assess specific prescriptions for bodily well-being that aim to promote well-being" (Cuomo 73). We recognize that when we are not healthy in body, we are not healthy in spirit, and vice versa. That is why recognizing principles of balance and wholeness are critical for GenAdmin. We are never simply our jobs; we're committed to doing our jobs and enjoying our jobs, and for us this means balancing our work, home, and personal lives, and allowing our personal lives to speak to and inform our professional lives (as discussed in Chapter 2). For Kate, practicing yoga brings her a peace of mind that helps her do her job better. Practicing yogis choose to align their bodies as a means to align their minds and lives. Practicing *ahimsa*, non-harm, works on and off the mat, for the self and others.

Second, "'flourishing' is a designation that can only be applied to something over a span of time" (Cuomo 74). We don't find the historical focus on WPA as victim or hero, for instance, as a past that will promote future flourishing without serious interrogation. It is not only our responsibility to see, but to *see concretely* so that we affect our pasts, presents, and futures. Intervening in that history by offering our interpretation of it and an alternative history via the resistant WPA is a two-fold way for us to intervene in the present to shape the future to promote flourishing. An orientation towards reconsidering history is part of our ethic, one that we hope emerges through our efforts to reframe and challenge WPA histories in this book. We hope readers take up suggestions and strategies as time passes.

We combine the third and fourth aspects because the recognition that flourishing is social and dialectical are so closely interwoven for us. As Cuomo writes, "Humans cannot flourish without other humans, ecosystems, and species, and nothing in a biotic community can flourish on its own" (74). Flourishing then is not selfish; our interests in theorizing GenAdmin serve us as individuals satisfied, even excited by this project, but that is largely because we believe it serves others as well—other WPAs but also our students, the teachers we educate, and the colleagues and administrators we work with on and across our campuses. We also hope it serves graduate students contemplating WPA careers or sWPAs reflecting on their careers. The dialectical element is crucial because "it does not make sense to say that an individual is flourishing in a community that is not flourishing . . . [and] a community cannot flourish unless a significant number of its members are flourishing" (Cuomo 75). As an example, Cuomo writes, "an economically prosperous society built on slavery cannot flourish, in an ethical sense" (75). Likewise, we know that writing programs built on the labor of poorly paid adjuncts cannot truly flourish, nor can faculty members living in a bullying culture, including one that furthers pre-tenure hazing. Furthering oppressions is simply not conducive to flourishing.

Fifth, flourishing is pragmatic in the sense that there are a number of creative ways to pursue flourishing, but that the consequences we aim for and actions we take must be assessed for their potential to contribute towards it (Cuomo 75). Shannon Sullivan helps clarify what this point means: "with Dewey's pragmatism, claims can be judged true or false based on the degree to which they promote flourishing in and through transactions with the world, not on the degree of their transparency to reality" (224). This aspect of flourishing refers to the pragmatic satisfaction of desires and needs rather than truth claims.

For instance, in designing a curriculum for first year students, we must consider not only the needs of the students but also the abilities and needs of the teachers. The teachers Kate works with are largely multidisciplinary TAs teaching for the first time, so even her textbook choices reflect their needs as new teachers as much as they reflect programmatic goals and student learning outcomes.

Sixth, flourishing depends on moral agents "who are capable of deliberating and making choices" and who value integrity and "self-directedness" (Cuomo 76). Cuomo draws on Claudia Card's research to define integrity: it "involves considerations of consistency, coherence, and commitment" (qtd. in Cuomo 76). We extend Cuomo's inclusion of moral agency to our more elaborated definition of epistemic responsibility above. Both concepts recognize individuals working in concert with others to actively support human and nonhuman flourishing and both concepts depend on individuals who, in bell hooks' words, are self-actualized. hooks argues in *Teaching to Transgress* that "teachers must be actively committed to a process of self-actualization that promotes their own well-being if they are to teach in a manner that empowers students" (15). She goes on to cite Thich Nhat Hanh saying, "if the helper is unhappy, he or she cannot help many people" (hooks 15). Kate remembers thinking, when she first read hooks in her TA practicum, that asking faculty to be self-actualized might be asking too much—because she wasn't sure she could achieve self-actualization and simultaneously because she felt like so many of her best mentors were/are already seeing that their own well-being matters. From her present vantage point, she, as we all are, is convinced that faculty do need to keep helping themselves to better help others (and themselves, too). It's somewhat intimidating to demand that we become self-actualized; however, given our emphasis on becoming, we are hopefully always in the process of personal development. Our articulation of GenAdmin identity best expresses and expands on the values and actions of moral agents in the context of writing program administration.

Seventh, and this is our contribution, we want to emphasize that flourishing is rhetorical. Part of our ethic means believing in the inventive, disruptive capabilities of rhetoric. It is clear from reading Cuomo's scholarship that an ethics of flourishing for ecological feminism is attuned to kairotic issues of time, space, and place. We also see the social, dialectical, process and change orientation of flourishing as rhetorical and pragmatic. As noted above, moral agents who deliberate and pursue various activities (including nonaction) seek to promote flourishing. Further, Cuomo's recognition that flourishing is not a universal concept or an ideal one implies its rhetoricity, and is illuminated here:

> the meaning of human, and women's, flourishing is uniquely contingent on contexts, histories, and the stories that shape lives and social realities. As far as the work of ethical theory and practice is concerned, useful and accurate notions of human flourishing can only emerge from richly contextualized, sometimes local, evaluations of what it means to be human, what people want and strive for, and what enables their living in ways they value in specific historical and cultural locations. (79)

Flourishing "is not a mere ideal" but a philosophical and rhetorical assertion of/practice of ethics (Cuomo 75). Promoting flourishing "include[s] attention to consequences, and assessments of which actions and institutions are likely to produce and contribute to flourishing" (Cuomo 75). A commitment to flourishing requires us to use our agency as responsible knowers to create rhetorical strategies that move us further towards our hoped-for consequences of writing programs and worlds free of oppression. A GenAdmin ethics, as a rhetorical, pragmatic, and feminist ethics, directs our sense of responsibility to our programs, our students, our discipline and our choices and actions as agents. The lives we lead and circumscribe in this book, and the discourse communication model we outline in Chapter 5, are ways of living and recommitting to our ethics. This, as is our effort to engage thoughtfully with our readers who navigate programs, professional collectives, and institutions, is our hope. In discovering, exploring, and questioning the signifier we have come to call GenAdmin, we hope to persuade others of the value of this stance and practice. Successfully persuading graduate students and colleagues that GenAdmin offers a way of knowing, thinking, and becoming writing program administrators can be a way to mitigate against those who refuse to consider this alternative identity as viable and fruitful for individuals, programs, and campuses, or simply a way of becoming in the world. We hope we offer others, especially gWPAs and jWPAs, a philosophy that might add a new, complex, and nuanced voice to the ongoing conversation.

A GenAdmin identity is productive for each of us, and so we hope we have given it substance and made it accessible to others who choose to see themselves and writing programs as sources of agency, as spaces of potential for flourishing.

Afterword

AGAINST IMPOSSIBILITY: A CLOSING (OPENING?) CONVERSATION

*Jeanne Gunner, Joseph Harris,
Dennis Lynch, and Martha Townsend*

As the four of us read *GenAdmin* and considered ways we might together create an afterword to it, we realized that we wanted to produce something different from the familiar sort of "commentary on" or "guide to" the work at hand. And we suspected that the authors hoped for something different from us, too, since they had after all asked us to collaborate in writing a companion piece to their book. Their request itself seemed to invite innovation.

So we looked for a format that would allow us to write in the spirit of *GenAdmin*, to continue the work it starts. We decided that each of us would write a brief response to four questions that emerged from our reading of the book, and to arrange our responses in dialogue with one another. What follows, then, is a kind of forum or symposium in which we grapple with *GenAdmin*'s theorizing of new identities and forms of work for WPAs.

What does it mean to have a philosophy of being a WPA or a philosophy of writing program administration?

Dennis: These could be construed as two quite different questions, one focused on the individual, one focused on the possibility of a systematically worked out position articulated for others. The first has echoes of what Heidegger calls "mineness" and reminds us of everyday uses such as "I have a philosophy of BBQing" or professional uses such as "Can you send us a statement of your teaching philosophy?" The second question can lead us to imagine an integrated, comprehensive, systematic investigation of first principles—with definitions and analyses of central concepts—not just expressed but argued for. That is, the second question begins to move us away from a position statement toward an argument in dialogue with other possibilities, intended not to represent one self to others but to engage others in mutual acts of interpretation and critique regarding writing program administration.

Joe: I'm glad that Dennis notes the importance of dialogue and critique, since that lets me begin by stating my only serious worry about *GenAdmin*—which is its somewhat uncritical endorsement of the term *administration*. Administrators supervise, manage, evaluate. That's their job, their role in the bureaucracy, and it's necessary work. But there are plenty of other—and I think more compelling—terms to use to describe the kinds of programmatic work that the authors here seem most interested in: *teach, direct, mentor, lead*. I was thus a little puzzled throughout my reading of *GenAdmin* by its ongoing stress on the institutional role of the administrator rather than on the intellectual work we hope to promote. Why isn't this *GenDirect* or *GenMentor*?

Marty: Or *GenTeach*, to recall the principle, practiced by those of a genuinely high-minded persuasion, that administration is a higher form of teaching? Although the authors use *GenAdmin* throughout the book, I appreciate that they also announce early on (in Chapter 1) that the term is actually a "placeholder." Given their ambitious goals for the book, in claiming a new philosophy and new ways of conceptualizing the profession, they seem to recognize the lesson that Haig Bosmajian's introduction to *The Language of Oppression* aims to show: that "the power which comes from naming and defining people has had positive as well as negative effects on entire populations" (1). By placing their focus on the more critical issue of elaborating their ideas rather than mounting an all-out campaign for a new term (indeed by acknowledging that WPAs are "constantly immersed in, and quite conscious of, rhetorical negotiations and choices," as they state in Chapter 5, and by insisting that "identity *is* rhetorical"), they leave open the possibility that others may arrive, perhaps through dialogic mediation, at a more appropriate label for the new generations of writing program administrators to come.

Jeanne: My sense is that, by articulating a philosophy of "becoming," the authors point toward what might be called a cellular notion of the writing program administrator, a way of seeing, knowing, and acting that encompasses a decentered range of positions. They resist—productively, I believe—a "meager" identity. By de-camping—finding multiple ways of being and relating rather than aligning with a particular theory, standpoint, or political orientation—they open up a WPA philosophy that is less a defensive posture defined *against* as much as it is a stance of critical inquiry. In this sense, *GenAdmin* presents us with a new WPA epistemology and, in its service, reframes the historical narratives that depend on binary thinking (literature/composition; tenured faculty/contingent worker; and, more recently, as the *GenAdmin* authors discuss, power narratives/victim narratives, WPA/jWPA, complicity/"shrill advocacy"). In the earliest generations of writing programs, the tasks defined the position, disallowing or at least discouraging philosophical considerations of program work. Philosophically, for the GenAdmin administrator, theory and practice are dialogic, though not equally so; as the text amply demonstrates through the absence of administrative "practices," the primary voice is philosophical.

Dennis: So perhaps the two questions might be read differently, both pointing toward philosophical efforts, one more narrowly focused than the other, or rather, one encompassing the other. To have a philosophy of being a WPA (as opposed to a philosophy of writing program administration) might mean merely to have a philosophy of identity, to have a philosophical basis for assuming an identity of a certain sort. Whereas to have a philosophy of writing program administration (as opposed to a philosophy of being a WPA) might mean that one has a systematically worked out basis for a full range of administrative practices, including but not limited to the practice of assuming or asserting a certain identity. In yet other terms, a philosophy of being a WPA might be coterminous with an ethics (and politics) of WPA-ing, whereas a philosophy of writing program administration might have epistemological and ontological dimensions, in addition to ethical (and political) ones.

Jeanne: If we take philosophy to be a reasoned belief system that accords meaning and value, then for WPA *GenAdmin* repositions this system and releases it from conventional grounding in disciplinary and institutional WPA "truths." The authors formulate GenAdmin philosophy at various points as the difference between "power" and "power to"; in the framing of writing programs as "complex activities systems"; in the value given to the hidden WPA curriculum; in separating WPA intellectual and professional work from a restrictive notion of its emanation from the WPA position; and hence the value placed on the philosophical concepts of posturing and positioning.

When, how, where, and why does one choose to be a WPA?

Joe: The authors of *GenAdmin* have an almost-shouted answer to this question: *In grad school!* I agree with them that grad school can be one place where you might begin to form a commitment to working with other writing teachers and shaping writing programs. But I don't think that grad programs in English or composition are the *only* places where you might decide to take on such work. The program I used to direct at Duke, for instance, hires postdoctoral fellows from a wide range of disciplines as teachers of academic writing. Several of these teachers—originally trained in disciplines like religion, history, engineering, and Latin American studies—have since gone on to direct writing programs at other schools. They're not compositionists, but they are directors of writing, and very good ones, too.

Dennis: I understand the intuitive dimension of the authors' argument that something significant has changed for those graduate students turned professional writing program administrators who not only applied and were accepted to rhetoric and composition graduate programs (of various kinds and locations) but who also had as a strong component of their coursework and other graduate experience direct and focused attention to writing program administration. Rhetoric and composition programs emerged late within English departments (and later as stand-alone departments or programs), and rhetoric and composition programs that have a special WPA focus, or a WPA area of concentration, emerged even later.

If, as Stuart Hall suggested, identities are formed or embraced "retrospectively" (Drew), then it might be hard to build much of an argument around the notion of having chosen, or not, one's identity at some particular moment in time. Everyone by this definition would be a latecomer to identity. The problem with building an argument about a new identity around "choice" might be related to constraining one's sense of identity to when and where without full consideration of how and why once accepts or assents to an identity or to an identification with certain ways of being. In this regard, it might be useful to remember Martha Nussbaum's comments on emotion as they relate to identity: "Emotion itself is the acceptance of, the assent to live according to, a certain story" (287).

Jeanne: The professional identity of a Miltonist, historian of rhetoric, or ESL specialist may coalesce retrospectively, or may evolve with the appearance and acknowledgment of published works, almost like Stephen Jay Gould's notion of punctuated equilibrium. Historically, for the WPA, however, choice of a special order has been the mechanism of identity. Colleagues moving into WPA positions spoke of serving a stint, being drafted, stepping into the breach, or other quasi-military metaphors that at one time were common ways of explaining administrative "service." That negative legacy is what distinguishes a commitment to WPA as an academic/scholarly specialty today as a *choice*. As the authors argue, it's also necessarily a matter of active choosing due to the negative professional pressure against junior WPAs.

What the authors emphasize that I see as particularly valuable is the validity of choosing (or retrospectively defining ourselves through) WPA as an academic/scholarly specialty. I haven't held the title of WPA for eight years, but I consider WPA work my field, research agenda, and intellectual home. *GenAdmin* speaks strongly to this construction of the WPA as a theoretical pursuit rather than a job, assignment, or posting. Much of the text works as a subversion of prior formulations of the field *as* the position ("junior" WPAs, field technicians, correction officers). It refutes the notion of graduate-level WPA study as managerial training. Like an anthropologist, a WPA may engage in fieldwork, but the work is embedded in theories, methods, and research. Its purpose is inquiry and knowledge production, and one becomes a WPA by participating, by choice, in cultural practices, stepping out to question the interpretive frames one is using.

Marty: But what if the "choosing" is reversed, in the sense that WPA-ing chooses the person? It is true, as Jonikka writes in the Prelude that in response to her compelling 2002 WPA conference presentation, I told her I had chosen to be a WPA. Had we conversed in more depth, though, I would have explained that I've long likened my work in higher education, and as a writing program administrator in particular, to a calling. Not an ecclesiastical calling, but a secular one. Not in service to a deity, but in service to students and fellow teachers. And not service in the traditional academic triad of teaching, research, and service, but service in the sense of using one's gifts and talents to fulfill a worthy mission. As the offspring of a clergyman, I observed and grew to understand the *obligations* of someone who has been called: to lead, guide, nurture, mentor, mediate, teach, inspire, and profess a set of beliefs. As I watched my father, I knew that what he was doing was something I also could—in fact, should—do. What my father felt about religion, I feel about higher education. For me, that identity wasn't formed "retrospectively"; it was formed early on, even though the specific instantiation occurred, as it did for these authors, in graduate school. In a very real sense, WPA work chose me, and the work has given meaning and purpose to my life.

What does it mean to see one's professional identity as a WPA in isolation from institutional contexts (in connection with portability)?

Dennis: It would be interesting to try to think of an identity that was formed with few or tenuous ties to a particular institutional context—one that was not at least formed in serious dialogue with a particular context with lasting and durable effects.

Joe: But don't most of us imagine our work identities in precisely these free-floating ways? Read the author bios at the close of our articles and books. They almost always describe individuals who are "Professors of Rhetoric" or "Professors of English" or whatever, and who teach *at* (rather than *for*) a particular university. And of course almost all of us, over the span of a career, end up teaching at several institutions—with the result that we end up identifying more with the values of "the discipline" or "the field" (or "WPA-ing?") than those of any particular institution we happen, at the time, to be working "at."

Dennis: It is also interesting to think about the relations between identity formation and the relative portability of identity. Is "GenAdmin" really a postmodern twist on the professional identities of older WPAs?

Portability—or transitoriness—has long been a feature of academic life, or more accurately of some academic lives. What would it mean, though, to build the possibility or expectation of such movement into the heart of one's professional identity as a WPA?

Joe: Yes, I think that is perhaps the boldest claim made in *GenAdmin*—that you might think of yourself as a career WPA in much the same way that most academics think of themselves as career teachers.

Marty: The idea of *not* being a career WPA seems odder to me than being an on-again/off-again WPA. So in that sense, the authors are giving welcome voice to my experience and identity. From a purely pragmatic point of view, rotating WPA positions deprive writing programs of the continuity they need to survive inevitable instability. (This assumes, of course, that the WPA is performing the job well.) If the WPA's professional identity derives from a commitment to the principles and precepts of higher education writ large, I could see that identity as free floating, unencumbered from ties to a specific local institution. The professoriate has long recognized that scholars' loyalties aren't to the specific department in which they're currently housed, but to the sub-discipline in which they work. I don't see the authors of *GenAdmin* as making a case to change that historical reality.

Jeanne: We've expended a lot of effort in forcing the map to be the terrain—to find WPA principles of a Platonic order, as the numerous WPA handbooks and guides and case-study collections show. I don't see *GenAdmin* as an attempt to rise above the local or to offer general precepts about administering writing programs. We're asked to see local conditions as themselves unstable, open to strategic change, and always contingent. That frees the WPA from a defining relationship with the institution. His or her strategies in a given situation emerge from and in the institutional context; they are particularized in time and place, and so they are not absolutes that can be made into abstract truths.

How seriously should a new WPA take the history of the profession, or the history of the institution (department, general education program, WAC initiatives) they step into?

Jeanne: Seriously enough to know it well, certainly, but the *GenAdmin* philosophy applies here as well, and so the answer is necessarily dependent on multiple contexts. But one of the notable characteristics of this text is the authors' extensive grounding of their arguments in the history of WPA literature. Their aim is the reframing of WPA history, an anti-foundationalist move. The comparison the authors draw between their position and that of third-wave feminists is apt. They reflect on the history and show it to us through new screens, revealing the limits of the historical frames we've constructed. They challenge us to throw off the chains of WPA history, to work from a philosophical perspective in all things, to see all things as philosophical propositions that are always open-ended. This standpoint transforms binary situations because no one thing, no event, discussion, "battle," or even collaborative endeavor takes on precedent-setting power or identity-determining implication. WPA and institutional histories (necessarily plural) thus have more or less importance depending on the situation—but knowledge of them seems critical still, and they in turn must be critically seen.

Joe: This question moves us in a different direction, toward the particular and the local. I've directed two university writing programs, and I experienced the two positions as almost completely different jobs—not different versions of the same job, but different jobs. At one university, I administered, making sure the courses were staffed and the teachers were following the curriculum that had been set up for them. At the other, I led a faculty who were responsible for designing their own courses—keeping them in dialogue with one another and with the goals of the program. I thus suspect that we need to avoid confusing having the same job title with doing the same kind of work—that a WPA is not a WPA is not a WPA. And I also suspect that there may be many situations, many programs, that it might be better *not* to step into.

Marty: I can't imagine any *professional* stepping into a new job not knowing the history of both the profession itself and the institution at which the job is situated. With regard to the former, *GenAdmin*'s authors make a significant contribution to the field through their substantial retelling, critiquing, and repositioning of WPA history and literature. Even as they criticize their forebears, the authors remain respectful; they enact the brand of rhetoric and ethics they seek to promulgate. Their commitment to the discipline is clear. I suspect that Harvey Weiner would approve of this book, even if he couldn't have predicted it. With regard to the latter, I recall my shock when, two decades ago, faculty on my campus drafted a new general education program without having a sense of the history of general education in the US. How, I wondered, could this body of well-intentioned leaders craft a new program without knowing the roots of the movement? WPAs have no less an obligation to understand the exigencies to which they are responding. *GenAdmin* offers them a new philosophical grounding for undertaking their work.

Dennis: I suspect it is a sign of significant change or development for any group of people moving toward a sense of collectivity when it begins to become concerned with its "history." It is a sign of professionalization. Such work of course sets in motion competing narratives, and to this extent I appreciate the effort of these authors to coin a new term—"GenAdmin"—that helps them tell a story, their story, our story, from a fresh perspective.

Regarding how seriously new WPAs need to take the history of the institutions they find themselves a part of, I could not imagine teaching a course—any kind of course—about writing program administration that did not ask class participants to reflect deeply on the institutional embeddedness of whatever administrative position they held or might hold (WC, WAC, or WP Director). Put otherwise, it would be a central "learning outcome" of any such course that students would develop the habit of attending first and foremost to institutional history, structure, and location—to the materiality of their job.

I would go so far as to say that our discipline (CCC/CCCC/WPA) has been remiss not to stress more than it has the varied—not universal but nevertheless persistent—relations between composition (first-year, advanced, WAC, WID, etc.) and general education as an enduring educational movement in this country.

And yet, would I go so far as to say that it is of the essence of WPA-ness, of what it means to be a WPA, that we are (they are) always already institutionalized? That WPA-ness is necessarily inextricable from its historicity and institutional embeddedness? Would I discourage a new WPA from imagining her or himself floating free from the institutional context and the history of whatever WPA position she or he happens to enjoy at any particular time, nor ever to carve out a sense of professional self largely or mostly independent of any particular place and time? Would I say categorically that doing so is unimaginable or always undesirable? No.

And, finally, to reflect . . .

Jeanne: We have spent decades theorizing about WPA work. The GenAdmin philosophy transcends that theory-work division and announces what they call in Chapter 1 the "viral potential" of WPA work. I welcome this challenge to a deterministic linear history and claim for a post-administrative WPA philosophy. As with Sid Dobrin's recent work, this text anticipates a next WPA phase, and it is intellectually exciting to see the generation of a new paradigm. And I say that as someone whose work has been much caught up in the old paradigm—my doubting game to *GenAdmin*'s believing game. In notes from an initial reading, I can trace my increasing openness to a GenAdmin position: from "need to problematize that; avoid smoothing out these conflicts" on a first page to "optimists, but no Candides" near the end.

Taking up doubting ways for a moment, though, I question how GenAdmin will apply in the context of the massive changes underway in higher education. Already the majority of faculty are contingent workers; for-profit institutions further reduce faculty roles; research is increasingly being privatized; outlets for scholarly work are shrinking—the litany is familiar. Is *GenAdmin* a philosophy only for an increasingly tiny elite? How will the changing material practices of higher education impinge on a philosophy of open-ended possibility, no matter how rhetorically agile one is? How much meaningful work, how much flourishing, will happen in such cynical places, such conditions of profit and (academic) loss? At what point does portability become commodification? Or I can position GenAdmin against what seems currently almost a WPA guild, whose interests, as Dobrin argues, are served by creating safe institutional places, insular and tribal communities that are increasingly atheoretical and ahistorical. How far in such straits will empathy take us?

Marty: I share Jeanne's concerns here. As much as I endorse these authors' new ideas and believe that WPA needs them, I worry that they're arriving at a time when academe's larger issues will override their value. I needed this book more than a decade ago when pursuing a bid for promotion and tenure. I had assembled the body of literature, already large then, that established WPA work as constitutive of a discipline for my promotion and tenure chair to review, only to have him ask, "What am I to make of this material?" This book might have helped convince him that WPA work has theoretical, philosophical grounding. My hope is that *GenAdmin* will help other WPAs coming up in the field now, not just for promotion and tenure, but for guidance and inspiration in their work.

Jeanne: And yet . . . this text, now, an unexpected turn, a dialogical history. As a member of an earlier generation in relation to GenAdmins, I feel like Ursula and Birkin at the end of D. H. Lawrence's *Women in Love*:

> "I don't believe it," she said. "It's an obstinacy, a theory, a perversity."
>
> "Well—" he said.
>
> "You can't have two kinds of love. Why should you!"
>
> "It seems as if I can't," he said. "Yet I wanted it."
>
> "You can't have it, because it's false, impossible," she said.
>
> "I don't believe that," he answered. (473)

In their epistemological responsibility and philosophy of active hope, impossibility is the one position that the authors of *GenAdmin* don't accept.

Works Cited

Bosmajian, Haig A. *The Language of Oppression*. Washington: Public Affairs P, 1974. Print.

Dobrin, Sidney I. *Post-Composition*. Southern Illinois UP, forthcoming 2012. Print.

Drew, Julie. "Cultural Composition: Stuart Hall on Ethnicity and the Discursive Turn." *JAC* 18.2 (1998): 172-196. Print.

Elbow, Peter. *Writing Without Teachers*. New York: Oxford UP, 1973. Print.

Lawrence, D. H. *Women in Love*. New York: Viking, 1960. Print.

Nussbaum, Martha C. *Love's Knowledge: Essays on Philosophy and Literature*. New York: Oxford UP. 1990. Print.

Notes

CHAPTER 1: TOWARDS A PHILOSOPHY OF GENERATION ADMINISTRATION

1. Although we recognize its source, we find the claim that junior WPAs are too inexperienced to be problematic for GenAdmin subjectivity. Our understanding of WPA work involves a conflation of abilities to theorize, experiment, network, act, assess, and build a community of teachers and students, a conflation which Horning and others would argue requires on-the-job experience or a position that is labeled "full professor." This perspective perpetuates an apprentice-expert model, which, though rarely unpacked in terms of its administrative significance, tells us that what we can do before tenure is fundamentally different from what we can do after tenure. Moreover, this argument does not fully embrace what we see as the larger purposes of WPA work—building knowledge about our goals of teaching students rhetoric and writing, developing writing teachers, and integrating sound rhetorical practices into the academic and personal lives of our students, colleagues, and selves. When our conception of WPA work—and the people working in those positions—is defined by the power afforded by tenure alone, we cut ourselves off from a more generative conversation that attends to the ways in which the WPA can not only create power or influence without tenure, but also improve the conditions in which s/he works. This in turn discredits the value and importance of discursive, rhetorical acts that all WPAs engage in because of their training as rhetoricians and their disposition to work toward meaningful, pragmatic programmatic change that supports student writers.

2. Throughout this book we offer *multiplicinarity* to connote the ways that our jobs require us to make decisions from and move between disciplines, positionings, and conceptions of power, in turn resulting in opportunities for us to shift episteme.

3. We see the following books as important precursors to this one in the ways they have shaped our thinking and the ways they serve as key texts in WPA seminars and in individual research: *Culture Shock and the Practice of Profession: Training the Next Wave in Rhetoric & Composition* (Anderson and

Romano, 2006), *The Writing Program Administrator's Resource* (Brown and Enos, 2002), *The Allyn and Bacon Sourcebook for Writing Program Administrators* (Ward and Carpenter, 2002), *The Writing Program Administrator as Theorist: Making Knowledge Work* (Rose and Weiser, 2002), *The Writing Program Administrator as Researcher: Inquiry in Action & Reflection* (Weiser and Rose 1999), *Kitchen Cooks, Plate Twirlers, and Troubadours* (George, 1999), *Resituating Writing: Constructing and Administering Writing Programs* (Janangelo and Hansen, 1995), *The Activist WPA: Changing Stories about Writing and Writers* (Adler-Kassner, 2008), *Developing Successful College Writing Programs* (White, 1998), *Composition and the Academy: A Study of Writing Program Administration* (Hartzog, 1986).

    4. Royster does not necessarily promote mapping metaphors as placeholders in the same way that Dobrin reacts to them. Barbara L'Eplattenier clarifies this point in her essay "Questioning Our Methodological Metaphors" by reminding us that—while limiting—mapping and landscaping metaphors are "powerful tools" that "carry implications, possibilities, and limitations" for historical research and the biases we bring to it (133). She cites Royster's definitions of "subject position" and "subjectivity" as critical to the researcher's ability to see the dynamism of the contexts they study and to make a space in which to discuss them (L'Eplattanier 137).

CHAPTER 2: LISTENING TO AND REWRITING HISTORY

    1. Primarily a social science, ethnomethodology is the study of how community members' interactions mediate and maintain their own social orders (Garfinkel). Practices are ethnomethodological if they involve analyzing discourse, observing nonverbal human interaction, or some other form of sociological data gathering, and we posit narratives this way for how they mediate and maintain social interaction (Smith) while also revealing those elements that disrupt and complicate the larger discourses they represent. They help broaden representations of our field beyond a limited canonization of experience that we think evades more complex (and localized) stories of origin and possibility, and they illustrate the productive tensions of a job where people become professionalized through their social interactions and by enacting while resisting disciplinary structures.

    2. Ruth Mirtz, Keith Rhoades, Susan Taylor, and Kim van Alkemade resist the limits of the victim or hero stories in "The Power of 'De-positioning': Narrative Strategies in Stories of Stopping" in favor of sharing a wider range of stories that reflect a multiplicity of positions: "Our stories of stopping are narratives of passage and choice, of development and change; but they are also narratives of limits, lines drawn in the sand, and the necessity, at times, to separate ourselves from work that we mostly love and respect" (80).

3. The conditions and paradigms fueling the debate about whether to accept or deflect a job with WPA expectations before tenure become moot for GenAdmin, not because we do not recognize that there are still environments where pre-tenure WPA work is unsustainable, but because we recognize we were hired into highly contextualized positions requiring that our rhetoric and composition identities necessarily be wrapped up in WPA work. Even if "WPA" is not an explicit part of the job description for this generation, the institutions hiring GenAdmin do so with the expectation that they have been prepared for WPA work, a circumstance that presents interesting possibilities for historians and philosophers and rhetorical theorists to see writing program work as intrinsically tied up in their scholarly identity, and/ or to further argue for WPA as a scholarly identity of its own.

4. For Bordelon, Buck's approach to rhetoric involved full participation, challenged unequal power relations, and translated into a pedagogy that promoted cooperative learning of fundamental patterns of discourse.

Interlude On Empathy

1. The *Oxford English Dictionary* online cites E. B. Titchener's use of the term in his 1909 *Lectures in Experimental Psychological Thought Processes* as one possible "rendering of [Theodore Lipps'] *Einfühlung*," something to be felt or acted on "in the mind's muscles" and typically "tak[ing] the form . . . of motor empathy" ("empathy, *n.*").

2. See, for example, the public report issued by Brown University's Steering Committee on Slavery and Justice (2006) and U.S. Senate resolution 26, apologizing for the wrongs of slavery (2009).

Chapter 3: Constructing Professional Identities

1. Most discussions of professionalization entail a slippage of terms. Sometimes, professionalization refers to the development of a discipline, which is how we're using it in this paragraph, but there are lots of other ways this word is used, including as a reference to the development of individuals as they become acculturated to and members of a particular profession. We see the terms professionalization, pre-professionalization, professionalism, and professional development all used in different texts, occasionally in reference to the same things, but often the differences are significant, so to avoid some of that slippage, we'd like to be clear about what do and do not mean. While we recognize the importance of the debate surrounding conversations about graduate student professionalization, we are not focusing in this chapter on what Enos and others have described as "pre-professionalization" with

an early emphasis on things like "graduate student publication, conference preparation, a strong teaching portfolio, [and] building and honing a network of contacts" through which "students are encouraged to do everything their professors do" before they graduate (Enos, "Reflexive" 60). What we are theorizing here is the process through which administrative identities are created, over time, through philosophical, intellectual, and administrative inquiry.

2. We do not offer this genealogy as an "attempt to validate through bloodline" or as a mere attempt at the type of historical validation of "WPA" Dobrin warns against in "Freedom and Safety." Instead, we are attempting to account for how a GenAdmin philosophy might have been able to emerge, and we contend that our theorization of WPA identity is possible in large part because of the legitimation of our disciplinary becoming.

3. Though we have relied heavily on Sue McLeod's 2007 history, specifically pages 63-78, we construct this timeline by also drawing on firsthand knowledge of some events as well as primary documents such as the "President's Message" and "Announcements" of events in early *WPA* journal issues. Other WPA histories include Amy Heckathorn's 1999 dissertation, "The Struggle Towards Professionalization: The Historical Evolution of Writing Program Administrators" and Barbara L'Eplattenier's and Lisa Mastrangelo's 2004 edited collection, *Historical Studies of Writing Program Administration: Individuals, Communities, and the Formation of a Discipline.*

4. See "Moving Up the Administrative Ladder" by Susan H. McLeod and "Writing Program Administration as Preparation for an Administrative Career" by David Schwalm in *The Writing Program Administrator's Resource.*

5. The list is summarized from Rose and Weiser's discussion in "Beyond 'Winging It': The Places of Writing Program Administration in Rhetoric and Composition Graduate Programs" (163-64).

6. See also Johanna Atwood Brown's "The Peer Who Isn't a Peer: Authority and the Graduate Student Administrator" in *Kitchen Cooks, Plate Twirlers and Troubadours* (120-25).

Chapter 4: Becoming WPAs

1. To be sure, WPAs are always already defined by exterior units made up of a variety of stakeholders with diverse understandings of writing, writing programs, and administration. A becoming philosophy of writing program administration is not grounded in the choice among the identities available to us, a choice that would more closely approach a philosophy of being. It does emerge from the choice to be engines of dissensus who continually learn to manage such an identity. GenAdmin WPAs will not always be the dissensual ones, the rabble-rousers, the gad-flies replacing one set of administrative

metaphors with another one. To be an engine of dissensus is to find ways to create spaces where dissensus can happen, give stakeholders opportunities to question and disagree in ways that are heard. We want to land punches, sure, but we also want to operate by dodging, weaving, distracting, playing the short game always with an eye towards the long one. Being defined by others as an administrator or anything else does not necessitate that the WPA under definition relinquish a becoming identity.

2. In the opening to "WPAs and Identity: Sounding the Depths," Christopher Burnham and Susanne Green remark that identity "has been largely overlooked within WPA literature" despite the preponderance of identities WPAs assume and the negative effects such variety has on the "whole cloth" of academic life (175). While it may be accurate that WPA literature doesn't often explicitly turn its critical gaze on teaching and administrative identities, we argue that identity has been an implicit site of struggle since the emergence of WPA. How to "manage" these identities, how to understand the "who" we are as WPAs, informs the majority of our book titles, our categorization of article collections, our assumed and disseminated metaphors, and our mentoring initiatives.

3. Even in several well-known critiques of writing program administration from within rhetoric and composition, echoed in the 2003 *Chronicle of Higher Education* interview between Lynn Worsham and Scott McLemee, we see a number of pivotal value points that have contributed to the formation of WPA multiplicinarity.

4. While we do not necessarily understand rhetoric and composition to be a sub-discipline of English studies or WPA a sub-discipline of rhetoric and composition, we understand the relationship between English, rhetoric and composition, and WPA to be synergistic and complex.

CHAPTER 5: ENACTING GENADMIN DISCOURSE

1. In fact, these categories need to equip us to ask and answer the following questions for the discipline: What makes our version of *negotiation* different from others that precede this book? How do we understand and articulate our institutional place? How does the *topos* work, i.e., do we drive it, or do we respond to extant forces in its construction? And finally, what defines our role in enacting it if we do not ascribe to predetermined or static WPA identities?

2. Our very investment in theorizing a twenty-first century identity for writing program administrators, and in improving working conditions for rhetoric and composition scholars and administrators in these geospatial contexts, still points to a vested interest in what—if not stringent arguments for "disciplinarity"—will help us to achieve them.

3. For Gunner, this perceived "moral authority" often causes others to react negatively to our questions and concerns, and often dictates how and why many view writing programs as highly partitioned sites for problem-identified students, such as basic writers, ESL writers, and other commodified bodies. This in turn reveals the limitations of metaphoric narratives for helping writers (or WPAs) convey *ethos*. Gunner's anecdote of being a newly appointed WPA earlier in her career and voicing legitimate concern about the nature and function of auxiliary writing components to courses in other disciplines does resonate with us, inasmuch as she discovered her authority was *ethos*- rather than discipline-based ("Cold Pastoral" 37). She discovered that her own goal to "participate in establishing a shared sense of community" with colleagues was quickly and automatically perceived as a moral challenge to entrenched ideologies surrounding the class, role, and function of writing programs (Gunner 37).

4. Carolyn Miller argues for genres as ethnomethodological classifications—ones that "seek to explicate the knowledge that practice creates" (156). Anis Bawarshi supports the notion that genres simultaneously communicate and generate knowledge and are active in the sense that they shape how we know and act when we encounter genre systems. He shares Miller's premise that genres are more than organizational or literary "tools"—they are "symbiotically maintained rhetorical ecosystems ... within which communicants enact and reproduce specific situations, actions, relations, and identities" (Bawarshi 39, 82), sometimes resisting or transforming those actions and identities (Bawarshi 45).

5. Egon Guba and Yvonne Lincoln argue for the use of post-hoc programmatic documents in gathering research data about writing programs because of their unobtrusiveness, non-reactivity (223), availability, and penchant for being organized in a typological fashion. Thus, programmatic documents are valuable in their potential for reanalysis and metaanalysis (Guba and Lincoln 227), which can be attractive to researchers who want to study social structures or observe social interactions without interfereing or being obtrusive (Guba and Lincoln 233). They can measure "traces of activity in these texts" (Guba and Lincoln 263). And even as she considers the limits of using curricular documents to enact reform, Christine Ross emphasizes the importance of instituting change on external levels—and in external documents—to ensure that teaching faculty and administrators do more than just believe epistemologically that they have changed for lack of an explicit theory of practice (303). Tracing the evolution of the collaboratively authored *Student Guide* at the University of California-Irvine, Ross points to a shocking lack of (or "failed") reform because of how "dominant discourses, beliefs, and practices" reproduced themselves in each draft (303). While the document itself underwent revisions, the tensions created by those revisions

went unnoticed as they operated in contradiction to the program's theoretical underpinnings (308).

6. Though we realize our terminology resonates with Richard Miller's 1994 *College English* article, in which he applies Pat Bizzell's discussion of "contact zones" to academic discussions of the student writing generated in these zones, or spaces or sites of ideological clash, we draw on geospatial notions of "fault-lines" (Miller, "Fault Lines") as a way of charting or locating those vulnerable areas where we can best articulate clashes between our own humanistic orientations (to GenAdmin as a philosophy and practice) and the non-humanistic expectations that often surround WPA work.

7. Based on interviews of collaborating scholars in rhetoric and composition across the U.S., Morris identified four events/areas/sites/ecologies that serve as clusters of activity: researcher influences, material considerations, institutional effects, and causal factors. Morris found that scholarly identifications led to patterns that then transformed the situation itself and the environment it perpetuated. For example, collaborators might ask themselves why they collaborated on a certain project, yielding reasons such as shared values, an interest in cutting-edge work, its theoretical importance, or the ease of putting it together based on previous work. Having identified factors in all four areas or sites, collaborators can reflect, realize that they have a shared apparatus, and use that apparatus to transform how they work or continue to value co-authored work in the academy.

8. To the students creating this game, this was a solution to the limitations of metaphoric narratives for helping writers to convey ethos, and for helping readers to identify with the author or subject. It led to greater understanding of the reader's own experience for familiarizing him or herself with the landscape, or to theorize knowledge as knowing how to work in a particular institutional context ("Praxis and Allies").

9. They draw on Les Perelman and Lucie Olbrechts-Tyteca's "convergence-seeking discourse" (as quoted in Mallin and Anderson 126) and to ultimately propose what they call "reflective listening" (Mallin and Anderson 129).

10. In *Nicomachean Ethics*, Aristotle defines *phronêsis* as a virtue of "practical thought" (or "practical wisdom"). And we might be tempted to link it to the kind of thought or intellect or habit of mind that Kenneth Burke says demonstrates our ability to use language as a "symbolic means of inducing cooperation" (*Rhetoric* 43). Even still, we argue, these definitions need not exclude the practical potential of *sophia*.

INTERLUDE ON ADVOCACY

1. We model our effort to resee and rewrite gaps after Hephzibah Roskelly and Kathleen J. Ryan's work in "Places of Possibility, Sites of Action: Reseeing the Gaps between High School and College Writing Instruction," where they bring together Wolfgang Iser's research on reading to show how we can see gaps "as invitations" with Freire's notion of turning limit situations into opportunities to act via mediation. They write: "Freire would have learners rely on mediation, a method that brings into relationship the many divisions and gaps students encounter. Mediation is no softening of positions, or compromise of ideology; it is instead an action that brings together disparate ideas by considering what is and what might be. It insists that learners themselves bridge gaps, perceive themselves as active, engaged participants who pull together ideas and remake them as they work and reflect" (Roskelly and Ryan 54).

2. The AAUP Statement on the productive role of gadflies reads as follows: "Gadflies, critics of institutional practices or collegial norms, even the occasional malcontent, have all been known to play an invaluable and constructive role in the life of academic departments and institutions. They have sometimes proved collegial in the deepest and truest sense" (par. 4).

3. Given the ways our discipline is feminized, we feel a sense of caution with this term because of the challenges women in leadership positions face and the connotations of the word "shrill." In *Women's Ways of Making It in Rhetoric and Composition*, Michelle Ballif, Diane Davis, and Roxanne Mountford write that a "female is required to 'play like a man,' exhibiting assertiveness and confidence; yet, she is also asked to exhibit the typically female behaviors of graciousness and collegiality . . ." (88). Kenji Yoshino effectively names these conflicting demands in *Covering: The Hidden Assault on Our Civil Rights*. He writes: "If women are not 'masculine' enough to be respected as workers, they will be asked to cover. If they are not 'feminine' enough to be respected as women, they will be asked to reverse cover" (Yoshino 149). We wonder if a woman who expresses anger is seen as shrill where a man might be seen as holding his position.

CHAPTER 6: RE-THEORIZING A GENADMIN ETHICS

1. In defining this term, we fuse together Aristotle's deployment of "doing good" (*Nicomachean Ethics* 1095a 15-22) with Jacobs' "enacting hope," which in turn requires that we accept Rowland and Womack's now-familiar interpretation of Aristotle's "rhetoric" as simultaneously amoral art and im/moral product (13). However, we also ascribe more dialectical qualities to rhetoric than Rowland and Womack claim to see in Aristotle's system. In

doing so, we suggest *eudaimonia* as a pragmatic activity for the way it helps us to situate knowledge "not in what the universe is, but in how it works. . . . [T]o find in what order things generally precede and follow one another" (Burke, *Philosophy* 382).

2. We find Karlyn Kohrs Campbell's definition of agency particularly compelling: it "(1) is communal and participatory, hence, both constituted and constrained by externals that are material and symbolic; (2) is "invented" by authors who are points of articulation; (3) emerges in artistry or craft; (4) is effected through form; and (5) is perverse, that is, inherently, protean, ambiguous, open to reversal" (2). Moreover, Renegar and Sowards' definition of contradiction as agency augments complexity as a kind of *techne*. In "Contradiction as Agency: Self-Determination, Transcendence, and Counter-Imagination in Third Wave Feminism," Renegar and Sowards argue that contradictio[n] foster[s] a sense of agency for some third wave feminist writers and their readers that enables them to understand their identities, diversity, and feminism on their own terms and to explore new possibilities and options for everyday experiences and activism" (2). They define contradiction as "not just a statement of opposition, but . . . a term that includes a myriad of other strategies such as ambiguity, paradox, multiplicity, complexity, anti-orthodoxy, opposition and inconsistency" (Renegar and Sowards 6). Contradiction, a strategic choice of third wave feminists who employ it to "resist normative standards for consistency and clarity in the development of identities" (Renegar and Sowards 7) reflects the multiplicity we value for GenAdmin identity.

3. In addition to our own model of GenAdmin discourse, we appreciate Kathryn Valentine's efforts to practice administration that doesn't assert authority on resistant writing consultants but rather revises her perspective on that relationship so that it centers on the prospects of consultants "develop[ing] identities of participation" through agency via negotiation (151).

4. Twale and De Luca also rely on Barash's (2004) premise that incivility is most accurately interpreted from the perspective of the recipient of these behaviors, not the perpetrator(s) (3). In other words, if you feel mistreated, you are being mistreated, a principle underlying more critical discernment of victimization behaviors: "feeling victimized can be a cause for further victimization, that is, victims may display more vulnerability" (Twale and De Luca 26).

5. It also is a critique that comes of out of uninterrogated place of privilege. Rather than critique the lack of privilege of the untenured WPA, what might we gain from critiquing the privilege and corresponding lack of awareness? See, for example, the WPA-L thread on this topic initiated by Doug Downs in Fall 2009.

Works Cited

AAUP. "On Collegiality as a Criterion for Faculty Evaluation." *American Association of University Professors*. Web. 29 Apr. 2010.<http://www.aaup.org/AAUP/pubsres/policydocs/contents/collegiality.htm>.

Adler-Kassner, Linda. *The Activist WPA: Changing Stories about Writing and Writers*. Logan, UT: Utah State UP, 2008. Print.

—. "Keeping Your Writing Life Alive While Doing WPA Work." Council of Writing Program Administrators Conference. Minneapolis. July 2009. Address.

Adler-Kassner, Linda, and Susanmarie Harrington. "Reframing the Accountability Debate." *Inside Higher Ed*. 23 Apr. 2009. Web. 27 Oct. 2009.

Anderson, Dana. *Identity's Strategy: Rhetorical Selves in Conversion*. Columbia, SC: U of South Carolina P, 2007. Print.

Anderson, Virginia, and Susan Romano. Introduction. *Culture Shock and the Practice of Profession: Training the Next Wave in Rhetoric and Composition*. Ed. Virginia Anderson and Susan Romano. Cresskill, NJ: Hampton P, 2005: 1-15. Print.

Anson, Chris, Jeanne Gunner, and Thomas P. Miller. "Portraits of a Field." *The Promise and Perils of Writing Program Administration*. Ed. Theresa Enos and Shane Borrowman. West Lafayette, IN: Parlor P, 2008. 79-91. Print.

Aristotle. *Metaphysics: Books I-IX*. Trans. Hugh Tredennick. Cambridge: Harvard UP, 1933. Print.

—. *Nicomachean Ethics*. Trans. H. Rackham. Cambridge: Harvard UP, 1934. Print.

Aronowitz, Stanley, and Henry A. Giroux. *Education Still Under Seige*. 2nd ed. Westport, CT: Bergin & Garvey, 1993. Print.

Atwill, Janet M. *Rhetoric Reclaimed: Aristotle and the Liberal Arts Tradition*. Ithaca: Cornell UP, 1998. Print.

Augustine. *On Christian Doctrine*. Trans. D. W. Robertson, Jr. Upper Saddle River, NJ: Prentice Hall, 1958. Print.

Austin, Ann. "Preparing the Next Generation of Faculty: Graduate School as Socialization to the Academic Career." *The Journal of Higher Education* 73.1 (2002): 94-122. Print.

Baker, Anthony, Karen Bishop, Suellyn Duffey, Jeanne Gunner, Rich Miller, and Shelley Reid. "The Progress of Generations." *WPA: Writing Program Administration* 29.1-2 (2005): 31-57. Print.

Ballif, Michelle, Diane Davis, and Roxanne Mountford. *Women's Ways of Making It in Rhetoric and Composition*. New York: Routledge, 2008. Print.

Barash, David P. "Birds Do It, Bees Do It—Should Professors, Too, Strive to Communicate Sincerity?" *Chronicle of Higher Education* 16 July 2004: B9-10. Print.

Barnetson, Robert. "Performance Indicators and Chaos Theory." *Chaos Theory and Higher Education: Leadership, Planning, and Policy*. Ed. Marc Cutright. Baltimore, MD: Peter Lang, 2001. 145-58. Print.

Baumgardner, Jennifer, and Amy Richards. *ManifestA: Young Women, Feminism, and the Future*. New York: Farrar, Straus and Giroux, 2000. Print.

Bawarshi, Anis S. *Genre and the Invention of the Writer: Reconsidering the Place of Invention in Composition Studies*. Logan, UT: Utah State UP, 2003. Print.

Bazerman, Charles, Joseph Little, Lisa Bethel, Teri Chavkin, Danielle Fouquette, and Janet Garufis. *Reference Guide to Writing Across the Curriculum*. West Lafayette, IN: Parlor P, 2005. Print.

Belanger, Kelly, and Brian Grogan. "Leading from the Middle: Women Administrators and Rhetorics of Institutional Change." Feminisms and Rhetorics Conference. Michigan State University, East Lansing, MI. Oct. 2009. Address.

Bieber, Jeffrey P., and Linda K. Worley. "Conceptualizing the Academic Life: Graduate Students' Perspectives." *Journal of Higher Education* 77.6 (2006): 1009-35. Print.

Bishop, Wendy, and Gay Lynn Crossley. "How to Tell a Story of Stopping: The Complexities of Narrating a WPA's Experience." *WPA: Writing Program Administration* 19.3 (1996): 70-79. Print.

Bloom, Lynn Z. "I Want a Writing Director." *College Composition and Communication* 43.2 (1992): 176-78. Print.

—. "Making a Difference: Writing Program Administration as a Creative Process." *Resituating Writing: Constructing and Administering Writing Programs*. Ed. Joseph Janangelo and Kristine Hansen. Portsmouth, NH: Heinemann, 1995. 73-81. Print.

Bloom, Lynn Z., Donald A. Daiker, and Edward M. White, eds. *Composition Studies in the New Millenium: Rereading the Past, Rewriting the Future*. Carbondale, IL: Southern Illinois UP, 2003. Print.

—. *Composition in the Twenty-First Century: Crisis and Change*. Carbondale, IL: Southern Illinois UP, 1996. Print.

Bordelon, Suzanne. *A Feminist Legacy: The Rhetoric and Pedagogy of Gertrude Buck*. Carbondale, IL: Southern Illinois UP, 2007. Print.

Bousquet, Marc. "Composition as Management Science: Toward A University Without a WPA." *Journal of Advanced Composition* 22.3 (2002): 493-526. Print.
Bourdieu, Pierre. *In Other Words: Essays Towards a Reflexive Sociology*. Trans. Matthew Adamson. Palo Alto, CA: Stanford UP, 1990. Print.
Breland, Mary, Melissa Faulkner, Tarez Samra Graban, David Marado, Marc Pietrzykowski, Veronica Pantoja, Alison Pryweller, and Sundy Watanabe. Unpublished "Graduate Student WPA Identity and Position Statement." Council of Writing Program Administrators Conference. University of Alaska at Anchorage, Anchorage, AK, July 2005. Address.
Brereton, John C., ed. *The Origin of Composition Studies in American College, 1875-1925: A Documentary History*. Pittsburgh, PA: U of Pittsburgh P, 1995. Print.
Brown, Johanna Atwood. "The Peer Who Isn't a Peer: Authority and the Graduate Student Administrator." *Kitchen Cooks, Plate Twirler, and Troubadours*. Ed. Diana George. 120-25. Print.
Brown, Stuart C. "Applying Ethics: A Decision Making Heuristic for Writing Program Administrators." *The Writing Program Administrator's Resource: A Guide to Reflexive Institutional Practice*. Ed. Stuart C. Brown and Theresa Enos. Mahwah, NJ: Lawrence Erlbaum, 2002. 155-64. Print.
Brown, Stuart C., Andrea Lunsford, and Edward M. White. "Location and the WPA." *The Promise and Perils of Writing Program Administration*. Ed. Theresa Enos and Shane Borrowman. West Lafayette, IN: Parlor P, 2008. 126-34. Print.
Brown, Stuart C., and Theresa Enos, eds. *The Writing Program Administrator's Resource: A Guide to Reflective Institutional Practice*. Mahwah, NJ: Lawrence Erlbaum, 2002. Print.
Bruffee, Kenneth. "Editorial." *WPA: Writing Program Administration* 1.3 (1978): 6-12. Print.
Bullock, Richard. "When Administration Becomes Scholarship: The Future of Writing Program Administration." *WPA: Writing Program Administration* 11.1-2 (1987): 13-18. Print.
Burke, Kenneth. *The Philosophy of Literary Form*. 3rd ed. Revised. Berkeley, CA: U of California P, 1973.
—. *A Rhetoric of Motives*. Berkeley: U of California P, 1969. Print.
Burnham, Christopher. "Reflection, Assessment, and Articulation: A Rhetoric of Writing Program Administration." *The Writing Program Administrator's Resource: A Guide to Reflective Institutional Practice*. Mahwah, NJ: Lawrence Erlbaum, 2002. 303-14. Print.
Burnham, Chrinstopher, and Susanne Green. "WPA Identity: Sounding the Depths." *The Writing Program Interrupted: Making Space for Critical Discourse*. Ed. Donna Strickland and Jeanne Gunner. Portsmouth, NH: Boynton/Cook, 2009. 175-85. Print.

Bushman, Donald. "The WPA as Pragmatist: Recasting 'Service' as 'Human Science.'" *WPA: Writing Program Administration* 23.1-2 (1999): 29-43. Print.

Butler, Paul. "Composition as Countermonument: Toward a New Space in Writing Classrooms and Curricula." *WPA: Writing Program Administration* 29.3 (2006): 11-24. Print.

Caldwell-Colbert, Toy, and Judith Albino. "Women as Academic Leaders: Living the Experience from Two Perspectives." *Women and Leadership: Transforming Visions and Diverse Voices.* Ed. Jean Lau Chin, Bernice Lott, Joy K. Rice, and Janis Sanchez-Hucles. Malden, MA: Blackwell, 2007. 69-87. Print.

Cameron, Deborah, Elizabeth Frazer, Penelope Harvey, Ben Rampton, and Kay Richardson. "Power/Knowledge: The Politics of Social Science." *The Discourse Reader.* Ed. Adam Jaworski and Nikolas Coupland. London: Routledge, 1999. 141-57. Print.

Campbell, Karlyn Kohrs. "Agency: Promiscuous and Protean." *Communication and Critical/Cultural Studies* (Mar. 2005): 1-19. Print.

Charlton, Colin, and Jonikka Charlton, eds. *The Assemblage Project.* N.p., n.d. Web. 9 June 2011.

Charlton, Jonikka, and Shirley K Rose. "Twenty More Years in the WPAs' Progress." *WPA: Writing Program Administration* 33.1-2 (2009): 114-45. Print.

Cherryholmes, Cleo H. *Reading Pragmatism.* New York: Teachers College P, 1999. Print.

Code, Lorraine. *Ecological Thinking: The Politics of Epistemic Location.* New York: Oxford UP, 2006. Print.

—. *What Can She Know? Feminist Theory and the Construction of Knowledge.* Ithaca, NY: Cornell UP, 1991. Print.

Cope, Edward M. *An Introduction to Aristotle's* Rhetoric. London: Macmillan, 1867. Print.

Corder, Jim W. "Argument as Emergence, Rhetoric as Love." *Rhetoric Review* 4.1 (1985): 16-32. Print.

Crowley, Sharon. *Composition in the University: Historical and Polemical Essays.* Pittsburgh, PA: U of Pittsburgh P, 1998. Print.

Cuomo, Chris J. *Feminism and Ecological Communities: An Ethic of Flourishing.* London: Routledge, 1998. Print.

Cutright, Marc, ed. *Chaos Theory and Higher Education: Leadership, Planning, and Policy.* New York: Peter Lang, 2001. Print.

Deleuze, Gilles, and Felix Guattari. *What Is Philosophy?* Trans. Janis Tomlinson. New York: Columbia UP, 1986. Print.

Derrida, Jacques. *Writing and Difference.* Trans. Alan Bass. Chicago: U of Chicago P, 1981. Print.

Desmet, Christy. "Beyond Accommodation: Individual and Collective in a Large Writing Program." *Discord and Direction: The Postmodern Writing Program Administrator.* Ed. Sharon James McGee and Carolyn Handa. Logan, UT: Utah State UP, 2005. 40-58. Print.

Dew, Debra Frank. "Labor Relations: Collaring jWPA Desire." *Untenured Faculty as Writing Program Administrators: Institutional Practices and Politics.* Ed. Debra Frank Dew and Alice Horning. West Lafayette, IN: Parlor P, 2007. 110-133. Print.

Dew, Debra Frank, and Alice Horning, eds. *Untenured Faculty as Writing Program Administrators: Institutional Practices and Politics.* West Lafayette, IN: Parlor P, 2007. Print.

Dobrin, Sidney I. "Freedom and Safety, Space and Place: Locating the Critical WPA." *The Writing Program Interrupted: Making Space for Critical Discourse.* Ed. Donna Strickland and Jeanne Gunner. Portsmouth, NH: Boynton/Cook, 2009. 56-71. Print.

Dryer, Dylan B. "The Persistence of Institutional Memory: Genre Uptake and Program Reform." *WPA: Writing Program Administration.* 31.3 (2008): 32-51. Print.

Dunn, Patricia A. *Talking, Sketching, Moving: Multiple Literacies in the Teaching of Writing.* Portsmouth, NH: Heinemann, 2001. Print.

Ebest, Sally Barr. *Changing the Way that We Teach: Writing and Resistance in the Training of Teaching Assistants.* Carbondale, IL: Southern Illinois UP, 2005. Print.

—. "Gender Differences in Writing Program Administration." *WPA: Writing Program Administration* 19.3 (1995): 53-73. Print.

—. "The Next Generation of WPAs: A Study of Graduate Students in Composition/Rhetoric." *WPA: Writing Program Administration* 22.3 (1999): 65-84. Print.

Edgington, Anthony, and Stacy Hartlage Taylor. "Invisible Administrators: The Possibilities and Perils of Graduate Student Administration." *WPA: Writing Program Administration* 31.1-2 (2007): 150-70. Print.

Elshtain, Jean Bethke. "Feminist Discourse and Its Discontents: Language, Power, and Meaning." *Signs* 7.3 (1982): 603-21. Print.

"empathy, *n.*" *The Oxford English Dictionary*, 2nd ed. 1989. OED Online, March 2011. Oxford University Press. 1 March 2011 <http://www.oed.com:80/Entry/61284>.

Engeström, Yrjö. *Learning by Expanding: An Activity-Theoretical Approach to Developmental Research.* Jyväskylä, Finland: Orienta-Konsultit Oy, 1987. Print.

Enoch, Jessica. "Becoming Symbol-Wise: Kenneth Burke's Pedagogy of Critical Reflection." *College Composition and Communication* 56.2 (2004): 279-96. Print.

Enos, Theresa. "Reflexive Professional Development: Getting Disciplined in Writing Program Administration." *The Writing Program Administrator's Resource: A Guide to Reflexive Institutional Practice*. Ed. Stuart C. Brown and Theresa Enos. Mahwah, NJ: Lawrence Erlbaum, 2002. 59-70. Print.

Enos, Theresa, and Shane Borrowman, eds. *The Promise and Perils of Writing Program Administration*. West Lafayette, IN: Parlor P, 2008. Print.

Eubanks, Philip. "Poetics and Narrativity." *What Writing Does and How It Does It: An Introduction to Analyzing Texts and Textual Practices*. Ed. Charles Bazerman and Paul Prior. Mahwah, NJ: Lawrence Erlbaum, 2004. 33-56. Print.

Farris, Christine. "Too Cool For School?: Composition as Cultural Studies and Reflected Practice." *Preparing College Teachers of Writing: Histories, Theories, Programs, Practices*. Ed. Betty Parsons Pytlik and Sarah Liggett. New York: Oxford UP, 2002. 108-20. Print.

Foss, Sonja K., and Cindy L. Griffin. "Beyond Persuasion: A Proposal for an Invitational Rhetoric." *Communication Monographs* 62.1 (1995): 2-18. Print.

Fox, Tom. "Working Against the State: Composition's Intellectual Work for Change." *Rhetoric and Composition as Intellectual Work*. Ed. Gary Olson. Carbondale: Southern Illinois UP, 2002: 91-100. Print.

Freire, Paulo. *Politics of Education: Culture, Power, and Liberation*. Trans. Donaldo Macedo. Westport, CT: Bergin & Garvey, 1985. Print.

Fulwiler, Megan. "Notes from a New WPA." *The Promise and Perils of Writing Program Administration*. Ed. Theresa Enos and Shane Borrowman. West Lafayette, IN: Parlor P, 2008. 92-101. Print.

Garfinkel, Harold. *Studies in Ethnomethodology*. Malden, MA: Polity P, 1984. Print.

George, Diana, ed. *Kitchen Cooks, Plate Twirlers, and Troubadours: Writing Program Administrators Tell Their Stories*. Portsmouth, NH: Boynton/Cook Publishers, 1999. Print.

Gere, Anne Ruggles. "The Long Revolution in Composition." *Composition in the Twenty-First Century: Crisis and Change*. Ed. Lynn Bloom, Donald Daiker, and Edward White. Carbondale, IL: Southern Illinois UP, 1996. 119-32. Print.

Gillam, Alice M. "Taking It Personally." *Kitchen Cooks, Plate Twirlers, and Troubadours: Writing Program Administrators Tell Their Stories*. Ed. Diana George. Portsmouth, NH: Boynton/Cook, 1999. 65-72. Print.

Goldblatt, Eli. *Because We Live Here: Sponsoring Literacy Beyond the College Curriculum*. Cresskill, NJ: Hampton P, 2007. Print.

Goggin, Maureen Daly. "The Disciplinary Instability of Composition." *Reconceiving Writing, Rethinking Writing Instruction*. Ed. Joseph Petraglia. Mahwah, NJ: LEA, 1995. 27-48. Print.

Graban, Tarez Samra, and Kathleen J. Ryan. "From 'What Is' to 'What Is Possible': Theorizing Curricular Document Revision as In(ter)vention and Reform." *WPA: Writing Program Administration* 28.3 (2005): 89-112. Print.

Grimaldi, William M. A. *Studies in the Philosophy of Aristotle's Rhetoric*. Wiesbaden, Germany: Franz Steiner Verlag, 1972. Print.

Grimm, Nancy Barbara Conroy Maloney. "'The Way Rich People Does It': Reflections on Writing Center Administration and the Search for Status." *Kitchen Cooks, Plate Twirlers, and Troubadours: Writing Program Administrators Tell Their Stories*. Ed. Diana George. Portsmouth, NH: Boynton/Cook, 1999. 14-25. Print.

Guba, Egon G., and Yvonna S. Lincoln. *Effective Evaluation: Improving the Usefulness of Evaluation Results Through Responsive and Naturalistic Approaches*. San Francisco: Jossey-Bass, 1981. Print.

Gunner, Jeanne. "Cold Pastoral: The Moral Order of an Idealized Form." *Discord and Direction: The Postmodern Writing Program Administrator*. Ed. Sharon James McGee and Carolyn Handa. Logan, UT: Utah State UP, 2005. 28-39. Print.

—. "Collaborative Administration." *The Writing Program Administrator's Resource: A Guide to Reflective Institutional Practice*. Eds. Stuart C. Brown and Theresa Enos. 253-62. Print.

—. "Ideology, Theory, and the Genre of Writing Programs." *The Writing Program Administrator as Theorist*. Ed. Shirley K Rose and Irwin Weiser. Portsmouth, NH: Boynton/Cook, 2002. 7-18. Print.

Hairston, Maxine. "Thomas Kuhn and the Revolution in the Teaching of Writing." *College Composition and Communication* 33.3 (1982): 76-88. Print.

Hall, Donald E. *The Academic Community: A Manual for Change*. Columbus, OH: The Ohio State UP, 2007. Print.

Handa, Carolyn, and Sharon James McGee, eds. *Discord and Direction: The Postmodern Writing Program Administrator*. Logan, UT: Utah State UP, 2005. Print.

Haraway, Donna J. *Simians, Cyborgs, and Women: The Reinvention of Nature*. New York: Routledge, 1991. Print.

Hardin, Joe Marshall. "The Writing Program Administrator and Enlightened False Consciousness: The Virtues of Becoming an Empty Signifier." *The Writing Program Interrupted: Making Space for Critical Discourse*. Ed. Donna Strickland and Jeanne Gunner. Portsmouth, NH: Boynton/Cook, 2009. 137-46. Print.

Harris, Joseph. "Déjà Vu All Over Again." *College Composition and Communication* 57 (2006): 535-42. Print.

—. "Meet the New Boss, Same as the Old Boss: Class Consciousness in Composition." *College Composition and Communication* 52.1 (2000): 43-68. Print.
Harris, Joseph, and Charles Schuster. "Exploring WPA Identities." Council of Writing Program Administrators Conference. Denver, CO, 2008. Address.
Healy, Dave. "Writing Center Directors: An Emerging Portrait of the Profession." *WPA: Writing Program Administration* 18.3 (1995): 26-43. Print.
Heckathorn, Amy. "Moving Toward a Group Identity: WPA Professionalization from the 1940s to the 1970s." *Historical Studies of Writing Program Administration: Individuals, Communities, and the Formation of a Discipline.* Ed. Barbara L'Eplattenier and Lisa Mastrangelo. West Lafayette, IN: Parlor P, 2004. 191-219. Print.
—. *"The Struggle Toward Professionalization: The Historical Evolution of Writing Program Administrators."* Thesis. Texas Christian University, 1999. Print.
Herzberg, Bruce. "A Primer on Computer Literacy for WPAs and Writing Instructors." *WPA: Writing Program Administration* 6.3 (1983): 23-32. Print.
Hesse, Doug. "The WPA as Father, Husband, Ex." *Kitchen Cooks, Plate Twirlers, and Troubadours: Writing Program Administrators Tell Their Stories.* Ed. Diana George. Portsmouth, NH: Boynton/Cook, 1999. 44-55. Print.
Hollbrook, Sue Ellen. "Women's Work: The Feminizing of Composition." *Rhetoric Review* 9.2 (1991): 201-29. Print.
hooks, bell. *Teaching to Transgress: Education as the Practice of Freedom.* New York: Routledge, 1994. Print.
Horner, Winifred Bryan. "President's Message." *WPA: Writing Program Administration* 9.3 (1986): 5-6. Print.
Horning, Alice. "Ethics and the jWPA." *Untenured Faculty as Writing Program Administrators: Institutional Practices and Politics.* Ed. Debra Frank Dew and Alice Horning. West Lafayette, IN: Parlor P, 2007. 40-57. Print.
—. Introduction. "What Is Wrong with This Picture?" *Untenured Faculty as Writing Program Administrators: Institutional Practices and Politics.* Ed. Debra Frank Dew and Alice Horning. West Lafayette, IN: Parlor P, 2007. 3-12. Print.
Howard, Rebecca Moore. "Reflexivity and Agency in Rhetoric and Pedagogy." *College English* 56.3 (Mar. 1994): 92-99. Print.
Hult, Christine. "On Being a Writing Program Administrator." Council of Writing Program Administrators Conference. Portland, OR, July 1990. Address.
Hult, Christine, David Joliffe, Kathleen Kelly, Dana Mead, and Charles Schuster. "'The Portland Resolution': Guidelines for Writing Program

Administrators." *WPA: Writing Program Administration* 16.1-2 (1992): 88-94. Print.

Ianetta, Melissa, Linda Bergmann, Lauren Fitzgerald, Carol Peterson Haviland, Lisa Lebduska, and Mary Wislocki. "Polylog: Are Writing Center Directors Writing Program Administrators?" *Composition Studies* 34.2 (2006): 11-42. Print.

Ingraham, Lauren Sewell. "From Adjunct Wrangler to Autonomous WPA: The Surprising Benefits of Pretenure Writing Program Administration." *The Promise and Perils of Writing Program Administration*. Ed. Theresa Enos and Shane Borrowman. West Lafayette, IN: Parlor P, 2008. 290-97. Print.

The Lord of the Rings: The Fellowship of the Ring. Dir. Peter Jackson. New Line Home Video, 2002. DVD.

Jackson, Nell C., Vivian Stringer, and Joyce Wong. "Minority Women in Administration." American Alliance for Health, Physical Education, Recreation and Dance 101st Convention. Cincinnati Convention Center, Cincinnati, OH, Apr. 1986. Address.

Jackson, Rebecca, Carrie Leverenz, and Joe Law. "(Re)Shaping the Profession: Graduate Courses in Writing Center Theory, Practice, and Administration." *The Center Will Hold: Critical Perspectives on Writing Center Scholarship*. Ed. Michael Pemberton and Joyce Kinkead. Logan, UT: Utah State UP, 2003. 130-50. Print.

Jacobs, Dale. "What's Hope Got To Do With It? Toward a Theory of Hope and Pedagogy." *Journal of Advanced Composition* 25.4 (2005): 783-802. Print.

Janangelo, Joseph. "Theorizing Difference and Negotiating Differends." *Resituating Writing: Constructing and Administering Writing Programs*. Ed. Joseph Janangelo and Kristine Hansen. Portsmouth, NH: Heinemann, 1995. 3-22. Print.

Janangelo, Joseph, and Kristine Hansen, eds. *Resituating Writing: Constructing and Administering Writing Programs*. Portsmouth, NH: Heinemann, 1995. Print.

Jschik, Scott. "The Gen X Professor." *Inside Higher Ed*. Web. 5 Apr. 2006. 8 Dec. 2009. <http://www.insidehighered.com/news/2006/04/05/genx>.

Kennedy, Kristen. "The Fourth Generation." *College Composition and Communication* 59.3 (2008): 525-37. Print.

Kill, Melanie. "Acknowledging the Rough Edges of Resistance: Negotiation of Identities for First-Year Composition." *College Composition and Communication* 58.2 (2006): 213-35. Print.

Killingsworth, M. Jimmie. "Discourse Communities—Local and Global." *Rhetoric Review* 11.1 (1992): 110-22. Print.

Kinney, Kelly. "Fellowship for the Ring: A Defense of Critical Administration in the Corporate University." *WPA: Writing Program Administration* 32.3 (2009): 37-48. Print.

Kopelson, Karen. "Rhetoric on the Edge of Cunning; Or, The Performance of Neutrality (Re)Considered As a Composition Pedagogy for Student Resistance." *College Composition and Communication* 55.1 (2003): 115-46. Print.

—. "Sp(l)itting Images; or, Back to the Future of (Rhetoric and?) Composition." *College Composition and Communication* 59.4 (2008): 750-80. Print.

Lakoff, George, and Mark Johnson. *Metaphors We Live By*. Chicago: U of Chicago P, 1980. Print.

Lamonica, Claire C. "Neither Fish Nor Fowl: The Promise and Peril of Directing a Program on an Administrative Line." *The Promise and Perils of Writing Program Administration*. Ed. Theresa Enos and Shane Borrowman. West Lafayette, IN: Parlor P, 2008. 146-52. Print.

Langstraat, Lisa, and Julie Lindquist. "Learning Discipline: Disciplinary Grammars, Emotion Cultures, and Pragmatic Education." *Culture Shock and the Practice of Profession: Training the Next Wave in Rhetoric and Composition*. Ed. Virginia Anderson and Susan Romano. Cresskill, NJ: Hampton P, 2006. 19-41. Print.

Lauer, Janice M. "Composition Studies: Dappled Discipline." *Rhetoric Review* 3.1 (1984): 20-29. Print.

L'Eplattenier, Barbara. "Questioning Our Methodological Metaphors." *Calling Cards: Theory and Practice in the Study of Race, Gender, and Culture*. Ed. Jacqueline Jones Royster and Ann Marie Mann. Albany, NY: State University of New York P, 2005. 133-46. Print.

L'Eplattenier, Barbara, and Lisa Mastrangelo. "Why Administrative Histories?" *Historical Studies of Writing Program Administration*. Ed. Barbara L'Eplattenier and Lisa Mastrangelo. West Lafayette, IN: Parlor P, 2004. xvii-xxvii. Print.

L'Eplattenier, Barbara, and Lisa Mastrangelo, eds. *Historical Studies of Writing Program Administration: Individuals, Communities, and the Formation of a Discipline*. West Lafayette, IN: Parlor P, 2004. Print.

Lerner, Gerda. "Why History Matters." *Why History Matters: Life and Thought*. New York: Oxford UP, 1997. 199-211. Print.

Leverenz, Carrie Shively. "Theorizing Ethical Issues in Writing Program Administration." *The Writing Program Administrator as Theorist*. Eds. Shirley Rose and Irwin Weiser. Portsmouth, NH: Boynton/Cook, 2002. Print.

Logan, Shirley Wilson. "Why College English?" *College English* 69.2 (2006): 107-10. Print.

Lu, Min-Zhan. "Tracking Comp Tales." *Comp Tales*. Ed. Richard H. Haswell and Min-Zhan Lu. New York: Longman, 1999. 195-226. Print.

Lunsford, Andrea. "Women's Work: Remixing Theory, Practice, and Pedagogy." Conference on College Composition and Communication. Louisville, KY, Mar. 2010. Address.

Mallin, Irwin, and Karrin Varsby Anderson. "Inviting Constructive Argument." *Argumentation and Advocacy* 36.3 (2000): 120-33. Print.

Martín-Alcoff, Linda. "The Problem of Speaking for Others." *Who Can Speak?: Authority and Critical Identity*. Ed. Judith Roof and Robyn Wiegman. Urbana, IL: U of Illinois P, 1995. 97-119. Print.

Mathieu, Paula. *Tactics of Hope: The Public Turn in English Composition*. Portsmouth, NH: Boynton/Cook, 2005. Print.

May, Todd. "When is a Deleuzian Becoming?" *Continental Philosophy Review* 36.2 (2003): 139-53. Print.

McClure, Randall. "An Army of One: The Possibilities and Pitfalls of WPA Work for the Lone Compositionist." *The Promise and Perils of Writing Program Administration*. Ed. Theresa Enos and Shane Borrowman. West Lafayette, IN: Parlor P, 2008. 102-09. Print.

McKeon, Richard, ed. *Ethica Nicomachea: The Basic Works of Aristotle*. Trans. W. D. Ross. New York: Random, 1941. Print.

McLemee, Scott. "Deconstructing Composition." *The Chronicle of Higher Education*, 21 Mar. 2003. Web. 28 Apr. 2010. <http://chronicle.com/article/Deconstructing-Composition/6127>.

McLeod, Susan H. "The Foreigner: WAC Directors as Agents of Change." *Resituating Writing: Constructing and Administering Writing Programs*. Ed. Joseph Janangelo and Kristine Hansen. Portsmouth, NH: Heinemann, 2006. 108-16. Print.

—. "Moving Up the Administrative Ladder." *The Writing Program Administrator's Resource: A Guide to Reflective Institutional Practice*. Ed. Stuart C. Brown and Theresa Enos. 113-24. Print.

—. *Writing Program Administration*. West Lafayette, IN: Parlor P, 2007. Print.

Micciche, Laura R. "More than A Feeling: Disappointment and WPA Work." *College English* 64.4 (2002): 432-58. Print.

Miller, Carolyn R. "Genre as Social Action." *Quarterly Journal of Speech* 70.2 (1984): 151-67. Print.

Miller, Hildy. "Postmasculinist Directions in Writing Program Administration." *The Allyn and Bacon Sourcebook for Writing Program Administrators*. Ed. Irene Ward and William J. Carpenter. New York: Longman, 2002. 78-90. Print.

Miller, Richard E. "Critique's the Easy Part: Choice and Scale of Relative Oppression." *Kitchen Cooks, Plate Twirlers, and Troubadours: Writing Pro-*

gram Administrators Tell Their Stories. Ed. Diana George. Portsmouth, NH: Boynton/Cook, 1999. 3-13. Print.

—. "Fault Lines in the Contact Zone." *College English* 56.4 (1994): 389-408.

—. "From Intellectual Wasteland to Resource-Rich Colony: Capitalizing on the Role of Writing Instruction in Higher Education." *WPA: Writing Program Administration* 24.3 (2001): 25-40. Print.

Miller, Scott L., Brenda Jo Brueggemann, Bennis Blue, and Deneen M. Shepherd. "Present Perfect and Future Imperfect: Results of a National Survey of Graduate Students in Rhetoric and Composition Programs." *College Composition and Communication* 48.3 (1997): 392-409. Print.

Mirtz, Ruth, Keith Rhoades, Susan Taylor, and Kim van Alkemade. "The Power of 'De-Positioning': Narrative Strategies in Stories of Stopping." *WPA: Writing Program Administration* 25.3 (2002): 79-96.

Morris, Margaret. "That Third Hybrid Thing." Council of Writing Program Administrators Conference. Denver, CO. July 2008. Address.

Musashi, Miyamoto. *The Book of Five Rings*. Trans. Thomas Cleary. New York: Random House, 2000.

Perelman, Chaim, and Lucie Olbrechts-Tyteca. *The New Rhetoric: A Treatise on Argumentation*. Trans. John Wilkinson and Purcell Weaver. Notre Dame, IN: U of Notre Dame P, 1969. Print.

Peterson, Linda. "The WPA's Progress: A Survey, Story, and Commentary on the Career Patterns of Writing Program Administrators." *WPA: Writing Program Administration* 10.3 (1987): 11-18. Print.

Phelps, Louise Wetherbee. "Turtles All the Way Down: Educating Academic Leaders." *The Writing Program Administrator's Resource: A Guide to Reflective Institutional Practice*. Ed. Stuart C. Brown and Theresa Enos. Mahwah, NJ: Lawrence Erlbaum, 2002. 3-39. Print.

—. "Writing the New Rhetoric of Scholarship." *Defining the New Rhetorics*. Ed. Theresa Enos and Stuart C. Brown. Newbury Park, CA: Sage, 55-78. Print.

Porter, James E. "Developing a Postmodern Ethics of Rhetoric and Composition." *Defining the New Rhetorics*. Ed. Theresa Enos and Stuart Brown. Newbury Park, CA: Sage, 1992. 207-26. Print.

Porter, James E., Patricia Sullivan, Stuart Blythe, Jeffrey T. Grabill, and Libby Miles. "Institutional Critique: A Rhetorical Methodology for Change." *College Composition and Communication* 51.4 (2000): 610-42. Print.

Powell, Malea. "Rhetorics of Survivance: How American Indians *Use* Writing." *College Composition and Communication* 53.3 (2002): 396-434. Print.

"Praxis and Allies: The WPA Game." *Council of Writing Program Administrators*. Web. 29 Apr. 2010. <http://www.wpacouncil.org/praxis-allies-wpa-game>.

Purdy, Dwight. "A Polemical History of Freshman Composition." *College English* 48.8 (1986): 791-96. Print.
Qualley, Donna. *Turns of Thought: Teaching Composition as Reflexive Inquiry.* Portsmouth, NH: Boynton/Cook, 1997. Print.
Ratcliffe, Krista. *Rhetorical Listening: Identification, Gender, Whiteness.* Carbondale, IL: Southern Illinois UP, 2005. Print.
Readings, Bill. *The University in Ruins.* Cambridge, MA: Harvard UP, 1997. Print.
Reid, E. Shelley. "A Changing for the Better: Curriculum Revision as Reflective Practice in Teaching and Administration." *WPA: Writing Program Administration* 26.3 (2003): 10-27. Print.
Renegar, Valerie R., and Stacey K. Sowards. "Contradiction as Agency: Self-Determination, Transcendence, and Counter-Imagination in Third Wave Feminism." *Hypatia* 24.2 (2009): 1-20. Print.
—. "Liberal Irony, Rhetoric, and Feminist Thought: A Unifying Third Wave Feminist Theory." *Philosophy and Rhetoric* 36.4 (2003): 330-52. Print.
Rice, Jeff. "Conservative Writing Program Administrators (WPAs)." *The Writing Program Interrupted: Making Space for Critical Discourse.* Ed. Donna Strickland and Jeanne Gunner. Portsmouth, NH: Boynton/Cook, 2009. 1-13. Print.
Rickly, Rebecca J., and Susanmarie Harrington. "Feminist Approaches to Mentoring Teaching Assistants: Conflict, Power, and Collaboration." *Preparing College Teachers of Writing: Histories, Theories, Programs, Practice.* Ed. Betty P. Pytlik and Sarah Liggett. New York: Oxford UP, 2001. 108-20. Print.
Roach, Stephanie. "Why I Won't Keep My Head Down or Follow Other Bad Advice for the Junior Faculty WPA." *The Promise and Perils of Writing Program Administration.* Ed. Theresa Enos and Shane Borrowman. West Lafayette, IN: Parlor P, 2008. 109-17. Print.
Ronald, Kate, and Hephzibah Roskelly. "Untested Feasibility: Imagining the Pragmatic Possibility of Paulo Freire." *College English* 63.5 (2001): 612-32. Print.
Rebhorn, Wayne A. Foreword. *Rhetoric Reclaimed: Aristotle and the Liberal Arts Tradition.* Ithaca: Cornell UP, 1998. ix-x. Print.
Rorty, Richard. "Feminism and Pragmatism." The Tanner Lectures on Human Values. University of Michigan, Ann Arbor, MI. 7 Dec. 1990. University of Utah. Web. 15 Sept. 2006. < http://www.tannerlectures.utah.edu/lectures/documents/rorty92.pdf.>
Rose, Shirley K, and Irwin Weiser. "Beyond 'Winging It': The Places of Writing Program Administration in Rhetoric and Composition Graduate Programs." *Culture Shock and the Practice of Profession: Training the Next Wave in Rhetoric and Composition.* Ed. Virginia Anderson and Susan Romano. Cresskill, NJ: Hampton P, 2006. 161-77. Print.

—. "The WPA as Researcher and Archivist." *The Writing Program Administrator's Resource: A Guide to Reflective Institutional Practice.* Ed. Stuart C. Brown and Theresa Enos. Mahwah, NJ: Lawrence Erlbaum, 2002. 275-90. Print.
Rose, Shirley K, and Irwin Weiser, eds. *The Writing Program Administrator as Researcher.* Portsmouth, NH: Boynton/Cook Heinemann, 1999. Print.
—. *The Writing Program Administrator as Theorist.* Portsmouth, NH: Boynton/Cook Heinemann, 2002. Print.
Rose, Shirley K, and Margaret J. Finders. "Thinking Together: Developing a Reciprocal Reflective Model for Approaches to Preparing College Teachers of Writing." *Preparing College Teachers of Writing: Histories, Theories, Programs, Practices.* Ed. Betty P. Pytlik and Sarah Liggett. New York: Oxford UP, 2002. 75-85. Print.
Roskelly, Hephzibah, and Kate Ronald. *Reason to Believe: Romanticism, Pragmatism, and the Possibility of Teaching.* Albany, NY: State U of New York P, 1998. Print.
Roskelly, Hephzibah, and Kathleen J. Ryan. "Places of Possibility, Sites of Action: Reseeing the Gaps between High School and College Writing Instruction." *Closing the Gap: English Educators Address the Tensions Between Teacher Prep and Teaching at Secondary Schools.* Ed. Karen Keaton Jackson and Sandra Vavra. Charlotte, NC: Information Age Publishing, 2007. 43-58. Print.
Ross, Christine. "Education Reform and the Limits of Discourse: Rereading Collaborative Revision of a Composition Program's Textbook." *College Composition and Communication* 55.2 (2003): 302-29. Print.
Ross, W. David. *Aristotle: The Nicomachean Ethics: Translated with an Introduction.* Oxford: Oxford UP, 1925. Print.
—. *Aristotle "Metaphysics" A Revised Text with Introduction and Commentary.* 2 vols. Oxford: Clarendon, 1958. Print.
Rowland, Robert C., and Deanna F. Womack. "Aristotle's View of Ethical Rhetoric." *Rhetoric Society Quarterly* 15.1-2 (1985): 13-31. Print.
Royster, Jacquelyn Jones. "Disciplinary Landscaping, or Contemporary Challenges in the History of Rhetoric." *Philosophy and Rhetoric* 36.2 (2003): 148-67. Print.
—. "Rescue, Recover, and Inscription: Now What?" Conference on College Composition and Communication, Louisville, KY. Mar. 2010. Address.
—. *Traces of a Stream: Literacy and Social Change Among African American Women.* Pittsburgh, PA: U of Pittsburgh P, 2000. Print.
Russell, David. "Activity Theory and Process Approaches: Writing (Power) in School and Society." *Post-Process Theory: Beyond the Writing-Process Paradigm.* Ed. Thomas Kent. Carbondale, IL: Southern Illinois UP, 1999. 80-95. Print.

Ryan, Kathleen J. "Subjectivity Matters: Using Gerda Lerner's Writing and Rhetoric to Claim an Alternative Epistemology for the Feminist Writing Classroom." *Feminist Teacher* 17.1 (2006): 36-51. Print.

Ryan, Kathleen J., and Elizabeth J. Natalle. "Fusing Horizons: Standpoint Hermeneutics and Invitational Rhetoric." *Rhetoric Society Quarterly* 31.2 (2001): 69-90. Print.

Ryan, Kathleen J., and Tarez Samra Graban. "Theorizing Feminist Pragmatic Rhetoric as A Communicative Art for the Composition Practicum." *College Composition and Communication* 61.1 (2009): 277-99. Print.

Satterfield, Jay, and Frederick J. Antczak. "American Pragmatism and the Public Intellectual: Poetry, Prophecy, and the Process of Invention in Democracy." *Perspectives on Rhetorical Invention*. Ed. Janice Lauer and Janet Atwill. Knoxville, TN: U of Tennessee P, 2002. 148-62. Print.

Schell, Eileen E. "The Feminization of Composition: Questioning the Metaphors That Bind Women Teachers." *Composition Studies/Freshman English News* 20.1 (1992): 55-61. Print.

Schilb, John. *Rhetorical Refusals: Defying Audiences' Expectations*. Carbondale, IL: Southern Illinois UP, 2007. Print.

Schwalm, David E. "Writing Program Administration as Preparation for an Administrative Career." *The Writing Program Administrator's Resource: A Guide to Reflective Institutional Practice*. Ed. Stuart C. Brown and Theresa Enos. Mahwah, NJ: Lawrence Erlbaum, 2002. 125-36. Print.

Seigfried, Charlene Haddock. "Shared Communities of Interest: Feminism and Pragmatism." *Hypatia* 8.2 (1993): 1-14. Print.

Selber, Stuart. "Institutional Dimensions of Academic Computing." *College Composition and Communication* 61.1 (2009): 10-34. Print.

Shapiro, Ester, and Jennifer M. Leigh. "Toward Culturally Competent, Gender-Equitable Leadership: Assessing Outcomes of Women's Leadership in Diverse Contexts." *Women and Leadership: Transforming Visions and Diverse Voices*. Ed. Jean Lau Chin, Bernice Lott, Joy K. Rice, and Janis Sanchez-Hucles. Malden, MA: Blackwell, 2007. 88-105. Print.

Sirc, Geoffrey. "Box-Logic." *Writing New Media: Theory and Applications for Expanding the Teaching of Composition*. Ed. Anne Francis Wysocki, Johndan Johnson-Eilola, Cynthia L. Selfe, and Geoffrey Sirc. Logan: Utah State UP, 2004. 113-48. Print.

Skeffington, Jillian, Shane Borrowman, and Theresa Enos. "Living in the Spaces Between: Profiling the Writing Program Administrator." *The Promise and Perils of Writing Program Administration*. Ed. Theresa Enos and Shane Borrowman. West Lafayette, IN: Parlor P, 2008. 5-20. Print.

Slevin, James. "Engaging Intellectual Work: The Faculty's Role in Assessment." *College English* 63.3 (2001): 288-305. Print.

Smith, Dorothy E. "Textually Mediated Social Organization." *International Social Science Journal* 36.1 (1984): 59-75. Print.

Stewart, Kathleen. *Ordinary Affects*. Durham, NC: Duke UP, 2007. Print.
Stone, Elizabeth. *Black Sheep and Kissing Cousins: How Our Family Stories Shape Us*. New York: Penguin, 1988. Print.
Strenski, Ellen. "Recruiting and Retraining Experienced Teachers: Balancing Game Plans in an Entrepreneurial Force-Field." *Resituating Writing: Constructing and Administering Writing Programs*. Ed. Joseph Janangelo and Kristine Hansen, 1995. 82-99. Print.
Strickland, Donna, and Jeanne Gunner, eds. *The Writing Program Interrupted: Making Space for Critical Discourse*. Portsmouth, NJ: Boynton/Cook, 2009. Print.
Stygall, Gail. "Certifying the Knowledge of WPAs." *The Writing Program Administrator's Resource: A Guide to Reflective Institutional Practice*. Ed. Stuart C. Brown and Theresa Enos. Mahwah, NJ: Lawrence Erlbaum, 2002. 71-88. Print.
Sullivan, Shannon. "The Need for Truth: Toward a Pragmatic-Feminist Standpoint Theory." *Feminist Interpretations of John Dewey*. Ed. Charlene Haddock Siegfried. University Park, PA: Pennsylvania State UP, 2002. 210-35. Print.
Suzuki, D. T. *An Introduction to Zen Buddhism*. New York: Grove Publishing, 1964. Print.
Syverson, Margaret A. *The Wealth of Reality: An Ecology of Composition*. Carbondale, IL: Southern Illinois UP, 1999. Print.
Thayer, Robert L., Jr. *LifePlace: Bioregional Thought and Practice*. Berkeley, CA: University of California P, 2003. Print.
Tiernan, M. L. "Writing Program Administration and (Self)-Representation: Paradoxes, Anomalies, and Institutional Resistance." *Kitchen Cooks, Plate Twirlers, and Troubadours: Writing Program Administrators Tell Their Stories*. Ed. Diana George. Portsmouth, NH: Boynton/Cook, 1999. 162-73. Print.
Townsend, Martha A. "Professionalization Requires Sharing Our Understandings More Broadly." *The Promise and Perils of Writing Program Administration*. Ed. Theresa Enos and Shane Borrowman. West Lafayette, IN: Parlor P, 2008. 265-70. Print.
Twale, Darla J., and Barbara M. De Luca. *Faculty Incivility: The Rise of the Academic Bully Culture and What to Do About It*. San Francisco, CA: Jossey-Bass, 2008. Print.
Valentine, Kathryn. "'Acting Out' or Acts of Agency: WPA and 'Identities of Participation.'" *The Writing Program Interrupted: Making Space for Critical Discourse*. Ed. Donna Strickland and Jeanne Gunner. Portsmouth, NJ: Boynton/Cook, 2009. 147-54. Print.
Vico, Giambattista. "On Method in Contemporary Fields of Study." *Vico: Selected Writings*. Ed. and Trans. Leon Pompa. Cambridge: Cambridge UP, 1982. 33-45. Print.

Vivian, Barbara G. "Gertrude Buck on Metaphor: Twentieth Century Concepts in a Late Nineteenth Century Dissertation." *Rhetoric Society Quarterly* 24.3-4 (1994): 96-104. Print.
Ward, Irene, and William J. Carpenter, eds. *The Allyn and Bacon Sourcebook for Writing Program Administrators*. New York: Longman, 2002. Print.
Weiner, Harvey. "President's Message." *WPA: Writing Program Administration* 3.3 (1980): 7. Print.
Weiser, Irwin, and Shirley K Rose. "Theorizing Writing Program Theorizing." *The Writing Program Administrator as Theorist*. Ed. Shirley K Rose and Irwin Weiser. Portsmouth, NH: Boynton/Cook, 2002. 183-95. Print.
West, Cornel. *The American Evasion of Philosophy: A Genealogy of Pragmatism*. Madison, WI: U of Wisconsin P, 1989. Print.
White, Edward M. Preface. *Untenured Faculty as Writing Program Administrators: Institutional Practices and Politics*. Ed. Debra Frank Dew and Alice Horning. West Lafayette, IN: Parlor P, 2007. vii-ix. Print.
—. "Use It or Lose It: Power and the WPA." *WPA: Writing Program Administration* 15.1-2 (1991): 3-12. Print.
"WPA 2009: The Institutes." *Council of Writing Program Administrators*. 24 June 2009. Web. 28 Apr. 2010. <http://wpa2009.umn.edu/institutes/>.
Yancey, Kathleen Blake. *CWPA President's Newsletter* Jan. 2002: 1-8. Council of Writing Program Administrators. Web. Apr. 2010. <http://wpa-council.org/archives/newsletter/wpa-president-newsletter-01-2002.pdf>.
Yarbrough, Stephen R. *After Rhetoric: The Study of Discourse Beyond Language and Culture*. Carbondale, IL: Southern Illinois UP, 1999. Print.
—. *Inventive Intercourse: From Rhetorical Conflict to the Ethical Creation of Novel Truth*. Carbondale, IL: Southern Illinois UP, 2006. Print.
Yoshino, Kenji. *Covering: The Hidden Assault on Our Civil Rights*. New York: Random House, 2006. Print.

Index

active hope, 173–175, 177–178, 211
Adler-Kassner, Linda, 12, 73, 75, 118, 121, 126, 135, 214
Adler-Kassner, Linda: *The Activist WPA; Changing Stories about Writing and Writers*, 12, 53, 121, 135, 214
advocacy, 21, 53, 165, 181–182, 186, 203
agency, 10, 15, 18, 20, 31, 58, 61, 68, 88–89, 105, 109, 121, 134–135, 138, 143, 149, 159, 164, 173–174, 179, 186, 198–200, 221
Anderson, Dana: *Identity's Strategy; Rhetorical Selves in Conversion*, 138
Anderson, Virginia, and Susan Romano, eds: *Culture Shock and the Practice of Profession; Training the Next Wave in Rhetoric and Composition*, 9, 13, 76, 81, 118, 163, 213
Aristotle: *Metaphysics*, 106; *Nicomachean Ethics*, 106–107, 219, 220; *techne*, 106–108 Aronowitz, Stanley, and Henry A. Giroux: *Education Still Under Siege*, 112, 162
Assemblage Project, The, 22, 109
Association of American University Professors, 166, 183, 220

Atwill, Janet: on *techne*, 106–109; *Rhetoric Reclaimed*, 107
Augustine, Bishop of Hippo, 147
Austin, Ann: longitudinal study of doctoral programs, 75, 87

Baker, Anthony, 6
Ballif, Michelle, 190, 220
Baumgardner, Jennifer, and Amy Richards: *ManifestA; Young Women, Feminism, and the Future*, 44, 193
Bawarshi, Anis: on genre theory, 145, 218
becoming, xv, 12, 18, 58–59, 105–106, 109, 112–116, 119, 125, 127, 138, 157, 172, 198–199, 203, 216–217
Bergmann, Linda, 81
Berthoff, Anne, 109
Bieber, Jeffrey, and Linda Worley, 90–91
Bishop, Karen, 6
Bishop, Wendy, and Gay Lynn Crossley, 38, 40–42
Blakesley, David, 136
Bloom, Lynn: "I Want a Writing Director," 38, 40–42
Bloom, Lynn Z., Donald Daiker, and Edward White, eds: *Composition Studies in the New Millenium; Rereading the Past, Rewriting the Future*, 14

241

Bourdieu, Pierre: cultural capital, 102, 110, 146; force–field, 93
Brown, Stuart, 126, 172–173
Brown, Stuart, and Theresa Enos, eds: *The Writing Program Administrator's Resource*, 11 214
Bruffee, Kenneth, 62, 97–98
Buck, Gertrude: at Vassar, 49, 124, 127; student–centered pedagogy, 49, 215
Bullock, Richard, 178
bully culture, 126, 184–186, 189, 197
Burke, Kenneth, 112, 147, 154, 171, 219, 221; attitude, 112
Burnham, Christopher, and Susanne Green, 111, 217
Bushman, Donald, 15

Chronicle of Higher Education, The, 125, 217
Code, Lorraine, 174, 179
composition: feminization of, 41, 125, 190
Computers and Composition Online, 54
contact zones, 21, 148, 219
Cope, Edward M., 107
Council of Writing Program Administrators, xii–xv, 4, 7, 25, 51–52, 64, 70, 75, 80, 86, 92, 95–97, 148, 151
Crowley, Sharon, 48, 178

Davidson, Donald: interpretive charity, 147, 195
Deleuze, Gilles, 112–113, 116, 125, 157
Desmet, Christy: accommodation–resistance binary, 9, 135, 138
Dew, Debra Frank, and Alice Horning, eds: *Untenured Faculty as Writing Program Administrators*, 13, 35, 45, 119, 121
dialogic negotiation, 148, 157–170, 182
différance, 161
differends, 156
discourse communities: and M. Jimmie Killingsworth, 133, 145
discourse community, 35, 133, 145
discursive competence, 9, 20, 140, 142
Dobrin, Sidney, 16, 70, 97, 110–112, 210, 214, 216
Dryer, Dylan, 139
Duffey, Suellyn, 6
dwelling, 59, 140, 157

Ebest, Sally Barr, 66, 91
ecology, 179, 194–196, 198
empathy, 21, 40, 57–61, 134, 139, 148–149, 154, 184, 211, 215
Enoch, Jessica, 171
Enos, Theresa, 77, 80
Enos, Theresa, and Shane Borrowman, eds: *The Promise and Perils of Writing Program Adminisration*, 12–13, 35, 66, 126
ethos, 13, 136, 151, 158, 218–219
Eubanks, Phillip, 55
eudaimonia, 20, 107, 109, 172, 174, 180–181, 194–195, 221
exigence, 144, 151, 156, 209, 244
expertise, 20–21, 33, 41, 54, 65, 68, 71–72, 80, 95, 97, 99–103, 114–115, 118, 120–121, 137

Faludi, Susan, 193
Farris, Christine, 135
fault-lines, 148, 150, 219
feminism: and third wave, 44, 46, 208, 221
Finders, Margaret, 151

Foss, Sonya K., and Cindy L. Griffin, 154
Fox, Tom, 127
Freire, Paulo, 94, 172, 176, 220
Fulwiler, Megan, 126
FYC: and abolition, 48, 178; at Harvard, 48; technology in, 52–53, 71, 129, 146, 149

GenAdmin: as disciplinary identity, 17, 120; as discourse, 20, 58–59, 133–135, 138, 140–142, 151, 153, 158–163, 171, 180, 221; as epistemology, 159; as generational positioning, xi, xvi, 11, 18, 46; as historical positioning, xvi, 4, 11, 14, 36, 63, 136; as intellectual identity, 9, 29, 138; as invention, 14, 36, 121, 164; as philosophy, 8, 16, 18–19, 22, 38, 113, 116, 174, 176, 208; as placeholder, 5, 113, 202
genre uptake, 139
George, Diana, ed.: *Kitchen Cooks, Plate Twirlers, and Troubadours; Writing Program Administrators Tell Their Stories*, 35, 119, 125, 214, 216
Gillespie, Vincent, 117
Goldblatt, Eli, 53, 73
graduate education: explicit curriculum, 76–87; hidden curriculum, 87–90; WPA seminars, 80
Grassi, Ernesto: *Rhetoric as Philosophy*, 78
gravity, 93, 104, 157
gravity of disappointment, 136
Grimaldi, William, 107
Gunner, Jeanne, 6, 14, 70, 105, 136, 142–143, 145, 156, 164, 188, 201, 218
gWPA: graduate student Writing Program Administrator, xiii, 20, 27, 56, 64, 69, 86, 92, 95–96, 138, 153, 174, 219

Hairston, Maxine: paradigm shift in FYC, 51
Hall, Donald E.: *The Academic Community; A Manual for Change*, 37, 146, 179, 181–182; "shrill advocacy," 170–173
Handa, Carolyn, and McGee, Sharon James, eds: *Discord and Direction; The Postmodern Writing Program Administrator*, 11–12
Hansen, Kristine, 11, 214
Hardin, Joe Marshall, 70, 72, 105
Harrington, Susanmarie, 118, 135
Harris, Joe, 66, 70, 72, 166, 167, 201
Healy, Dave, 73
Heidegger, Martin, 78, 99, 181, 201
Hesse, Doug, 84, 125
Hill, Adams Sherman, 48, 49, 52
hooks, bell: *Teaching to Transgress*, 198
Horning, Alice, 5, 13, 43, 46, 119, 152, 193, 213
Hult, Christine 51, 62,
humanism, 15, 57, 140, 141, 147, 219
hybridity, xv, 15, 100, 105, 134, 138

identification, 7, 9, 10, 14, 15, 28, 42, 49, 63, 65, 66, 69, 83, 95, 96, 97, 104, 105, 106, 109, 118, 119, 121, 141, 174, 216
in medias res, 138
Ingraham, Lauren, 127
Institutes, WPA, 64, 95
invention, 21, 29, 33, 73, 107–109, 111, 113, 115, 118, 123, 127,

135–136, 141–143, 154–155, 157, 160–161, 175, 177, 198

Jackson, Nell C., 155
Jackson, Rebecca, 80
Jacobs, Dale, 172
Janangelo, Joseph, 11, 73, 133, 156, 161, 171, 178, 180, 181, 214
Janangelo, Joseph, and Kristine Hansen, eds: *Resituating Writing; Constructing and Administering Writing Programs*, 11, 214
job choice, 13
Jschik, Scott, 188
jWPA: junior Writing Program Administrator, 4–6, 13, 43, 45, 46, 56, 64, 66, 95, 121, 127, 138, 152, 153, 173–174, 183, 185, 186, 188–189, 192, 199, 203

kairos, 134
Kairos: Online Journal, 54
Kennedy, Kristen, 45
Kill, Melanie, 139
Killingsworth, M. Jimmie, 133, 145
Kinney, Kelly, 151
Kopelson, Karen, 17–18

Lakoff, George, and Johnson, Mark: *Metaphors We Live By*, 123–124
Langstraat, Lisa, 79
Law, Joe, 80
Lerner, Gerda, 36, 56, 174
Leverenz, Carrie, 80, 172–173
Lindquist, Julie, 79
locatability, 59, 134–135
Logan, Shirley Wilson, 79
Lu, Min-Zhan, 47
Lunsford, Andrea, 33, 61

Mallin, Irwin, and Karrin Varsby Anderson, 154, 219
Martín-Alcoff, Linda, 152–153
Mathieu, Paula, 172, 175–177
McClure, Randall, 126
McLemee, Scott, 72, 125–126, 217
McLeod, Susan, 10, 47–49, 54, 63–65, 121, 127, 216
mediation, 122, 140–142, 144, 147, 163, 167, 176, 182, 195, 202, 220
mentoring, xiii, 15, 26, 86, 90–96, 123, 142, 160, 169, 183, 188, 217
Micciche, Laura, 74, 136, 177
Miller, Carolyn, 218
Miller, Hildy, 190–192
Miller, Richard, 6, 47, 72, 73, 74, 178, 219
Miller, Thomas P., 37
MLA *Job Information List*, 63
moral authority, 138, 218
Morris, Margaret: consociational model for collaboration, 151, 219
multiplicinarity, xv, 7, 20, 60, 63, 91, 103, 114, 115, 157, 174, 213, 217

negotiation, 112, 117, 134, 148, 157– 161, 170, 182, 217, 221
North, Stephen, 50
Nussbaum, Martha, 78, 205

Olson, Gary: *Rhetoric and Composition as Intellectual Work*, 78

Phelps, Louise Wetherbee, 3, 68, 70
phronêsis, 159–160, 219
phronimos, 160, 196
Portland Resolution, The 1990, 43, 51–52, 64–65, 188
Post-administration, 112
Post-WPA, 66

Powell, Malea, 54–55
power: discursive, 9, 20, 140, 142; discursive, over managerial, 9, 20, 140, 142; in discourse, 9, 20, 140, 142; vertical, 117, 140, 191
pragmatism, xv, 12, 58, 109, 116, 154, 161, 197; and activism, 20, 140, 182; and change, 116; and disciplinarity identity, 111; and feminism, xiii, 114, 141, 159, 174, 179, 182; Classical American, 20, 176; pragmatic action, 58
professionalization, xii, 7, 11, 13, 19–20, 25, 37, 62–64, 67–70, 72, 74–76, 80, 90, 92, 96–97, 113, 150, 163, 181, 209, 215–216
Prometheus narratives, 108

Quintilian: *vir bonus*, xii

raison d'etre, 162
Ratcliffe, Krista: *Rhetorical Listening; Identification, Gender, Whiteness*, 130, 138, 155
Readings, Bill: *The University in Ruins*, 78, 110, 162, 195
Reid, E. Shelley, 6, 122, 144
reinvention, 76, 163
Renegar, Valerie, and Stacey K. Sowards, 35, 44, 46, 181, 221
resistance, xiv, xv, xvi, 9, 47, 49, 50–51, 53, 56, 58, 63, 102, 108, 112, 116, 120, 130, 134–135, 142, 148, 155–156, 162–163, 174, 182, 184, 187, 190
ressentiment, 117
rhetoric and composition: histories and theories, 50–51, 63, 102, 121, 169; institutional place of, 12, 14, 16, 69, 78, 169, 178; waves of disciplinary formation, 63, 117

rhetorical agility, 61, 134, 138–140
rhetorical listening, 130, 132, 153–156
Rickly, Rebecca, 135
Roach, Stephanie, 185–186
Ronald, Kate, 111, 142, 172, 176
Rorty, Richard, 140, 161
Rose, Shirley K, 24, 92, 123
Rose, Shirley K, and Irwin Weiser, 11, 42, 69, 70, 81, 84, 112, 214, 216
Rose, Shirley K, and Irwin Weiser, eds: *The Writing Program Administrator as Researcher: Inquiry in Action and Reflection*, 42, 146, 214; *The Writing Program Administrator as Theorist: Making Knowledge Work*, 11, 42, 112, 214
Roskelly, Hephzibah, 111, 142, 165, 172, 176, 220
Royster, Jacqueline Jones, 3, 16, 17, 61, 179, 180, 181, 214; disciplinary landscaping, 3, 16, 119, 164, 214

Satterfield, Jay, and Antczak, Frederick 140, 161
Schema Theory, 90, 91, 184
Schilb, John, 156
Schuster, Charles, 66
Scott, Fred Newton: at University of Michigan, 49
Selber, Stuart, 187
self-positioning, 15
Sommers, Nancy, 95
sophia, 159, 160, 219
sophist, 103, 160
Stewart, Kathleen, 104, 105
strategizing, 21, 39, 56, 129, 131, 132
Strickland, Donna, 14, 70, 105, 156

Strickland, Donna, and Gunner, Jeanne, eds: *The Writing Program Interrupted; Making Space for Critical Discourse*, 14, 70, 105, 156
Stygall, Gail, 80
Suzuki, D. T., 101
Syverson, Margaret, 194, 195

techne, 106–109
telos, 163
tikkun olam, 12, 126
Tompkins, Jane, 184
Townsend, Martha, xii, 66
Twale, Darla J., and Barbara M DeLuca: *Faculty Incivility; The Rise of the Academic Bully Culture and What to Do About It*, 126, 184, 186–187, 221

Valentine, Kathryn, 88–89, 221
victim narratives, 19, 37, 39-42, 56, 124, 203
Ward, Irene, and William J. Carpenter, eds: *The Allyn and Bacon Sourcebook for Writing Program Administrators*, 11, 214
West, Cornel, 140, 174
White, Edward, 38–39, 42, 45,119, 121, 126–127
Winterowd, Ross, 117
Worsham, Lynn, 72, 125, 217
WPA: Writing Program Administration, 14, 64, 216
WPA Mentoring Project, 92
WPA Survey, 2007, 80
WPA-L listserv, 36, 64, 66, 95, 117, 156, 176, 221
writing program administration: as epistemology, 3, 37, 119, 144, 150, 161, 177, 180; as ethnomethodology, 37, 214, 218
writing programs: as activity systems, 15, 34, 133, 143, 180, 181

Yarbrough, Steven, 140-142, 147, 195; discursive power, 140, 142
Yoshino, Kenji, 190, 220

Zen, 101

About the Authors

Colin Charlton is Associate Professor of Rhetoric and Composition at the University of Texas-Pan American. He coordinates developmental reading/writing classes, for which he also designed and runs an innovative STUDIO Teaching and Conferencing Center. His interests include collaboration, everyday innovative technology, writing pedagogy, multimodal design, and always, always learning from students in unexpected spaces.

Jonikka Charlton is Associate Professor of Rhetoric and Composition at the University of Texas-Pan American where she coordinates the first-year writing program. Her scholarship focuses on issues related to writing program administration, particularly WPA identity, preparation, and professionalization. Much of her work is collaborative and appears in the journals *WPA: Writing Program Administration*, *Basic Writing eJournal*, and *Profession*, as well as the recent book collection *Going Public*. Her current work is a book-length project based on empirical research about CWPA members written with Shirley K Rose to be published by Parlor Press.

Tarez Samra Graban is Assistant Professor of English at Indiana University where she teaches rhetoric, writing, public discourse, and pedagogy. She currently coordinates first-year composition for multilingual learners at IU-Bloomington, where she has implemented a curriculum entitled "Developing Textual Identities" and designed a proseminar for new instructors to the course. Additionally, she regularly teaches service-learning and advises both graduate and undergraduate students whose projects are at various intersections of histories and theories of rhetoric and composition, discourse studies, and emergent pedagogies. Her publications have appeared in *Writing on the Edge*, *CCC*, *WPA: Writing Program Administration*, *Rhetorica*,

Gender & Language, and in various edited collections. In 2011, she began working with Indiana University's Institute for Digital Humanities on "Beyond Recovery," the prototype for an historical knowledge base that represents obscure or partially processed information about the writing activities of women involved in the development of rhetoric and composition.

Kathleen J. Ryan is Associate Professor of English and the Director of Composition at the University of Montana. Kate has been a WPA since 1998, currently co-chairs the High Mountain WPA affiliate, and is beginning a three-year term as a member of the WPA executive board. Her teaching includes first year composition, advanced composition, and graduate courses in composition pedagogy. Her publications, broadly conceived, reconceptualize rhetorical studies to account for feminist exigencies, theorize administering writing programs humanely, and explore how subjectivity matters to acts of knowing/composing. She has published in *CCC*, *WPA*, *Rhetoric Review*, *Rhetoric Society Quarterly*, *Composition Studies* and *Feminist Teacher*. She recently co-edited *Walking and Talking Feminist Rhetorics: Landmark Essays and Controversies* (Parlor Press, 2010) with Lindal Buchanan. Her next book project centers on theorizing feminist rhetorical *ethoi*.

Amy Ferdinandt Stolley is Assistant Professor of English and Writing Program Director at Saint Xavier University, where she teaches first-year writing and courses in advanced argument, the teaching of writing, and digital writing. As the WPA at Saint Xavier, she has led the redesign of the first-year writing curriculum and has secured local grant monies to institute regular faculty development workshops, peer tutoring for developmental writing courses, and a year-long assessment of the writing program curriculum. She is currently at work on a project that studies how first-year writing students transfer their writing knowledge from high school to the first-year college writing classroom.

www.ingramcontent.com/pod-product-compliance
Lightning Source LLC
Chambersburg PA
CBHW030132240426
43672CB00005B/115